4

WORDSWORTH'S M

WORDSWORTH'S MIND AND ART

WILLIAM MINTO

ROGER SHARROCK

E. A. HORSMAN

W. J. B. OWEN

A. W. THOMSON

D. G. JAMES

EDWARD E. BOSTETTER

DONALD DAVIE

ANTHONY CONRAN

BERNARD BLACKSTONE

Essays edited by

A. W. THOMSON

BARNES & NOBLE, Inc.

NEW YORK

PUBLISHERS AND BOOKSELLERS SINCE 1873

First published in Great Britain, 1969
by Oliver and Boyd, Ltd
First published in the United States, 1970
by Barnes & Noble, Inc.

ISBN 0 389 03984 5

Printed in Great Britain by
Cox & Wyman Ltd, London, Fakenham and Reading

ACKNOWLEDGMENTS

Several of the essays in this collection have already been published elsewhere and for permission to reprint them here the following acknowledgments are due: D. G. James, "Visionary Dreariness", reprinted from *Scepticism and Poetry* (1937 and 1960) by permission of the author and Allen & Unwin Ltd.; Roger Sharrock, "Wordsworth's Revolt Against Literature", reprinted from *Essays in Criticism*, Vol. III (1953), by permission of the author and editors; Edward E. Bostetter, "Wordsworth's Dim and Perilous Way", reprinted from *P.M.L.A.*, Vol. LXXI (1956), by permission of the author and the Modern Language Association of America; and E. A. Horsman, "The Design of Wordsworth's *Prelude*", reprinted from the *Proceedings and Papers* of the Tenth Congress of the Australasian Universities Language and Literature Association (February 1966), by permission of the author and editor.

v

CONTENTS

A. W. Thomson

INTRODUCTION

Perhaps no single essay in Wordsworth criticism has been more important than Bradley's lecture of 1909, which finally made it clear where a major part of Wordsworth's strength lay. The purpose of Arnold's selection of thirty years before had been clearly stated: to make Wordsworth receivable as a classic by clearing away the irrelevances from a body of powerful work, and to save this work from being compromised by the attentions of the Wordsworthians. But in spite of the authority of the selection, Arnold's introductory essay was something of a simplification. Irving Babbitt suggested that its weakness was in the failure to define the quality of Wordsworth's inspiration, and this criticism is surely just. Perhaps the reason is that the volume was designed for a popular audience, or perhaps the limiting of Wordsworth's poetry to something with which most people could feel at home reflects a less conscious purpose. Of course, it is not Arnold whom Bradley has in mind when he speaks of those who "translate 'the soul of all my moral being' into 'somehow concordant with my moral feelings', or convert 'all that we behold' into 'a good deal that we behold'", and dismisses this as the road round Wordsworth's mind, not into it. But his comment, that Arnold was deficient in that kind of imagination which is allied to metaphysical thought, is difficult to misunderstand. And against the poet whose greatness is in his power of feeling the joy offered to us in nature and in "the simple primary affections and duties", against the poet of strong and peaceful affections and calm and meditative joy, Bradley sets that Wordsworth whom Arnold had helped to obscure, the Wordsworth of strangeness and paradox, the visionary Wordsworth in whose work there is inevitably a certain

1

hostility to "sense". The mind which fed upon its solitary anguish is hardly that of the Wordsworth who put by the cloud of mortal destiny. Like nearly everyone else, Bradley has some doubts about this phrase, but in general seems to understand Arnold to mean that Wordsworth turned away from the cloud. Perhaps the phrase cannot be explained, as F. R. Leavis explained it, by referring the concept to "Obermann" and the vision there of the Wordsworth whose "eyes avert their ken / From half of human fate". There may be a difference, after all, between the very deliberate act of putting something by – in its context, an act of great self-confidence – and that of simply averting one's gaze.

It is difficult, however, to overestimate the contemporary value of Arnold's introduction and selection. In spite of the simplified Wordsworth he suggested, and in spite of his apparent lack of interest in *The Prelude*, he was in no doubt about Wordsworth's greatness. He may or may not have had Bagehot in mind when he spoke elsewhere of the ridiculous elevation of Tennyson above Wordsworth. Of course in one sense Wordsworth, in Bagehot's essay on pure, ornate, and grotesque art, is taken, with Milton, as a kind of standard. And the "singleness of expression" Bagehot finds in him seems a telling phrase, until it becomes clear in another essay that, unlike Tennyson, the older poet is seen to have triumphed rather in character than in imagination, by putting all his mind into a single task.[1] "The mind of Wordsworth was singularly narrow; his range peculiarly limited; the object he proposed to himself unusually distinct." The claims of those adverbs, unlike those of the adjectives, are false; they do not progress, although they seem to pretend to. And despite his purity of style, the Wordsworth who emerges in the end is a strange figure, a sort of gaunt tortoise who, by sticking doggedly to his path, got there and triumphed as the banana-eating Tennyson, for all his greater powers, had as yet failed to do.

It is easy to be wise after what seems to have been the event, and perhaps, in introducing an anthology of this sort, one should be concerned with other things than matters of general agreement. Before coming to what seems to be most valuable in recent

[1] "Tennyson's Idylls", in Vol. II, *The Collected Works of Walter Bagehot*, ed. Norman St John Stevas. London (The Economist) 1965. The editor accepts this essay as Bagehot's.

criticism of Wordsworth, I should like to glance at two critical studies which, for one reason or another, are misleading. Salvador de Madariaga's remarkable essay appeared in 1920, but since yesterday's light is not necessarily today's darkness, and since Madariaga in fact makes out a strong case against Wordsworth, it is worth while considering it here. There is an odd kind of resemblance between Madariaga's approach and that of Irving Babbitt, seen from this date. Babbitt is mainly interested in what he considers to be a doctrine of spontaneity and wise passiveness; Madariaga finds throughout Wordsworth's poetry a too conscious control; the common factor in these analyses appears to be the general impressiveness of the thesis in each case, and the weakness of the actual evidence. It would be tedious now to answer Babbitt's criticisms in "The Primitivism of Wordsworth"; the essay is less an analysis of Wordsworth than part of the general deployment of a thesis which is to be illustrated at this point by reference to Wordsworth. Madariaga's chapter "The Case of Wordsworth", in *Shelley and Calderón*, is a more impressive performance altogether. Its starting-point is the admission that Arnold's prophecy, that Europe as well as England would yet recognise Wordsworth, had not been fulfilled, and the proposal to show what the Spanish mind would make of something so typically English as Wordsworth's poetry. The attack has little to do with a heresy of wise passiveness, and indeed one of its main prongs is the argument that Wordsworth's restless intellect dominated his creative soul. Madariaga speaks of the cold glare of Wordsworth's eye, which, like a general's intent on victory, contemplates the agitation below, and goes on to say that as a poet he was not sufficiently disinterested, that he was neither whole-hearted enough nor trustful enough: "at bottom he is too utilitarian, too much in a hurry". The purpose of his poetry is too much with us: the centre of gravity of his poems is beyond them, and the centre of gravity of his work as a whole is in teaching rather than poetry. "It is a genre which admirably fits the national taste for a literature in which no particular essence predominates, which is thoughtful though not philosophical, well written though not poetical, edifying though not avowedly moral, mixed and vague like life, healthy, serious, and above all useful." There could be, perhaps, no more deadly praise than this; it is as if exasperation had taken a sudden vengeance on a long habit of unwilling admiration for the English and their works. The final statement, that the quality which multiplies Wordsworth's voice in his own country deadens it abroad, is sometimes hard to resist.

But though the case for the prosecution is brilliantly stated, some of the evidence is as shaky as Babbitt's. The criticism, for example, of the opening line of the Intimations *Ode* as a mere statement of fact suggests that Madariaga has not really considered the importance of the flux and reflux in the first four stanzas of the *Ode*, and has not understood what is happening in the opening stanza, and notably in the monosyllabic deliberation of its last line: that is, that Wordsworth, for his own purposes, starts from a desperate limiting of his problem to the simple fact of loss. Madariaga's occasional tendency to turn to the advantage of his main argument what can be picked up on the surface is very evident in his remarks about "Resolution and Independence" and "The Ruined Cottage". For example, the line "Far from the world I walk, and from all care" means very nearly the opposite of what it seems to say; the depression is not a mere surfeit of joy; and Wordsworth does not suppress all painful thoughts and feelings about the leech-gatherer – indeed the line "Yet still I persevere, and find them as I may" expresses as much painful thought about the old man's distress as we find in the *Journal* of Dorothy, whose head here, as so often, is seen peeping over the witness-box. The vision of the cold glare of Wordsworth's overseeing eye is more impressive than the rather distant thunders of Babbitt. But the illustrations of both Babbitt and Madariaga have a way of rising up and bearing witness against them. And on the whole recent criticism of Wordsworth is better because it sticks more closely to the poetry: we are more ready now to take Wordsworth's poetry as poetry, and not, say, as the raw material for a system of philosophy, or as an illumination of the problems of his life and of what we take to be his character. In at least one recent study, however, the question of how far our knowledge of Wordsworth's life adds to our understanding of his poetry seems to me to have been confused. Lascelles Abercrombie pointed out that it is because we can never be sure of the poet's motive that criticism is so ready to consult biography, and added a significant reminder of something which both Fausset and Read overlooked: that is, that the central

habit of experience in which poetry has its origin may be something quite different from anything the poet's mere biography can
show us. "To this central habit of the poet's experience," Abercrombie says, "this essential spirit of the man as poet, all our intelligent interest in his art urges us, sooner or later, to penetrate."
There is no doubt here where the emphasis is, but in F. W.
Bateson's *Wordsworth: a Re-interpretation* it frequently appears elsewhere. This study of Wordsworth has been widely read, but it
contains (together with some incidental weaknesses) at least one
important argument which seems to me to be false.

Although the book has been severely criticised, some of its
virtues are obvious: it is extremely readable, it contains a good
deal of biographical material very conveniently arranged, and it is
chiefly concerned with the Wordsworth whom Bateson rightly
believes to be the Wordsworth who matters: that is, not the
Wordsworth whose ideas have been so frequently abstracted, but
"the . . . Wordsworth who loved and suffered and feared". The
case for what is called a tragic intensification in the relationship
between Wordsworth and his sister is skilfully made,[2] and Bateson
has recently produced evidence of contemporary gossip on the
same theme.[3] And many of the comments on Wordsworth's
relationship with his audiences are very much to the point. But
the simplification of one central division into what occasionally
seem to be opposing football teams of Romantic-subjective and
Augustan-objective tendencies, and such irresponsibility as the
comment on the supposed prescription in the Intimations *Ode* to
"become again as a little child", must cause some misgivings. Nor
(to take an example almost at random) need it be clear to anyone
that it was Annette who seduced Wordsworth, merely because she
was four years older than Wordsworth, and because Wordsworth's
French was not good: the subsequent drama of the question
"what was it about Annette that Wordsworth found so difficult to
resist", is perhaps ill-advised. My main concern, however, is with
the argument contained in the preface to the second edition.
Bateson states that in the better poems of the English Romantic
poets it is always recognisably the historical poet who is speaking,

---

[2] See, however, W. J. B. Owen's comments on this in *The Review of English
Studies*, Vol. VII (1956), pp. 90–2.

[3] *Essays in Criticism*, Vol. XVII, No. 2 (April 1967).

and that their poetry is impoverished and falsified if the autobiographical elements which pervade it are excluded or ignored.
The reply to T. S. Eliot's criticism of Bateson's arguments – that
he felt no need for any light upon the Lucy poems beyond the
radiance shed by the poems themselves – is peculiar. Restricted to
the Lucy poems (it is, in effect, no restriction at all) the argument
can be summarised as follows: (i) the Lucy poems do not make
complete sense unless we know who Lucy was (ii) Eliot has dis-
agreed, but has also said elsewhere that we must have intellectual
satisfaction from religion (iii) poetry resembles religion (iv) we
must, therefore, have intellectual satisfaction from poetry (v) about
this intellectual satisfaction not very much more need be said than
that it is not sentimental satisfactions: roughly, it should mean that
the poems must now make sense (vi) they cannot now make sense
unless we know who Lucy was. The alternatives offered to the
kind of understanding which is recommended are, contentment
with the "surface meaning", and the peculiarly limited stylistic
satisfaction which Wordsworth affords. There is a fair amount
which could be said against the charge of limited stylistic satisfaction, but the unnatural harshness of a choice which makes Lucy-
mongering the crowning privilege is probably obvious enough.
Nor is Bateson justified in using *The Prelude* as a kind of keystone
to these arguments, by presenting it either as Wordsworth's post-
mortem on his dead genius, or as a model of how to make intelligent guesses about Wordsworth and his poems, and so as a
justification by example of the urgent need to know what Wordsworth did not consciously know about himself and Lucy. These
are harsh things to say about a book which many have found
stimulating. And it is only fair to say that Bateson argues more
persuasively elsewhere, as, for example, towards the end of his first
chapter. But even there some odd assumptions are made. "Since
the poems are either the direct or the symbolic expression of his
personal feelings, moods and intuitions their interpretation must
depend upon a reconstruction of the affective undercurrents of his
personality." It is hardly too much to say that the word "interpretation", so far as this context is concerned, has died.

But in spite of its obvious faults, Bateson's book does differ from
a good deal of earlier work in that it is mainly concerned with
Wordsworth's poetry. Sometimes, in the case of the English

critics, one may regret that this concern seems to oblige them to be brief. J. F. Danby's *The Simple Wordsworth* and Colin Clarke's *Romantic Paradox* are both rewarding, and in particular Danby's analysis of some of the shorter poems is brilliant: the quality of both these studies makes one wish that their range had been wider. One kind of attention which Wordsworth's poetry is beginning to receive is perhaps best exemplified by Clarke's study, by William Empson's chapter in *The Structure of Complex Words*, by Donald Davie's chapter in *Articulate Energy*, and by the epilogue to John Jones's *The Egotistical Sublime*. The epilogue to this study in solitude and relationship, and in what Jones calls the poetry of indecision, suggests the beginning of an inquiry into Wordsworth's language. Of particular value is the suggestion that the double movement of the effect of language on mind and that of mind on language is an aspect of that principle of sympathy in nature which was so important to Wordsworth. Once again (it is, of course, ungracious to complain) this part of Jones's study seems tantalisingly brief. This cannot be said of recent American criticism of Wordsworth. And one of the most interesting aspects of the work of American scholars in this field is the attention they have paid to *The Prelude*. The fine comparative edition of de Selincourt undoubtedly provided an incentive, but the bulk of the work done on *The Prelude* over the last thirty years or so, from R. D. Havens to A. F. Potts, and from Potts to Ferry, Lindenberger, and Hartman, seems to have been American. In the natural course of things, Havens's massive study of 1941 has been partly superseded, and much of Potts's book is taken up with discussion of parallels and possible sources. But in the recent books by David Ferry and Geoffrey H. Hartman, *The Prelude* is again taken as central, and Herbert Lindenberger's *On Wordsworth's Prelude* is, of course, only indirectly concerned with the other poems.

Ferry's *The Limit of Mortality* is one of the most perceptive studies of Wordsworth to have appeared, and it is interesting to compare some of his arguments with those of older critics. His contention, that Wordsworth is in a certain sense the most remote of our great poets from the ordinary reader, is one which most readers now would be prepared to listen to, and it is as far from the opinion of Madariaga as it is from that of Arnold. Ferry finds in Wordsworth a sacramental view of nature as a symbol for

eternity, which is continually being thwarted by a "mystical yearn-
ing" which tends towards a destruction of all articulation, and so
of poetry itself. At the heart of this concept of Wordsworth is the
idea of a poet who, as Ferry says, sometimes turns on his own
symbolism and devours it. Like the analysis of Wordsworth's
inability to settle for optimism or pessimism in his view of man's
state, or of what precisely was meant by love of nature leading to
love of man, this suggests a far more complex Wordsworth than
an earlier public had bargained for. The account of the tension
between the sacramental and the mystical in the last three books of
The Prelude, and of the opposing visions of order and confusion
within the great vision on Snowdon, is almost disquietingly per-
suasive. Ferry's acknowledgment that *The Prelude* is Wordsworth's supreme achievement, and his insistence on the deep sense
of confusion in its climax, is perhaps a fair reflexion of contemporary thinking about Wordsworth.[4] The same understanding of
power and deep confusion in Wordsworth appears in a more
recent study, of ampler scope: Geoffrey H. Hartman's *Wordsworth's
Poetry 1787–1814*. The unusual range of Hartman's study gives
point to his contention, that the Romantic poets are not often read
in a wide enough context. Like Harold Bloom, Hartman makes
extensive use of the term "apocalyptic", and his use of it to describe, among other things, "any strong desire to cast out nature
and to achieve an unmediated contact with the principle of things"
suggests some affinity with Ferry's approach.[5] Both Ferry and
Hartman, of course, are concerned with Wordsworth's imagination, and with certain unusual and even paradoxical aspects of his
dealings with nature, which, to say the least of it, have not always
been apparent. Something of Wordsworth's mistrust of the
imagination was suggested by Charles Williams in 1932, when he
declared that his poetry could not sufficiently trust itself. Williams
went on to say that there was a sense in which Wordsworth was
compelled to avoid his own Solitaries, and related the abdication

[4] For another point of view, see Douglas Bush, in *Wordsworth: Centenary
Studies Presented at Cornell and Princeton Universities*, ed. Gilbert T. Dunklin,
London, 1963: "we read *The Prelude* more as a document than as a poem . . .
only fractions of it (are) great poetry". Professor Bush describes his paper as
"a minority report".

[5] See also Hartman's *The Unmediated Vision. An Interpretation of Wordsworth,
Hopkins, Rilke, and Valéry*, Newhaven, 1954, London, 1955.

of the pure poetic authority in his verse to the fact that when he passed through his crisis of despair, it was by some other authority than the purely poetic that he was revived. I am not sure that I fully understand Williams here, but I believe his suggestion, that the poetry could not sufficiently trust itself, arises from a profound understanding of Wordsworth's problems as a poet. The closely documented account which Hartman gives of Wordsworth's dealings with nature and the mind, his analysis of what he calls the myth without myth and of Wordsworth's long and lonely struggle "to save nature for the human imagination", is fascinating, even where one differs. Professor Horsman, in the present collection, disagrees with Hartman's interpretation of one very important passage in *The Prelude*, and I am myself a little uncertain about some of his comments on the induction to Book 1 and to the poem. But the authority of this study, as of Ferry's, is unmistakable. That Wordsworth is receiving critical attention of this quality is a sign of a new admiration for him. And no doubt it will be shared in time by a wider public.

I have included in this collection William Minto's essay of 1889, "Wordsworth's Great Failure", partly, I suppose, as a concession to that feeling for the historical which is probably never very far from the minds of editors of anthologies of this sort, and partly because it anticipates some later ideas about Wordsworth. The essay has been slightly shortened, and some of the references have been corrected.

William Minto

WORDSWORTH'S GREAT FAILURE[1]

. . . The whole dramatic interest of Wordsworth's poetic life
centres in the work – the formally incomplete work – of which the
fragment entitled *The Recluse* was meant to be the prologue . . .
The great philosophical poem to be called *The Recluse* was never
completed. There would have been no great harm in affixing the
title to this fragment if the design had been lightly entered on and
lightly abandoned. But so far was this from being the case, that
the history of the unfinished *Recluse* is the history of Wordsworth's
poetic life: his conception of this grand purpose and life-long
striving to fulfil it being the central line that gives unity and
dramatic interest to his career. It was this project that brought him
to Grasmere, and the failure of it tortured many hours and days
and weeks of his fifty years' residence in the Lake Country. The
dominant significance of *The Recluse* in Wordsworth's life is
pushed out of sight when the title is appropriated for a fragment
which represents only two or three months of joyous enthusiastic
labour in the first heat and confidence of the enterprise, before the
mirage that lured him on had faded, and glad anticipations had
given place to despondency and a cheerless sense of impotence. . . .

That Wordsworth entertained the idea of writing a poem to be
called *The Recluse* is one of those things that everybody knows
but few think worth attending to, one of those things that might
tempt an epigrammatist to say that what everybody knows nobody
knows. Yet whoever does attend to it, may find a new and previously unsuspected interest in the poet's personality: it is the clue
to an inner life that contrasts strangely with the popular concep-

[1] Reprinted, in a shortened form, from *The Nineteenth Century*, September,
1889. Book I of *The Recluse* was first published in 1888.

tion of the man and his career. The popular conception is that Wordsworth, his *Lyrical Ballads* being received with a universal shout of ridicule, shut himself up in the Lake Country, and worked out his own ideas with serene indifference to the opinions of the critics; that he had unbounded faith in himself and confidence of ultimate triumph; that work after work as it issued from his peaceful retreat was pursued with merciless rancour; that still the poet held on his way unmoved, doing exactly what he intended to do; and that at last, in spite of infinite calumny and detraction, the world recognised his greatness and crowned his latter days with honour. This is the drama of Wordsworth's life as generally conceived, and while it passes current and unquestioned one would be sorry to drag to light any cold realities likely to impair by the slightest chip or blemish so noble a figure in the history of our literature. If damaging facts lay concealed among the records of his life, it would be almost a duty to continue to ignore them. Fortunately no such compromise between truth and beneficent fiction is necessary in Wordsworth's case. The popular conception, though it is tinged with romance, is right in the main. It cannot help assimilating the real Wordsworth to its favourite simple type of a good man struggling against villains, and so does injustice to his critics: it must have its sacrifice: but the honour that it renders to the poet is no more than his due. The truth is not quite so simple, but it is not less heroic and it is certainly much stranger. Truth would substitute for the serene, steadfast, clear-eyed demigod the more picturesque and interesting figure of a man, full of contradictions and uncertainties, often harassed by doubts and despondencies, impulsive and extravagant in his hopes, indefinite in his plans, stumbling along more under the guidance of circumstance than of deliberate choice, and yet withal possessing

> A mind and heart,
> Though sensitive, yet, in their weakest part,
> Heroically fashioned.[2]

The idea of *The Recluse* would seem to have originated in one of those joyous, discursive, suggestive talks with Coleridge at Alfoxden and in its neighbourhood, which did so much to clear the elder poet's aims and inspire him with confidence in himself. At

[2] Sonnet to B. R. Haydon, 4–6.

least, the first trace we have of the idea is in a letter written from Alfoxden during this memorable and fruitful companionship, a letter addressed to Mr Losh, a Cumberland friend, and dated 11 Mar. 1798: "I have been tolerably industrious within the last few weeks," Wordsworth wrote: "I have written 1300 lines of a poem which I hope to make of considerable utility. Its title will be *The Recluse; or, views of Nature, Man, and Society.*" The idea, however it originated, was warmly taken up by Coleridge, and it is something of a paradox to find this habitual procrastinator, who allowed so many of the projects of his own fertile brain to remain in the condition of glorious dreams, appearing in the character of an urgent monitor, again and again whetting the blunted purpose of his more industrious friend. We next hear of the design in the summer of the following year, after Wordsworth's return from Germany. "I am anxiously eager," Coleridge wrote to him, "to have you steadily employed on *The Recluse* . . . My dear friend, I do entreat you to go on with *The Recluse*; and I wish you would write a poem, in blank verse, addressed to those, who, in consequence of the complete failure of the French Revolution, have thrown up all hopes of the amelioration of mankind, and are sinking into an almost epicurean selfishness, disguising the same under the soft titles of domestic attachment and contempt for visionary *philosophes.* It would do great good, and might form a part of *The Recluse*, for in my present mood I am wholly against the publication of any small poems." Still, however, Wordsworth would seem to have procrastinated. He was deliberating that summer, in his wisely passive way, over the choice of a permanent home, and perhaps put off working at *The Recluse* till he should be fairly settled. In October of the same year Coleridge renewed his exhortations: "I long to see what you have been doing. O let it be the tail-piece of *The Recluse* for of nothing but *The Recluse* can I hear patiently." Grasmere was fixed on, and the poet and his sister went there on St Thomas's Day, 1799. When they had been a month there, Coleridge, still urgent, wrote again: "I grieve that *The Recluse* sleeps." Then Wordsworth seems to have set to work in earnest, and writing down "*The Recluse. Book First, Part First. Home at Grasmere*", to have laboured with continuous and prosperous industry till he had completed, not the philosophical poem, but the introductory canto . . .

The springtime of 1800 was occupied with this "prelusive song", a description in an impassioned strain of the Recluse's Home, and the spirit in which he settled there – all his powers bent upon the vast design of harmonising the human soul with the universe, probing the mind in his solitude to discover the secret of a perfect union between Man and Nature, not ignoring, or passing by without "authentic comment", the discordant passions of humanity, but striving to "win the vacant and the vain to noble raptures," while he proclaims:

> How exquisitely the individual Mind
> (And the progressive powers perhaps no less
> Of the whole species) to the external World
> Is fitted: – and how exquisitely, too –
> Theme this but little heard of among men –
> The external World is fitted to the Mind.[3]

I cannot agree with the opinion that this canto of the Recluse's Home and his aspirations, is inferior to *The Prelude*. It is really a fragment of that impassioned history, written throughout in the same exalted vein; the verse is of the poet's prime, and the feeling is more whole-hearted and buoyant, being crossed by no disturbing currents of regret or misgiving. It is this, indeed, that constitutes the pathetic interest of the canto – that the poet, when he wrote it, was standing on the top of golden hours, possessed by a noble ambition, and confident that its execution was within his grasp. There is no trace of misgiving, unless we are to find it in the very pains that he took to satisfy himself by the explicit enumeration of his advantages that he had made no mistake in his choice of residence, and that he ought to be grateful for the impulse that had directed him to Grasmere.

But this happy mood was soon dispersed when he proceeded to the formal construction of a poem charged with the weight of so sublime an argument. To feel in moments of rapt ecstasy that there is a natural harmony between man's soul and the universe, to enjoy the solemn transport of the mystic in communion with the spirit of the world, is one thing; a very different thing it is to establish for the common heart the reality of this harmonious correspondence by formal exposition of it, carried through all the

[3] "Prospectus" of *The Excursion*, 63–8.

circumstances of human life. This cannot be done without some kind of poetic machinery, and such machinery Wordsworth had now to invent. How slowly and painfully he fared in this quest may be traced in the journal of his sympathetic sister, Dorothy. During the summer of 1800, after writing his Recluse's Prologue and Invocation, he turned aside to prepare a new edition of his *Lyrical Ballads*, and to write his famous preface of defence and introduction. Dorothy, who, among other enthusiastic services, was her brother's copyist, wrote "the last sheet of Notes and Preface" on the 30th of September, 1800. On the 5th of October she was busy with an "addition". Then on the 6th of October there is an entry showing that the poet had gone back at once on his *magnum opus*: "After tea read *The Pedlar*" (Coleridge being present). There can be no hesitation in identifying the Pedlar with the Wanderer of the *Excursion*. To anyone who compares the Invocation of *The Recluse* with the account of the Wanderer's character, as founded and moulded by Nature, the continuity of idea is at once apparent. A common packman is chosen as a hero, to show that Nature, even in the humblest life, with the smallest help from books and fortune, can build up a character of the most enlightened wisdom and serene and gracious temper. Thereby is illustrated the adaption of the human lot to the poorest of human creatures; and it is obvious also how the "vagrant merchant" would suit the purposes of a poet embarked on a comprehensive survey of man and society, and bent especially upon exploring and exhibiting the life of the poor as rich in opportunities of ennobling emotions. In *The Pedlar*, then, which Wordsworth read to Coleridge in October 1800, we have beyond doubt his first idea of a dramatic machinery for his philosophic poem. . . . There are constant references in the Grasmere Journals to *The Pedlar* as a subject of weary and unprofitable application. On the 30th of January he "worked at *The Pedlar* all the morning [and] kept the dinner waiting till four o'clock. He was much tired." Two days after he is at it again and tires himself, and the day after that again. At the end of a week he reads it, and Dorothy thinks it done: but no, it is "uninteresting, and must be altered. Poor William!" A few days later Dorothy writes it out, "they hope, for a final writing"; they read the first part and are delighted with it, "but William afterwards got to some ugly place, and went to bed tired out". Next day he is "sadly tired, and working still at *The Pedlar*"; and on the day after that, when she recopies it, he is still unsatisfied, and they have "an affecting conversation". Another morning finds him still "at work at *The Pedlar*, altering and refitting"; he reads part of his *Recluse* to Dorothy, trying, perhaps, to recover something of the glowing confidence of the Prologue. In the course of a fortnight, when he is still brooding over it, Dorothy is "so unlucky as to propose to rewrite *The Pedlar*": "William got to work, and was worn to death". This was on the 3rd of March; on the 8th of July, the journal records, "William was looking at *The Pedlar* when I got up. He arranged it, and after tea I wrote it out – 280 lines."

Two years later we still find Coleridge sighing, "Oh, for one hour of *The Recluse*", and prophesying immortality for it "as the first and finest philosophical poem, if only it be (as it undoubtedly will be) a faithful transcript of his own most august and innocent life, of his own habitual feelings and modes of seeing and hearing". Meantime, the poet seemed to make but little progress, and he gave vent to his own sense of baffled endeavour in the first book of *The Prelude*.[4] It was to deliver himself from this bondage of self-distrust that he began *The Prelude* – a review of what Nature had done from his childhood upwards to qualify him for the office of poet. This, at least, was his original motive. Whether he did not lose sight of it as he went on, and virtually anticipate the illustration of the leading ideas of his "philosophy", I will not undertake to say. What is in point as regards the history of his cherished project of a philosophical poem, is that, when after sixteen months of fairly continuous labour *The Prelude* had been completed, he still looks before him with heaviness of heart.

> I finished my poem about a fortnight ago [he wrote to Sir George Beaumont on 3 June, 1805]. But it was not a happy day for me; I was dejected on many accounts; when I looked back upon the performance it seemed to have a dead weight about it, the reality so far short of the expectation; it was the first long labour that I had finished, and the doubt whether I should ever live to write *The Recluse*, and the sense which I had of this poem being so far below what I seem'd capable of

[4] I, 124–31, 227–40, 255–61.

executing, depressed me much . . . This work may be considered as a sort of *portico* to *The Recluse*, part of the same
building – which I hope to be able, ere long, to begin with in
earnest; and if I am permitted to bring it to a conclusion, and
to write, further, a narrative Poem of the Epic kind, I shall
consider the *task* of my life as over.

He returned to *The Recluse* with a certain impetus from this
retreat *pour mieux sauter*: but the impetus did not carry him far. He
wrote again to Sir George Beaumont in August[5] that he had
returned to *The Recluse* and written seven hundred lines, adding
significantly that if only he had Coleridge by him to talk with he
would go on swimmingly. But towards the close of 1806 we find
him writing to Sir Walter Scott: "I am going to the Press with a
Volume which . . . I publish with great reluctance; but the day
when my long work will be finished seems farther and farther off."

Coleridge returned in 1807; *The Prelude* was read to him, and
received, as everybody knows, with an inexpressibly touching
mixture of enthusiasm for his friend, and remorse over his own
wasted powers. Soon after this Wordsworth settled down to *The
Excursion* and worked at it with stubborn determination till it was
completed. The rest of the project was then allowed to go to sleep,
though its sleep was occasionally broken by uneasy compunc-
tions . . . In spite of the poet's own statement in the preface to *The
Excursion* that it was but a part of *The Recluse*, Dorothy maintained
that *The Excursion* was by itself an independent and complete
work. Whether or not this was a pious opinion on this faithful
sister's part to mitigate her brother's self-reproaches, there is a
good deal to be said for it. *The Excursion* is an attempt to carry out
the same central idea in a complementary but practically independent form.

Enough has been adduced to show how large a place in Wordsworth's life was occupied by his unfinished project of "a philosophical poem to be called *The Recluse*". It is easy to understand
why so little attention has been paid to it by his biographers. The
popular conception of his character had been fixed by a public
career of more than half a century before the world had any means
of knowing how seriously he had taken this ambition. By 1850,

---

[5] Of 1806.

when *The Prelude* was published, which was the first open evidence of the fact, people were not disposed to accept Wordsworth as a poet of unfulfilled ambition – a self-dissatisfied poet whose achievement in one great particular fell short of his aspiration. On the contrary, he had become fixed in the public mind as a very type of self-confidence, not to say self-complacency; as a poet who had pre-eminent reason to be satisfied with his own work, of all men least cause to sigh over "things incomplete and purposes betrayed", seeing that he had maintained a belief in himself against the ridicule of a whole world of critics, and held the field in his old age without having once lowered his flag. That such a man should have suffered from a sense of his own defects, that with all his persistence and all his success the great "determinate aim" of his poetic life was unachieved, was as incredible at the time of Wordsworth's death as the possibility of his attaining the rank then held by him would have seemed forty years earlier.

Wordsworth, as we all know and acknowledge, was not baulked of his noble ambition to be of service to mankind in the sacred office of poet: but, undoubtedly, he did not succeed as he hoped and strove to succeed in being the exponent of a final philosophy of life. The word philosophy is used with such latitude that it is easy enough to argue to the contrary, as many good Wordsworthians do, with every appearance of triumphant demonstration. Philosophy means love of wisdom: true wisdom is to let insoluble problems alone.

> One impulse from a vernal wood
>   Will teach you more of man,
> Or moral evil and of good,
>   Than all the sages can.[6]

Have we not here a sound philosophy?

> Spontaneous wisdom breathed by health,
>   Truth breathed by cheerfulness?[7]

But this happy arrest of the meddling intellect was not the poet's permanent mood; it was not the mood in which he invoked the Muse to aid him in showing forth the mutual fitness of Man and Nature, or the mood in which, as his sister's records show, he

[6] "The Tables Turned", 21–4.   [7] *Op. cit.*, 19–20.

spent days and nights of perplexed and exhausting labour. For philosophy in the ordinary sense, in the sense in which Coleridge used the word when he confidently anticipated for *The Recluse* that it would be the first and only philosophical poem, we search Wordsworth's published works in vain. When *The Excursion* was published, Coleridge did not conceal his disappointment, and frankly wrote to his friend to explain what he had expected from their conversations on the subject. A poem constructed on such a plan as Coleridge sketched would have had some claim to be called philosophic: but we may be sure it would not have been accepted as a final philosophy, and we may doubt whether it would not have been even in Coleridge's hands open to the reproach that what was poetry was not philosophy, and what was philosophy was not poetry. For himself, at any rate, in *The Excursion*, Wordsworth, as his friend pointed out, practically abandoned all claim to be the exponent of a philosophy when he repudiated system, and professed only to present commonplace truths in an interesting light. In spite of this disclaimer, Charles Lamb, attracted by the poet's bold undertaking to exhibit the harmony between the external universe and the human soul, seems to have made an attempt to extract a coherent "scheme of harmonies" from *The Excursion*. But his essay had an untoward fate. It was written for the *Quarterly*, and Gifford exercised his editorial right with such savage freedom, and cut out so much of the "scheme of harmonies" that – so Lamb wrote – "without conjuration no man could tell what he was driving at". Unfortunately, Lamb kept no copy of his original draft, so that his exposition is irrecoverably lost. This loss can never be too much regretted, for Lamb's essay, even as it stands, is the most sympathetic and illuminating criticism that *The Excursion* has ever received. We must regret the loss, but at the same time it must be admitted that a metrical philosophy that needs a prose interpreter is as a philosophy but half sung. After all, if a clue is needed to the philosophy of *The Excursion* – and many readers have said in their haste that they could not understand what the Wanderer was driving at – the best clue is to be found in the Savoyard Vicar's profession of faith. In his natural religion Wordsworth is the pupil of Rousseau, and, as a philosopher, is hardly the equal of his master. Wordsworth's ambition to write a philosophical poem – and we have Coleridge's testimony as well as the proof of the Wanderer's discourses that a reasoned philosophy was his original design – was unquestionably a mistaken ambition. It was persevered in *invita Minerva*. Haydon, who was a believer in phrenology, took an opportunity of doing for the poet what Lamb proposed to do with a candle for the collector of customs, and, after examining his "bumps", pronounced him deficient in *lucidus ordo* and in the constructive faculty – a perfectly true diagnosis in whatever way it was arrived at. No one who has felt the divine charm of Wordsworth's "high and passionate thoughts" will ever be disposed to deny him the veneration due to a great moral teacher; but it was not by expounding an ethical system that he established his claim on our gratitude. It was his perplexed attempts to give a systematic form to his precepts, as if they were rules of universal application, that tempted Mary Lamb to say that "it would seem by his system that a liver in towns had not a soul to be saved". One could wish that some of those who profess to see a system of ethics in Wordsworth's poetry, implicit or explicit, would deal with this criticism.

The philosophical poem was a mistaken ambition, and yet Nature, kinder to the poet than his own deliberate volition, guided him to the fulfilment of all that was poetically practicable in the aspiration of *The Recluse*. Nature did not, after all, betray the heart that loved her. She treated her worshipper with a sort of benevolent irony, broke the word of promise to the ear, but kept it to the hope, answered the prayer, but not in the terms of the petitioner. The little occasional poems, for which Coleridge was inclined to reproach him *relatively* as he would himself have said, as being a desertion of his grand ambition, and which were intended by himself only to fill niches and recesses in the great temple – trifles to be executed while he waited for strength to build the main structure – were really themselves the fulfilment of his dream, the poetic expression of "the sensations and opinions of a poet living in retirement . . ." Nature's invitation to Grasmere was not a mockery and a snare. He gained his ambition while seeming to lose it. If he could not construct a philosophic poem such as he vaguely dreamed of, he could hold on doggedly in the vain endeavour to his chosen home, and by the mere fact of thus localising himself, give a certain unity of effect to his work, and make for himself as distinctive a position in literature as if he had achieved a great regular work in any of the recognised forms, epic, dramatic or didactic. It was an age of grand ambitions, in art as well as politics, and Wordsworth was like other children of his age in having one. Though it was not literally fulfilled, he was probably, like Scott, in the case of his more worldly dream, carried farther than he might have been by a humbler aim. Without this ambition and the consecration of his powers to it, he would never have taken such a hold of the public imagination, because without it his life and work would have been wanting in any principle of unity.

There was no treachery in Nature's invitation to Grasmere as regarded the substance of the poet's ambition. But, in moving him to fix his home in that quiet retreat, Nature may be accused of having behaved with a certain jealousy towards her worshipper, as if her object had been to attach him firmly and surely to her exclusive service, at a time when he showed a disposition to be unfaithful. For the great mass of readers, Wordsworth is simply the poet of Nature. But this, as readers of *The Prelude* know, was not his own conception of himself. According to that conception, the disinterested worship of Nature was only a passing stage in his development; it was only in his youth that he loved natural objects with passion and rapture for their own sake; in his mature age, the love of Man was paramount: Man was the centre of his interests. Indeed, one of the main purposes of *The Prelude* was to explain his change of attitude, and show how Nature herself had aided in the transition, love of Nature passing into love of Man by a continuous and harmonious process of expansion. The drift of the history given in the impassioned language of *The Prelude* was put by him in plain prose in a conversation recorded by Crabb Robinson. "He did not," he told Robinson (Diary for the 17th of August, 1837), "expect or desire from posterity any other fame than that which would be given him from the way in which his poems exhibit Man – in his essentially human character and relations – as child, parent, husband: the qualities which are common to all men, as opposed to those which distinguish one man from another." Wordsworth said this in 1837, when his poetic work was done; but it was not an afterthought: the same idea is to be found in *The Prelude*, and it appears also in the letter to Fox which he sent along with a copy of the 1800 edition of his poems. It represents, in fact, the persistent purpose of his life, to exhibit Man as a being formed for a happy and noble life, and capable in all conditions of realising his destined end. Can he be said to have fulfilled this purpose? Only very partially. It is not as the poet of Man but as the poet of Nature that the world took Wordsworth, continues to take him, and is justified in taking him.

> The sounding cataract
> Haunted me like a passion: the tall rock,
> The mountain, and the deep and gloomy wood,
> Their colours and their forms, were then to me
> An appetite.[8]

How often have these lines been quoted as expressing the very essence of the spirit of Wordsworth! Nobody can read a page of his poetry without recognising the truth of the description. How many are aware that in those words he intended to describe a state of mind that was his only in his youth and immaturity, and that, according to his own belief about himself, the animating principle of his poetry was not this passionate interest in the beauty and the grandeur of the world of sense, but a sober conviction that –

> Nature for all conditions wants not power
> To consecrate, if we have eyes to see,
> The outside of her creatures, and to breathe
> Grandeur upon the very humblest face
> Of human life.[9]

The insight into this great truth and the imaginative power to make it visible to others was in Wordsworth's own belief, as expressly proclaimed in the thirteenth book of *The Prelude*, the peculiar faculty that had been vouchsafed to him. Poets, like prophets, have each their own peculiar faculty, and this was his, to discern a new world beneath life's every-day appearances, and transmit it in his verse to other minds. Was he right in this judgment of his own faculty? The claim is so far from being self-evident, that the full meaning of it is not apparent without some study. "The Idiot Boy", "The Thorn", "Goody Blake", the "Lines on Wilkinson's Spade", the sonnet on "Steamboats and

[8] "Tintern Abbey", 76–80.   [9] *The Prelude*, XIII, 283–7.

Railways", are examples of his efforts to "breathe grandeur upon the very humblest face of human life". Personally I am among the number of those who would not say that he has failed even in these poems: for me he succeeds in investing even so humble an instrument of human life as Wilkinson's spade with a certain grandeur. But I confess that it was through other poems that I learnt to see with his eyes even such humble objects as the Idiot Boy and Martha Ray bathed in consecrating light; and to confess this is as good as to admit the almost universal judgment that as poems these essays are failures. The taste for them is a taste that few, very few, acquire: in their case the poet has succeeded with very few in creating the taste by which they are to be enjoyed. Where, then, are we to look for the successes of what the poet held to be his peculiar faculty? "The Affliction of Margaret", "Ruth", "The Leech Gatherer", "The Sailor's Mother", "Simon Lee", "Michael", "The Brothers". His unequivocal successes can almost be counted on the fingers. If with Wordsworth himself we take his poetic mission to have been "to exhibit Man in his essentially human character and relations – as child, parent, husband", irrespective of station and worldly circumstance, and thereby promote the brotherhood of man, we must take amount as well as quality into consideration in any estimate of the degree of his success, and on that ground we are bound to refuse him a high place among the world's benefactors, however much we honour the nobility of this ambition.

Wordsworth probably deceived himself in his judgment of what constituted his peculiar faculty. That he had an eye for spiritual dignity in unlikely places, in familiar vulgar life where people are not in the habit of looking for it, amidst "Nature's unambitious underwood", we all know: but to make this visible to others required a power of creating character of which he has given no proof. The men and women of the Pastor's tales in *The Excursion*, the hapless Lover, the Miner, the Prodigal, the Matron, the Mother, though the incidents of their stories are touching, and the sentiments of their narrator are noble and elevating, have no distinct individual life, and take no hold on the memory: even the Pedlar, on the portraiture of whom he lavished so much pains, remains a very imperfect creation. The Pedlar's wisdom does not come to us like Uncle Toby's, or the Vicar of Wakefield's, recommended by love or veneration for the man; it is only out of respect for his author that we give him a hearing, and very impatient or very languid is the hearing that most readers accord. The faculty of creating character, if Wordsworth had it, was certainly never developed into an efficient art. Rather he would seem to have deliberately studied the effacement of individuality in his sketches of human life, treating each life as an instance merely of some good or evil quality, some trait of moral beauty or depravity, a harmony or a discord with the central Good. It is not without design that the characters of *The Excursion* are all nameless, destitute even of that first and most rudimentary attribute of individuality, a separate and distinctive name. His method in this respect is the very opposite of that of Dickens, with whom a comparison is not inapposite inasmuch as the great novelist more than any other man fulfilled the poet's aspiration to spread abroad a vital sympathy with the "human kindnesses and simple joys" to be found in humble life. If Wordsworth had possessed this faculty, he could not have taken a worse course with a view to giving it exercise than settling down to the life of a recluse in a quiet valley. Theoretically life in such a confined scene might yield to his loving observation types of all the higher human affections, but practically the field was too narrow and obscure to yield types that would permanently impress all mankind. Thus, if Wordsworth had really been capable of fulfilling his conscious ambition as an artist, we might justly have charged Nature with betraying him in moving him to settle at Grasmere. But as it was, Nature judged his powers more wisely than he did, and with benign intention guided him to the field most proper for their fruitful exercise.

Seclusion, however, was not an unmixed benefit to Wordsworth, and it is a singular fact, not a little at variance with customary assumptions, that much of his best poetry was written during those intervals when he emerged from his seclusion. We are accustomed to think of the Recluse poet as drawing his strength from solitary communion with Nature. Now if this were so in an unqualified sense, we should expect to find that the more and the longer he was alone in his home by Grasmere or at Rydal Mount, the richer, the more perfect, and the more abundant would his poetry be. The contrary, strange to say, is the case. If we look to his biography, and mark out the periods of continuous occupation unbroken by change of scene, change of company, or change of work, we find that they coincide with periods of comparatively flat and dull poetic activity. All Wordsworth's best work, as I have elsewhere pointed out, was done either before he settled down to the seclusion of his native regions, or during some break in the monotony of that seclusion, a tour in Scotland, or on the Continent, the presence at his quiet home of some stimulating visitor, or the excitement of preparing for publication. The powers of the Recluse were at their highest not in his seclusion, but when he was in contact with his fellow-men. Solitude may have restored and husbanded his strength, and quiet secluded meditation may have helped him to lay more solid foundations, but communion with man seems to have been necessary to quicken his blood and raise his spirits to the intensity of successful composition. It would be wrong, then, to give to solitude all the merit of Wordsworth's poetry, to count this as being all on one side in any question of the comparative value of solitary retirement and social intercourse. The truth would seem to be that Wordsworth was seldom long in solitude without becoming restless and beginning to pine for change, and that he would have travelled much more than he did but for the simple reason that he could not afford it. In his sixtieth year he wrote to Sir W. R. Hamilton that "wandering was his ruling passion, as writing was Southey's". It is a paradoxical confession to come from a Recluse, but there is abundant evidence that the words were not merely the expression of a passing mood, but indicated a restlessness of disposition that was habitually suppressed because circumstances would not permit of its indulgence. If we are to give the words all the weight that they seem capable of bearing, solitude with Wordsworth, settled solitude at least, confinement to one scene, was against the grain: he sequestered himself in his native region not from free choice, but from necessity and a strong sense of duty.

Probably one reason why Wordsworth's solitude was comparatively so unproductive in work of superlative excellence, is to be found in the fact that when he was at home duty was ever urging him to persevere with his uncongenial and impracticable philosophic poem, and that he fatigued and harassed his powers with unprofitable endeavour. This depressing burden he left

behind him when he set out on tour, and he wrote with corresponding elasticity and freedom, "trances of thought and mount-
ings of the mind". In view of the strength with which his verse
soared on many such occasions, one can imagine him saying in the
words of *The Prelude*:

> It is shaken off,
> That burthen of my own unnatural self,
> The heavy weight of many a weary day
> Not mine, and such as were not made for me.[10]

It has often been remarked that although Wordsworth's long life
extended to 1850, all his best work, with few exceptions, was done
before 1808. He did not cease to write: he produced at least as
much again in quantity: but there is a conspicuous falling off in
quality. No external influence has been suggested to account for
this; nothing has been spoken of but the premature diminution of
his energy, or the hardening or stiffening of his faculties. We
should probably not do wrong to connect it with the slow progress of the task on which his will was set as the great work of his
life. To this task he addressed himself with resolute determination
very soon after the publication of two thin volumes of minor
pieces in 1807. These two volumes represent him in the very
prime of his powers: they contain the "Ode to Duty", the "Intimations of Immortality", "Resolution and Independence", "West-
minster Bridge", and the most powerful and inspiring of his
political sonnets. This 1807 edition, indeed, is the *merum sal* of
Wordsworth's genius; it is the most impressive single appeal that
he ever made to the public, and remains still the best of all intro-
ductions to his poetry, better in its arrangement as it stands than
any selection that has yet been made or could be made for the
purpose. In it he would seem to have put his best before the
public in the most attractive order that he could devise; and, that
done, to have braced himself for the great work at which he had
already made so many unprosperous and disheartening attempts.
The result of several years of strenuous labour was *The Excursion*.
The decline in his powers that has been so universally remarked
coincides with his final entrance upon this unhappy task in full
determination not to turn aside to right-hand or left till he had

[10] *Op. cit.*, I, 20-3.

c

carried it through. It seems to me a most probable supposition that he broke his spirit over it: that his vitality was sapped, the elasticity of his mind irretrievably impaired by a long continuance of comparatively joyless effort, by "long-lived pressure of obscure distress". He was far from being a self-complacent workman: the severe standard that he applied to the work of his contemporaries was applied with no less severity to his own work; no man knew better than himself that the sober moralising of his interlocutors did not always, to use his own words, "fulfil poetic conditions". He said this of "The Happy Warrior": how much more must he have felt it about many of the discourses of the Wanderer! And if he was disheartened on the completion of *The Prelude*, which is sustained throughout at a much higher poetic level, proceeds on a much simpler plan, and engaged him for less than half the time, we can hardly suppose that he looked back with satisfaction on *The Excursion*, a fragment, after all, of the projected *magnum opus*, a fragment after five years of continuous labour and seven more of vain beginnings and tentative bits. We must remember, too, that when *The Prelude* was completed, it was hailed with unbounded enthusiasm by Coleridge, and was not submitted to the cold criticism of an unsympathetic world. *The Excursion* was given to the world, and was received with protest and derision, while among the few friendly voices that came to encourage "the lonely Muse", Coleridge's was not heard, but, on the contrary, was raised to express disappointment. Wordsworth would have been more than human if he had passed through such an ordeal with the buoyancy of his powers unimpaired. The magnificent sonnet to Haydon, "High is our Calling, Friend", shows with how manly a spirit he bore his fate, but his undaunted faith in his mission, and the firm self-assertion with which he met the hostile critics who refused him what he felt to be his due, must not be confounded with serene indifference.

The result of any study of the history of *The Recluse* project must be to qualify considerably the conception of Wordsworth as a man of clear inflexible purpose, of steady, happy, self-satisfied industry, calmed and strengthened by the influence of Nature to pursue his aims with something of the self-absorption and indifference of Nature's own procedure. Persistency of purpose was undoubtedly his in an heroic degree, but to represent the relation between his conscious aims and his achievement as one of perfect harmony is to do violence to the facts. His conscious aims were vague and perplexed, and to a large extent perverse and unsuited to his powers. Nature laid her hand on him and guided him more wisely than he would have guided himself. His unconscious self was, under the guidance of Nature and circumstance, a greater poet than his conscious self aimed at being. There is no more striking instance in history of the narrowness of a great man's vision in laying plans for himself, or of the familiar truth that his ends are shaped for him, "rough-hew them how he will".

D. G. James

VISIONARY DREARINESS[1]

I

The passage in Book II of *The Prelude* in which Wordsworth
writes of the activity of the imagination in the life of the child
clearly derives its substance from Coleridge. The "first poetic
spirit of our human life" is Coleridge's "primary imagination",
the condition of perception. The mind of the child, we are told,
is "prompt and watchful, eager to combine / In one appearance,
all the elements / And parts of the same object, else detach'd / And
loth to coalesce".[2] The "else detach'd and loth to coalesce" rings
indeed of associationism, as well as of the doctrine of the imagination creative in knowledge which Kant asserted and Coleridge
adopted. Wordsworth, indeed, was not a philosopher, either by
inclination or natural ability; and we can allow for confusion in
whatever of philosophical theories he undertook to present. In
any case, what Wordsworth, despite confusion in his thought, was
most clearly concerned to assert was the activity of the mind in
knowledge, not a bare receptivity to associated elements. And in
speaking of this task of primary creation in perception, Wordsworth
again follows Coleridge, for when he says that the power of
imagination

> Even as an agent of the one great mind,
> Creates . . .[3]

[1] Reprinted from *Scepticism and Poetry*, London (Allen & Unwin) 1937 and
1960, pp. 141–69.
[2] This is, of course, almost a travesty of Coleridge's view, which did not
suggest that the child is a more or less conscious creator.
[3] *The Prelude* (1805), II, 272–3.

we are hearing Coleridge's "the primary imagination I hold to be . . . a repetition in the finite mind of the eternal act of creation in the infinite *I am*".

Wordsworth, however, does not represent the imagination as working alone in this act of creation; other parts of the child's personality are involved; above all, his active response to his mother and those around him. The child is not an "outcast" working alone. His creation of a world of objects is not his alone; the co-operation of society is necessary to complete the activity of his own original powers. The child "claims manifest kindred with an earthly soul"; the "discipline of love" is ever present, and he quickly learns the active and emotional responses to objects of those who live with him. And in saying this Wordsworth no doubt gives a fuller psychological account of the primary imagination than Coleridge. He is quite right in insisting on the importance of social co-operation, and in refusing to view the creativeness of the imagination in the making of its world as the activity of the isolated mind. It is in all strictness true that the child's affections for and dependence on others are of the most vital importance to the activity of the imagination. The entire life of the child is involved in its creativeness, and not merely an abstract faculty. The imagination, the primary organ of knowledge, is part and parcel of a personality reaching in a hundred ways to an environment of people, in what psychologists are accustomed to call "intersubjective intercourse". The knowledge of other minds and of objects as responded to by other minds, is made possible only through the affectionate ministration of his mother and others; without this life of action and emotional response the imagination could never obtain a foundation for its activity. This point is of the greatest importance for Wordsworth's scheme; it means that he viewed the imagination not as a power divorced from the full activities of life, but as dependent on them, the flower of personality in all its activities and responses, deriving its health from a total well-being of mind. He says in the second book of *The Prelude* that the imagination can only grow through the ministration of affection and love; and at the conclusion of the poem he says that intellectual love and imagination cannot act or exist without each other, cannot stand "dividually".

In human life, Wordsworth tells us, the imagination grows from

this humble beginning into the sublimest faculty of man, a faculty
which he describes at length in two famous passages in *The Prelude*.
Of imagination he says, at the end of the poem, that it is

> but another name for absolute strength
> And clearest insight, amplitude of mind,
> And reason in her most exalted mood.
> This faculty hath been the moving soul
> Of our long labour: we have traced the stream
> From darkness . . .
>   . . . follow'd it to light
> And open day, accompanied its course
> Among the ways of Nature, afterwards
> Lost sight of it, bewilder'd and engulph'd,
> Then given it greeting, as it rose once more
> With strength, reflecting in its solemn breast
> The works of man and face of human life,
> And lastly, from its progress have we drawn
> The feeling of life endless, the great thought
> By which we live, Infinity and God.[4]

And it is of the imagination in this last sense that he speaks in the
other passage:

> Imagination! lifting up itself
> Before the eye and progress of my Song
> Like an unfather'd vapour; here that Power,
> In all the might of its endowments, came
> Athwart me; I was lost as in a cloud,
> Halted, without a struggle to break through.
> And now recovering, to my Soul I say
> I recognise thy glory; in such strength
> Of usurpation, in such visitings
> Of awful promise, when the light of sense
> Goes out in flashes that have shewn to us
> The invisible world, doth Greatness make abode,
> There harbours whether we be young or old.
> Our destiny, our nature, and our home
> Is with infinitude, and only there;

4 *Op. cit.*, XIII, 168–73, 175–84.

With hope it is, hope that can never die,
Effort, and expectation, and desire,
And something ever more about to be.[5]

Wordsworth, then, with Coleridge, viewed the imagination as an essential unifying agency in all perception: but it was also something more. For it is the imagination, "so called/through sad incompetence of human speech", which also gives order and unity to life through its sense of an infinitude which is beyond "the light of sense". The imagination, failing to apprehend nature and man as a self-contained whole, beholds the world as pointing beyond itself to an infinite unknown. In its "struggle to idealise and unify" the imagination, starting from its beginnings in the perception of the child, advances to the sense of an infinitude and of "unknown modes of being". The highest reaches of the imagination are of a piece with the simplest act of perception, and issue from the demand for unity which is the life of the imagination. There is a passage in *The Prelude* in which Wordsworth develops this thought. It occurs after his description of his ascent of Snowdon, in which he describes the moon "naked in the Heavens", shining upon a huge sea of mist through which "a hundred hills their dusky backs upheaved"; while from below

Mounted the roar of waters, torrents, streams
Innumerable, roaring with one voice.[6]

In this scene Wordsworth beheld

The perfect image of a mighty Mind,
Of one that feeds upon infinity.[7]

The resemblance between the scene and the "mighty Mind" is then expounded. In the scene nature exhibited a "domination upon the face of outward things –"

So moulds them, and endues, abstracts, combines,
Or by abrupt and unhabitual influence
Doth make one object so impress itself
Upon all others, and pervade them so
That even the grossest minds must see and hear
And cannot chuse but feel.[8]

[5] *Op. cit.*, VI, 525–42.
[6] *Op. cit.*, XIII, 58–9.
[7] *Op. cit.*, XIII, 69–70.
[8] *Op. cit.*, XIII, 79–84.

The thought appears to be that in the scene before him the effect
of the moon was to create so strange and "unhabitual" a spectacle
that the "grossest mind" could not but be affected. The appearance
of the moon created a new and astonishing world. Such a creation
by nature of a strange and new world is the "express resemblance",

> a genuine Counterpart
> And Brother of the glorious faculty
> Which higher minds bear with them as their own.[9]

Here is Coleridge's "secondary" imagination having expression
in verse. "Higher minds"

> from their native selves can send abroad
> Like transformation.[10]

They are "ever on the watch", "willing to work and to be
wrought upon";

> in a world of life they live,
> By sensible impressions not enthrall'd,
> But quicken'd, rouz'd, and made thereby more fit
> To hold communion with the invisible world.
> Such minds are truly from the Deity,
> For they are Powers; and hence the highest bliss
> That can be known is theirs, the consciousness
> Of whom they are habitually infused
> Through every image, and through every thought,
> And all impressions. . . .[11]

And hence, he adds, come "religion, faith, sovereignty within, and
peace at will". The creativity of the imagination in perception,
quickened in the life of the poet, leads on to, and is of a piece with,
the sense of a transcendent world. It was clearly Wordsworth's
view that the free development of the imagination is bound up
with a perception of the world as in itself fragmentary and unified
only in what is beyond itself. Such an imagination, operating in
and through "recognitions of transcendent power", is the condition of "freedom" and "genuine liberty", of an abiding reconciliation of emotion and peace.

[9] *Op. cit.*, XIII, 88–90.   [10] *Op. cit.*, XIII, 93–4.
[11] *Op. cit.*, XIII, 102–11.

2

Such was, we may believe, the essence of Wordsworth's doctrine
of the Imagination. But he did not continuously enjoy such an
imaginative life; for at the time of the Revolution he had not
integrated into his imaginative scheme recognition of the world's
suffering, pain, and evil. He responded to the Revolution with
overwhelming enthusiasm; and the effect upon him of the attitude
of the English Government, and then of the subsequent course of
the Revolution, was catastrophic. It may appear surprising to us,
when we consider the strongly religious character of his earlier
imaginative life, that he should have been absorbed so completely
in hopes of what he called

> Saturnian rule
> Returned, – a progeny of golden years
> Permitted to descend, and bless mankind.[12]

Certainly his sense of life was not so clear-eyed as was that of
Keats, who from the outset rejected any hopes of earthly happiness for mankind. Yet the fact remains that it seemed to Wordsworth that his view of life demanded, as a condition of its validity,
"Saturnian rule returned". Shocked, therefore, by what happened, he felt that the failure of the Revolution was destructive of
his imaginative life, and his confidence in what Keats was to call
the "truth" of the imagination. What happened, therefore, was a
revulsion from the imaginative way of life and a search for a
touchstone which could stand unshaken by circumstance. He
therefore fell back upon the discursive intelligence, and en-
deavoured to create, by its exercise, a way of life and an attitude to
the universe in which he might have a permanent confidence.
Later, Wordsworth was to formulate what he came to think was
the true relation of the discursive intelligence to the imagination.
But this he did only after he had recovered his belief in the
imagination. The faltering of his spirit before the facts of life
which he experienced during the course of the seventeen nineties found him unprepared by reflection on the relation of the
imagination to the intellect; and he was all the more inclined
to abandon the imagination because of the respect which, when

[12] *The Excursion*, III, 756–8.

at Cambridge, he had felt for mathematical inquiry. From such
studies

> I drew
> A pleasure quiet and profound, a sense
> Of permanent and universal sway,
> And paramount belief.

And he goes on to say:

> specially delightful unto me
> Was that clear synthesis built up aloft
> So gracefully.[13]

He sets this "clear synthesis" in opposition to the turgid condition
in which the mind is

> beset
> With images, and haunted by herself.[14]

Hence, when the passionate strength of his imagination was
weakened, it was inevitable that his mind should revert to the
clearness and certainty of intellectual inquiry which formerly he
had most intimately known in the field of greatest abstraction,
namely, mathematics. He turned naturally at this juncture to the
exercise of the intelligence, but no longer to the intelligence in its
activity of making

> an independent world,
> Created out of pure intelligence,[15]

but to the intelligence which seeks to discover a "clear synthesis"
of the world in its multiplicity, the concrete world of perception,
feeling, will, and also to arrive at clear principles of knowledge
and behaviour. In his first stage of doubt and despair he cheered
himself by taking to mind

> those truths
> That are the commonplaces of the schools . . .
> Yet, with a revelation's liveliness,
> In all their comprehensive bearings known
> And visible to philosophers of old.[16]

But after the Terror he spoke

---

[13] *The Prelude*, VI, 129–32, 161–3.　　[14] *Op. cit.*, VI, 159–60.
[15] *Op. cit.*, VI, 166–7.　　[16] *Op. cit.*, X, 191–2, 194–6.

>   with a voice
> Labouring, a brain confounded, and a sense,
> Death-like, of treacherous desertion, felt
> In the last place of refuge – my own soul.[17]

And from this point on he could no longer cheer himself with
the platitudes of ancient philosophy. If he was to recover, it would
be, he then knew, by hard reflexion compelled upon him by his own
experience, by a philosophy sprung from the necessity of destroy-
ing, if might be, his sense of "treacherous desertion" in his soul,
and built up as a permanent bulwark against further collapse of his
inner life.

>   Evidence
> Safer, of universal application, such
> As could not be impeached, was sought elsewhere.[18]

What he needed were

>   speculative schemes –
> That promised to abstract the hopes of Man
> Out of his feelings, to be fixed thenceforth
> For ever in a purer element.[19]

The result of this incursion into philosophy was disastrous – it
gave him over, not to a "clear synthesis", but to "despair".

>   So I fared,
> Dragging all precepts, judgments, maxims, creeds,
> Like culprits to the bar; calling the mind,
> Suspiciously, to establish in plain day
> Her titles and her honours; now believing,
> Now disbelieving; endlessly perplexed
> With impulse, motive, right and wrong, the ground
> Of obligation, what the rule and whence
> The sanction; till, demanding formal *proof*,
> And seeking it in every thing, I lost
> All feeling of conviction, and, in fine,
> Sick, wearied out with contrarieties,
> Yielded up moral questions in despair.[20]

[17] *Op. cit.*, X, 412–15.   [18] *Op. cit.*, XI, 203–5.
[19] *Op. cit.*, XI, 224–7.   [20] *Op. cit.*, XI, 293–305.

This rejection of philosophy was absolute, and there was no going back to it. No one ever had greater motive for philosophy than Wordsworth – it was a matter of life and death, an intellectual search behind which a passionate need was present. No doubt what training he had had in mathematics reinforced his sense of need in endeavouring to extract from philosophical reflexion a degree of clarity, of "clear synthesis" which philosophy is notoriously slow to supply, and set a standard of proof which he found philosophy incapable of sustaining. The demand for "formal proof", arising both from his mathematical training and from the insistence of his personal need, was inevitably left unsatisfied. He might seek escape in abstract science

> Where the disturbances of space and time –
> Whether in matters various, properties
> Inherent, or from human will and power
> Derived – find no admission.[21]

But this was merely escape, and he knew it. What certainties abstract science could supply were irrelevant to his need. Thus, with the total collapse of his belief in the "holiness of the heart's imagination", and the exasperation and despair to which philosophy brought him, he was completely adrift. A crisis had arisen in which he was helpless. The imagination carried within it no criterion of its truth; philosophy could supply no criterion of its truth or afford proof of that for which he hungered. All effort, all conscious direction of his energies, was stopped. There was nothing more he could do. He could but abandon effort; and in that abandonment remain.

In the third book of *The Excursion* Wordsworth retells this story, at least in part, in the character of the Solitary. The Solitary in *The Excursion* is the Wordsworth of his crisis, and is sharply set over against the Wanderer who is the Wordsworth who was afterwards matured and confirmed in his belief in the Imagination. In the Solitary, the rejection of life has gone to extreme lengths, paralysing action. Imagination and intellectual inquiry are not for him:

> Ah! What avails imagination high
> Or question deep? –[22]

[21] *Op. cit.*, XI, 330–3.   [22] *The Excursion*, III, 209–10.

and with this goes the extreme of despair:

> Night is than day more acceptable; sleep
> Doth, in my estimate of good, appear
> A better state than waking; death than sleep:
> Feelingly sweet is stillness after storm,
> Though under covert of the wormy ground![23]

The Solitary indeed, unlike Wordsworth, had known private grief: but it drove him to that state of agitated inquiry which was Wordsworth's after the Reign of Terror:

> Then my soul
> Turned inward, – to examine of what stuff
> Time's fetters are composed; and life was put
> To inquisition, long and profitless!
> By pain of heart – now checked – and now impelled –
> The intellectual power, through words and things,
> Went sounding on, a dim and perilous way![24]

From this condition he was restored by the hopes he fixed in the French Revolution: but the outcome was to plunge him more deeply than ever into the condition from which he had just escaped; a complete atrophy of his mental life set in.

> My business is,
> Roaming at large, to observe, and not to feel
> And, therefore, not to act – convinced that all
> Which bears the name of action, howsoe'er
> Beginning, ends in servitude – still painful,
> And mostly profitless.[25]

3

The Borderers is the one considerable work which dates from this period in Wordsworth's life. It has, therefore, a great significance as an additional comment upon his inner life at this time. *The Borderers* is a tragedy, for these few years were indeed Wordsworth's "tragic period"; and that he should have written what at no other period of his life he attempted to do – a tragedy – offers us the possibility of an illuminating comparison with those plays

[23] *Op. cit.*, 277–81.   [24] *Op. cit.*, 695–701.   [25] *Op. cit.*, 891–6.

of Shakespeare which convey the condition of Shakespeare's mind when he, like Wordsworth, knew a sense of "death-like, treacherous desertion". For our present purpose it is of more immediate importance to notice how the story of *The Borderers* is connected with the story of Wordsworth's own life and with the story of the Solitary. Both Oswald and Marmaduke are men to whom a grave wrong has been done; the sense of "death-like, treacherous desertion" has been theirs. Oswald and Marmaduke alike, through deception by others, have been made responsible for an innocent man's death. And the words of Marmaduke,

> the firm foundation of my life
> Is going from under me;[26]

and those of Oswald when, narrating his story to Marmaduke, he says

> for many days,
> On a dead sea under a burning sky,
> I brooded o'er my injuries, deserted
> By man and nature;[27]

alike spring from the condition which was also Wordsworth's condition. In all "desertion" is the key word; an unfair, cruel blow had been struck at one utterly undeserving of it, who trusted and believed his environment. The Solitary, Oswald, and Marmaduke are all the Wordsworth of this time. Indeed, Oswald uses words which are identical with those of the Solitary after the death of his wife and children:

> three nights
> Did constant meditation dry my blood;
> Three sleepless nights I passed in *sounding on,*
> *Through words and things, a dim and perilous way.*[28]

All three are men of nobility of imagination; all had known "rainbow arches", "highways of dreaming passion",

> What mighty objects do impress their forms
> To elevate our intellectual being.[29]

Thence had they been brought back to

[26] *The Borderers,* 547–8.   [27] *Op. cit.,* 1697–1700.
[28] *Op. cit.,* 1772–5.   [29] *Op. cit.,* 1809–10.

the unpretending ground we mortals tread.[30]

But while the Solitary, Marmaduke, and Oswald are one in these respects, the response of each to this identical situation is different. In the Solitary there occurs a revulsion from feeling, and therefore from action, a permanent numbing of sensibility; in Oswald it leads to deliberate evil; in Marmaduke to resignation and the life of religion, "in search of nothing that this earth can give".

There can be little doubt that it is Oswald who, though the villain of the piece, voices most of Wordsworth's thought and feeling of the time. In the play Wordsworth symbolises his own state as one suffering an unjust blow struck at a trusting and confident nature. Sensitive to the forms of nature, Oswald's disgust with humankind struck at his sense of our high "intellectual being"; what he now knew of

The World's opinions and her usages[31]

could not be reconciled in one personality with the life of the imagination and the contemplation of objects which "impress their forms to elevate our intellectual being". The latter, "a thing so great", must "perish self-consumed". Personality under these circumstances becomes split in two, a condition which, in Oswald's case, resolved itself, so far as it resolved itself at all, by a total rejection of moral sense. And though in part his treatment of Marmaduke was animated by resentment of a universe of experience which had betrayed him, a resentment which he vented on the conspicuous virtue of Marmaduke, it was also inspired by a certain inverted idealism, a pure assertion of the will, which sought to issue in an enlargement of "Man's intellectual empire". This pure, disinterested assertion of the will, concerned to maintain itself in disregard of good, became in the heart of Oswald a demand for a pure freedom, free from the soft claims of shame, ignorance, and love.

We subsist
In slavery; all is slavery; we receive
Laws, but we ask not whence those laws have come;
We need an inward sting to goad us on.[32]

That "inward sting" had come to Oswald as it had come to

[30] *Op. cit.*, 933.   [31] *Op. cit.*, 1816.   [32] *Op. cit.*, 1856–9.

Wordsworth. In the Solitary, Wordsworth later envisaged a person whom the "inward sting" had failed to goad into activity, leaving, after its first pain, a permanent numbness, a lasting extension of the chilling of life which he himself had for a while known. In Oswald, writing from the midst of this period of his life, he envisaged the other alternative, in which the sting became a "goad".

This condition of intellectual hate, of living in rebellion and a pure assertiveness, which was to be in later years a theme for the novels of Dostoevsky, never, it is probable, took considerable possession of Wordsworth's mind. It must, indeed, have occurred with unusual vividness to his imagination – *The Borderers* shows that it did. Yet over against Oswald is Marmaduke, embodying so different an attitude from that of Oswald that if what we have is what Wordsworth actually wrote in the years 1795 and 1796,[33] we are compelled to believe either that Wordsworth was never in the gravest danger of the pure rebellion of Oswald, or that, at the time of writing, he was recovering in some degree the previous condition of his mind. It is true that Marmaduke, believing, at Oswald's prompting, in the depravity of Herbert, reacted as Wordsworth at the time of the Terror had done, with a despair which believed the "world was poisoned at the heart"; yet he was able to say

> there was a plot,
> A hideous plot, against the soul of man:
> It took effect – and yet I baffled it,
> In *some* degree.[34]

Which he can say, a little priggishly indeed, because he killed Herbert, not with his sword but by leaving him exposed to cold and hunger, out of regard for a higher judgment than his own. And, instead of a goad to enraged activity, his action becomes an inducement to the way of religious humility and expiation:

> A Man by pain and thought compelled to live,
> Yet loathing life.[35]

[33] And we have Wordsworth's word for it that in all essentials it is. (For the composition of *The Borderers*, the date 1796–97 has been suggested: see the *Poetical Works*, eds. de Selincourt and Helen Darbishire, Vol. 1, p. 343.)

[34] *The Borderers*, 2112–5.   [35] *Op. cit.*, 2319–20.

There are three issues of this experience which is represented differently in the guise of fiction in *The Borderers* and *The Excursion*, yet in essence identical with that which Wordsworth himself suffered – first a lasting atrophy of the imagination and intellectual life, secondly a fierce effort to live a life in the greatest degree lawless, and thirdly the way of religious humility. Wordsworth was to re-discover the last. But, inevitably, he could not be the same; although, in all essentials, he was to find again the attitude to life which he asserted in the famous passage in Book VI, it had now become an attitude far more inclusive, an imaginative grasp of life richer and more comprehensive than formerly it was. For where formerly it was a vision of life irrelevant to and without knowledge of evil, crime, and suffering, it must now incorporate that knowledge into itself and be reconciled with it. Wordsworth now knew the unmitigated reality of evil and pain. Somehow, before he could be a man again, these facts must become part of a single imaginative grasp of things. He had known the bitterness of mind of a Stavrogin, the extremity of revolt; to forget this and to ignore the facts and realities from which such a condition takes its origin would necessarily mean a loss of integrity and self-respect. If his imaginative life, as formerly he knew it, was to return, it must be inclusive of all his experience and to that degree must be changed. To be led back

> through opening day
> To those sweet counsels between head and heart
> Whence grew that genuine knowledge, fraught with peace,[36]

was what was necessary to him, a "genuine knowledge" which might occur out of, and as a reconciliation of, the conflict of head and heart. Formerly his strong imaginative life was a natural growth, unimpeded by perplexity and conflict. That condition, indeed, could not last; it was too simple, too easily come by. Terror in some form was bound to come. And having come, it destroyed, or at least overcast, the vitality of his imaginative vision; and his head, saturated with realisations which in his youth did not exist for him, was unable to give liberation. Out of this condition he could not release himself. The vitality and energies of the imagination do not operate at will; they are fountains, not

[36] *The Prelude*, XI, 352–4.

machinery. And from his intellectual inquiry came no knowledge. Such a condition is, in a sense, final. There was no more that Wordsworth could do. Life was cut off from him,

> inwardly oppressed
> With sorrow, disappointment, vexing thoughts,
> Confusion of the judgment, zeal decayed,
> And, lastly, utter loss of hope itself
> And things to hope for![37]

Here is the nadir of descent from that view of the imaginative life of which he said:

> With hope it is, hope that can never die,
> Effort, and expectation, and desire,
> And something ever more about to be.[38]

4

After reviewing the restoration of his imaginative vitality, Wordsworth, although he has paid tribute to Dorothy and Coleridge for all they meant to him, insists upon the loneliness in which the imagination is nourished:

> Here keepest thou in singleness thy state:
> No other can divide with thee this work:
> No secondary hand can intervene
> To fashion this ability; 'tis thine,
> The prime and vital principle is thine
> In the recesses of thy nature, far
> From any reach of outward fellowship,
> Else is not thine at all.[39]

This "singleness of state" Wordsworth must have felt to an extreme degree during this period of his life, exhausted as he must have been by a sense of his own helplessness. Yet, in his helplessness, it was his early imaginative life which stood him in greatest stead; and what returned to him was not, at first, the joyous and abounding vitality of his earlier years, but recollection

---

[37] *Op. cit.*, xii, 3–7.   [38] *Op. cit.*, vi, 606–8.
[39] *Op. cit.*, xiv, 211–18.

of two incidents which from this time on were to be a type of symbol very frequent throughout his poetry. It is worth while pausing to comment at length upon them; for, in looking back, he realised, through the memory of these incidents, that his imagination in years gone by had been acquainted with something of the desolation which in greater degree he had since known. Both the incidents relate to death, and to a natural scene associated in each case with death. In the first he describes how he had stumbled upon an old and mouldering gibbet, and saw, carved out in the turf near by, the name of a murderer who had been hanged there. He fled "faltering and faint, and ignorant of the road". In his terror he climbed to a point whence he saw

> A naked pool that lay beneath the hills,
> The beacon on the summit, and, more near,
> A girl, who bore a pitcher on her head,
> And seemed with difficult steps to force her way
> Against the blowing wind. It was, in truth,
> An ordinary sight; but I should need
> Colours and words that are unknown to man,
> To paint the visionary dreariness
> Which, while I looked all round for my lost guide,
> Invested moorland waste, and naked pool,
> The beacon crowning the lone eminence,
> The female and her garments vexed and tossed
> By the strong wind.[40]

The second incident, of identically the same quality, describes his ascent to a crag from which he could see two roads, along either of which he was feverishly and impatiently awaiting horses whereby he might return home.

> 'twas a day
> Tempestuous, dark, and wild, and on the grass
> I sate half-sheltered by a naked wall;
> Upon my right hand couched a single sheep,
> Upon my left a blasted hawthorn stood.[41]

Some days afterwards his father died; the event at once carried back his imagination to

[40] *Op. cit.*, XII, 249–61.   [41] *Op. cit.*, XII, 297–301.

> The single sheep, and the one blasted tree,
> And the bleak music from that old stone wall.[42]

And his imagination of the scene became for him a fountain whence he drank. Wordsworth clearly attaches an enormous importance to these two incidents; and to his recollection of them at this period of his life. Recalled from a time when his imagination was strong and growing, they had a peculiar significance for him now. They contained, he came to see, a dissolvent of his present condition, a "renovating virtue". They had left "power behind", and

> feeling comes in aid
> Of feeling, and diversity of strength
> Attends us, if but once we have been strong.[43]

"If but once we have been strong." Wordsworth recalled that not once, but twice, he had been strong, and had found imaginative vision in which strong feelings of revulsion and pain had been absorbed or had purgation. What, then, was the secret of the power of these incidents upon his troubled mind?

In the second incident, the scene came to have "visionary dreariness" only after his father's death; his response to it while waiting for the horses was negligible – he was merely impatient to be gone. It became, in all truth, an object to his imagination only after sorrow had come. In the first, the desolate scenery had stirred him as he fled in terror from the thought of the hanged murderer. In both cases the scene was bare, wild, swept with wind and mist, untouched by gentleness or softness of colour; in both were features marked by a curious stillness; in the one, the naked pool, the beacon, the girl bearing a pitcher on her head; in the other, the sheep, the tree, the stone wall – all set around with tempest and vast expanse. It is this which, in each case, held his imagination, reconciled peace with tempest, calm with emotion, an "emblem of eternity", an overwhelming sense of "something ever more about to be". It is no wonder that in the revulsion and numbness of mind at the time he recalled this experience:

> I should need
> Colours and words that are unknown to man,
> To paint the visionary dreariness.[44]

[42] *Op. cit.*, XII, 319–20.　　[43] *Op. cit.*, XII, 269–71.　　[44] *Op. cit.*, XII, 254–6.

Here, we may be sure, more than even the ministrations of Coleridge and Dorothy, were places of power which on revealing themselves in the "recesses of his nature", renewed his imagination. He knew then that he was no further changed

> Than as a clouded and a waning moon.[45]

His past had reappeared to succour him. And from this time on his imagination, in all its variety of activity, centred around, as its highest objects of contemplation, images of a like type, men and women who knew the extreme of desolation and suffering, creatures of curious impassivity, who in the midst of "dreariness" seem to be almost terrifying intimations of "otherness". In speaking of the restoration of his imaginative life he made special mention of the two incidents which we have quoted, incidents dating back to early years: but it is to be noticed that in the poem are recounted two other incidents, of a like kind, incidents which no doubt had been brought back vividly to his mind when he had realised the significance of the incidents relating to the gibbet and his father's death. They are to be found in Book IV and Book VII. That in Book IV describes a soldier whom he met on a road, in moonlight:

> He was alone,
> Had no attendant, neither Dog, nor Staff,
> Nor knapsack; in his very dress appear'd
> A desolation, a simplicity
> That seem'd akin to solitude. Long time
> Did I peruse him with a mingled sense
> Of fear and sorrow. From his lips, meanwhile,
> There issued murmuring sounds, as if of pain
> Or of uneasy thought; yet still his form
> Kept the same steadiness; and at his feet
> His shadow lay, and mov'd not.[46]

Here, again, is desolation, and again a terrifying acquiescence:

> and when, erelong,
> I ask'd his history, he in reply
> Was neither slow nor eager; but unmov'd,

[45] *Op. cit.*, XI, 344.   [46] *The Prelude* (1805), IV, 415-25.

And with a quiet, uncomplaining voice,
A stately air of mild indifference,
He told, in simple words, a Soldier's tale. . . .[47]

and throughout the telling of his story there was in all he said

a strange half-absence, and a tone
Of weakness and indifference, as of one
Remembering the importance of his theme
But feeling it no longer.[48]

In the seventh book Wordsworth describes a beggar whom he
saw in London, on his chest a label telling who the man was and
his story:

My mind did at this spectacle turn round
As with the might of waters, and it seem'd
To me that in this Label was a type,
Or emblem, of the utmost that we know,
Both of ourselves and of the universe;
And, on the shape of the unmoving man,
His fixèd face and sightless eyes, I look'd
As if admonished from another world.[49]

So it is with the Leech Gatherer "from some far region sent";
in all alike is the extremity of suffering and desolation coupled with
composure, unmoving and awful.

There can be no doubt that it was in the contemplation of such
scenes and personages as this that Wordsworth's imagination
reached its highest limit. He could never, to reiterate Keats, have
seen these scenes and these men as he describes them had he not
"committed himself to the Extreme"; and certainly his ability to
recall them from his past and to contemplate them marks the full
restoration of his powers. It was not, indeed, that he effected such
a restoration; his restoration was a gift to him from his early
imagination which in its young strength had been able to encompass and grasp all that the scenes described in Book XII represented.
In them sweet counsels between heart and head are re-established;
a finality of desolation is incorporated into a supreme object of

---

[47] *Op. cit.*, IV, 440–5. [48] *Op. cit.*, IV, 475–8.
[49] *Op. cit.*, VII, 615–22.

imaginative contemplation, reconciled with vision, and suggestive "of unknown modes of being". There is a sense in which, humanly speaking, such imaginative vision is final. It is the stage to which Keats's young Apollo had come when he cried:

> Names, deeds, grey legends, dire events, rebellions,
> Majesties, sovran voices, agonies,
> Creations and destroyings, all at once
> Pour into the wide hollows of my brain,
> And deify me.[50]

In all these passages the greatest dreariness and dereliction is melted into the visionary, and lost in it; suffering, known in the extreme, is invested, more than aught else could be, with the sense of something "ever more about to be", so that the soldier, telling the story of his life, spoke as one who, "remembering the importance of his theme", yet felt it no longer.

Once Wordsworth had reached this phase in the growth of his imagination, it became true of him that knowing too well the importance of the story of human life and suffering, he felt it no longer. For over the abyss hung the world of vision. It was not that he became insensitive to the spectacle of human evil and pain, but that over it lay suspended the firmament of otherness. The overwhelming sense of the unknown, the unforeseen, which visited him when he had crossed the Alps, was now with him in his contemplation of the deepest suffering and apparent dereliction. And in the attainment to this sense in the face of pain and destitution lay the full restoration of his imaginative power. His imagination had now encompassed with the feeling of Infinity not only the world of nature, but the world of man. The importance of that world he could never indeed deny, or wish to deny; but he could "feel it no longer" in the same degree. "So still an image of tranquillity, so calm and still" could he now maintain in himself that

> what we feel of sorrow and despair
> From ruin and from change, and all the grief
> That passing shows of Being leave behind,
> Appeared an idle dream.[51]

In other words, Wordsworth had come to see the error which he

[50] Keats, *Hyperion*, III, 114–18.   [51] *The Excursion*, I, 949–52.

had made in thinking that his early view of the life of imagination was bound up with a return of "Saturnian rule". Actually, as he came to see, in recollecting those early days, his experience had contained within itself the answer to the questions which in his time of crisis he asked and could not answer. And indeed it was not that his early imaginative powers were inadequate to meeting that crisis; instead, he had allowed himself to become absorbed in a passionate social idealism to a degree which blinded him to the power and adequacy of his imagination to include in its synthesis the whole world of human suffering. He thought, overwhelmed by a disappointment accompanied by a sense of human evil greater than than anything he had known before, that his life was destroyed, and all foundations for the future destroyed. But in reality, all that was necessary was the exploration in memory of his former days of imaginative vitality. "The days gone by return upon me"; and those days proved "hiding-places" of his power. It was not that his imagination had failed him, but that he had failed his imagination. Natural as it was that, when a very young man, he had abandoned himself to revolutionary ardour, yet it was the recollection of his imaginative experiences, above all those which were vitally associated with pain, terror, and sorrow, which saved him. Then he was able to see that his imagination, which in his younger days could invest dreariness with vision, might do so again. It was not that his revolutionary ardour had been misplaced or mistaken; no one, I think, would judge that it was. What had been misplaced was the effort, however unconsciously made, by his imagination, to circumvent the fact of evil and suffering – the refusal to see them as inevitable to human life. But the result of his revolutionary experiences was more than ever to thrust them before his eyes, even to the point of paralysing his powers. Then there was no escape; and he was delighted and surprised to find that in himself and "days gone by" lay the power to encompass all the degradation of human life with his imagination. He was thus able to see the French Revolution as the "weak functions of one busy day" set over against the "slowly moving years of time, with their united force", the years of effort and suffering which even no return of "Saturnian rule" could blot out for an imagination which in its contemplation of life seeks to maintain its integrity.

Within the soul a faculty abides,
That with interpositions, which would hide
And darken, so can deal that they become
Contingencies of pomp; and serve to exalt
Her native brightness.[52]

What had come to him was an extension of the power of imagination which he had enjoyed in his youth. If he rejected that power
for a while, the circumstances of that rejection proved but "contingencies of pomp". "The sense of possible sublimity", which
he had known in the presence of nature, to which he felt the soul
aspires

With faculties still growing, feeling still
That whatsoever point they gain, they yet
Have something to pursue,[53]

he now felt with, if possible, a still greater force, his mind "caught
. . . as with the might of waters", in the presence of what is,
humanly, a total dereliction. The infinity of the soul's aspiration,
so that however far it moves and grows there is always a "something", the vast unknown dimly apprehended before it, became
now the "main theme of his song"; a "something" so real that in
comparison sorrow, despair, ruin, change, and grief are but "the
passing shows of Being", an "idle dream". The triumph of his
imagination, or better, the restoration to him of imaginative
power, was the apprehension, however dim, of "Infinitude" as the
necessary complement and completion not only of the beauty of
nature, but of the extremity of suffering. Now that this realisation,
or this imaginative grasp of reality, had been made in his mind, it
was natural and indeed inevitable that the dogmas of Christianity
should increasingly appear to his mind as a consummate convey-
ance of all that he had learnt; and his increasing humility before
Christianity is surely a mark not of the decay, as is so often rashly
thought, of his imagination, but of the consummation of it. His
gratification in realising that all that he had learnt, by "proof upon
the pulses", in the loneliness of his imagination, "in singleness of
state", was embodied in the tradition of Christianity must indeed
have been tempered with a sorrowful and healthy humiliation. He
was no longer

[52] Op. cit., IV, 1058–62.   [53] The Prelude, II, 320–2.

Voyaging through strange seas of Thought, *alone*; [54]

he was no longer

sounding on,
Through words and things, a dim and perilous way; [55]

he had found community. His greatest poetry is indeed the story
and expression of his lonely voyaging. But if his imagination in
those later days found adequacy and rest in forms of expression not
his own, it is not for critics to assume, as they have been so quick
to do, that his life degenerated at its source.[56]

5

Of the relation of poetry to religion we shall try to speak in a later
chapter.[57] There is occasion, however, at this point to observe the
attitude which, after the restoration of his mental health, Wordsworth adopted towards science, an attitude which showed that
Wordsworth never arrived at a harmonised view of human experience. Holding the view of the imagination which I have tried
to set out earlier in this essay, Wordsworth never tired of setting
over against the direct creativity of the imagination

that false secondary power
By which we multiply distinctions, then
Deem that our puny boundaries are things
That we perceive, and not that we have made.[58]

In the same passage, immediately preceding that in which he writes
of the imagination in the earliest years of the mind, we find the
following lines, in which Coleridge is addressed:

[54] *Op. cit.*, III, 63.   [55] *The Borderers*, 1774-5.
[56] Some time after the above was written, a reference in an article on A. C.
Bradley in *The Times Literary Supplement* (23 May 1936), led me to read (what,
to my shame, perhaps, I had not formerly read) Bradley's lecture on Wordsworth in *Oxford Lectures*. The reader who feels that in the above section I
have over-emphasised one aspect of Wordsworth's imaginative life may be
advised to read Bradley's remarkable lecture.
[57] See Chapter VIII of *Scepticism and Poetry*, of which this essay forms
Chapter V.
[58] *The Prelude*, II, 216-19.

to thee
Science appears but what in truth she is,
Not as our glory and our absolute boast,
But as a succcedaneum, and a prop
To our infirmity.[59]

It is difficult not to be puzzled by these lines, written by one who
at a time of the greatest "infirmity" sought a "succedaneum" and
a "prop" in intellectual and scientific inquiry, and signally failed
to find one. During that time he despaired, as we have noticed, of
philosophy; science, by its very security "from disturbances of
space and time", might be an escape: but by its very irrelevance to
his life, "to human will and power", it could not conceivably help
him. Whether, therefore, in the passage quoted he means by
"science" the discursive intelligence in all its operations, or
physical science in a strict sense, it is difficult to see how he could
write of it as a "succedaneum" or "prop". For it was precisely as
a succedaneum, something we fall back upon, a substitute source
of power, that it had failed him. If his experience was an adequate
guidance, it was neither our glory, absolute boast, succedaneum
nor prop. Yet he continued to cleave to this sentimental view of
science. In the fourth book of *The Excursion*, in other respects one
of the very greatest pieces of Wordsworth's work, his attitude to
intellectual inquiry is childish and condescending, mistaken in
thought and false in feeling. Go, he says,

demand
Of mighty Nature, if 'twas ever meant
They we should pry far off yet be unraised;
That we should pore, and dwindle as we pore,
Viewing all objects unremittingly
In disconnexion dead and spiritless . . .
waging thus
An impious warfare with the very life
Of our own souls![60]

Certainly, if the exercise of the intelligence necessarily implied an
atrophy of imaginative powers, one could understand such an
outburst. But it is only a superficial view of the intellectual life

[59] *Op. cit.*, II, 211-15.   [60] *The Excursion*, IV, 957-62, 966-8.

which implies that this is so. Wordsworth writes in resentment of the life of intellectual inquiry. But why? Wordsworth should surely have seen that there is as urgent a practical and moral necessity to exercise the intelligence to the full extent of its powers as to exercise the powers of the imagination. And later, we find the following:

> Science then
> Shall be a precious visitant; and then,
> And only then, be worthy of her name:
> For then her heart shall kindle; her dull eye,
> Dull and inanimate, no more shall hang
> Chained to its object in brute slavery . . .

nor:

> Shall it forget that its most noble use,
> Its most illustrious province, must be found
> In furnishing clear guidance, a support
> Not treacherous, to the mind's *excursive* power.[61]

This is the height of nonsense. Such a condescending attitude to science is merely silly; and condescendingly to justify science at all by holding that it can, if it behaves itself nicely, give evidence and support to the "excursive power" is not only utterly mistaken but false to Wordsworth's own experience. It is monstrous to seek to justify science and philosophy by any other than intellectual values; it is still more monstrous that Wordsworth should thus ignore all that his experience had most clearly taught him. Had he reflected a little more he would have seen, what indeed he should have seen from his own experience, that science is simply irrelevant to the problems of life. Wordsworth no doubt was right to give pride of place to the imagination: but it is merely an insult to science patronisingly to offer it second place, and that on condition that it furnishes "clear guidance" and "a support not treacherous" to the creative imagination. The fact is that science can no more offer clear guidance or reliable support to the imagination than it can offer false guidance or doubtful support to the imagination; and there was a time in Wordsworth's life when he saw this, compelled on him as it was by the very anguish of his experience. And

[61] *Op. cit.*, IV, 1251–6, 1260–3.

equally his enjoyment of mathematics should have saved him from such mistaken condescension to the intellectual life. The Arab of his Cambridge dream was concerned to save mathematics as well as poetry from the general deluge. And there was no reason why Wordsworth should not combine in his reflexion both a knowledge of the essential irrelevance of science and mathematics to the problem of life, and a recognition of their worth and joys. This, however, he failed to do, however nearly we may judge, in reviewing his story, he came to succeeding. He was right in his perception that what knowledge science can give is "secondary" and abstract. But he was not true enough to his own experience to conclude with a recognition of what is, from the point of view of the imaginative life, the unimportance of scientific knowledge.[62] Had he gone the whole length of this realisation he would not have been tempted to such a pompous patronage of science nor sought from science "aids and supports". The imagination, he tells us in the Preface to the *Lyrical Ballads*, is, in contrast to the detachment of science, part and parcel of our life "as enjoying and suffering beings", the apprehension by personality, in action and emotion, of the world. "If the time should ever come," he goes on to say, "when what is now called science, thus familiarised to men, shall be ready to put on, as it were, a form of flesh and blood, the Poet will lend his divine spirit to aid the transfiguration." This is, indeed, eloquent; but such a transfiguration is as undesirable as it is impossible, an absurd fiction created for an eloquent argument more passionate than careful. He says rightly that science must seek to view all objects unremittingly

In disconnexion dead and spiritless;[63]

but this "deathly and bloodless" condition is for science a condition of its life; and to resent it, or wish it changed, is the merest peevishness. And equally foolish is it to expect science to offer "props and stays"; for as Wordsworth himself recognised, science simply is not concerned with the values which are "flesh and

[62] That this is so is shown by the fact that the issue between a mechanistic and purposive view of the universe stands today precisely where it did when Socrates read the works of Anaxagoras. Similarly, despite a widespread illusion to the contrary, it is absurd to suggest that Freud's psychology has in the slightest degree affected the agelong conflict of freedom *versus* determinism.

[63] *The Excursion*, IV, 962.

blood" to the life of personality. Though one hesitates to quarrel with a statement which has won such universal quotation and respect, it is nevertheless difficult to see how poetry is the "breath and finer spirit of all knowledge", and how it is the "impassioned expression which is in the countenance of all science". At a later date Wordsworth was to deplore the viewing of things in "disconnexion dead and spiritless" and to urge that to do so is to "wage an impious warfare on the soul". The countenance of activity such as that would hardly bear the "impassioned expression" which Wordsworth claims poetry to be. And Wordsworth cannot have it both ways. It is merely rhetoric to say that science is really a poetical affair. On the other hand, it is equally absurd to say, as Wordsworth says in *The Excursion*, that science is a kind of demoralising "prying".

Wordsworth's mature view of human nature failed to embrace a clear comprehension of the relation of the imaginative to the intellectual life. But on the other hand, his perception of the relation of imagination to morality was clear and sure. Here at least he stood on sure ground. He grounded his moral sense in the contemplative life which gives release from immersion in action and emotion. And in *The Prelude*, at least (and he did not see fit to change it in the later version), it is the discipline of the contemplative life lived in intimacy with nature which he sets over against the formal discipline of religious observances as the condition of moral health. It is in the potency of "a mere image of the sway" of solitude that the self which is the seat of true morality finds itself. The moral life, that is to say, flows naturally from the discipline of quietude. In such a discipline, he held, is the condition of a true morality, springing not from imposed precept, and proof therefore against "shock of accident". Such morality therefore cannot be sought for itself; it is a product of a life animated by

> The universal instinct of repose,
> The longing for confirmed tranquillity,[64]

which is, indeed, the life of the imagination, craving peace

> Not as a refuge from distress or pain,
> A breathing-time, vacation, or a truce,
> But for its absolute self.[65]

[64] *Op. cit.*, III, 397–8.　　　　　[65] *Op. cit.*, III, 383–5.

And in such a life the forms of nature, a world of life at peace, are the paramount and lasting influence. Sought for their own beauty, they give the imagination freedom from the urgency of will and emotion, creating thereby "stability without regret or fear".

Roger Sharrock

WORDSWORTH'S REVOLT
AGAINST LITERATURE[1]

Wordsworth's was a revolt of a nature and importance which perhaps no literary revolt had before. It was a revolt against literature, or the literary element in poetry, an assertion of the supreme value of life at all costs in poetry.[2]

Wordsworth's revolt against the poetic diction of the later eighteenth century, and the expository convenience of this for the purposes of the literary historian, have obscured the more icono-clastic notes of the *Preface* of 1800. Helen Darbishire reminds us that the revolt was directed, not against the excesses of any one literary tradition, but against "the literary element in poetry". Critics, readers, and parodists of Wordsworth have, of course, been aware of the *consequence* of this iconoclasm: the aridity of poetic speech found in *Lyrical Ballads*, and less frequently in later poems. This, indeed, has become the crux of Wordsworthian criticism. Some have deplored the aridity, and attributed to it the bathos and prosing of the less successful ballads; they have usually followed Coleridge's dangerous implication that Wordsworth is most him-self as a poet when he forgets his theories. Remembering J. K. Stephen's irreverent sonnet, we may label them the Two Voices school of Wordsworth critics. Others have felt that the theories did not necessarily result in inferior poetry; penetrating further towards an understanding of his central ideas, they have found something of this unliterary starkness and simplicity in the highest moments of his work. But the critical principles involved have

[1] Reprinted from *Essays in Criticism*, Vol. III, 1953, pp. 396–412.
[2] Helen Darbishire, *The Poet Wordsworth*. Oxford, 1950, p. 53.

remained unexplored. If we look again at the more curious passages in the *Preface*, where Wordsworth, a poet, expresses a profound dissatisfaction with literature, we can learn some of the reasons for both the successes and failures among his attempts to create a poetry freed from literary shackles.

The following is perhaps the most striking passage:

> While [the Poet] describes and imitates passions, his situation is altogether slavish and mechanical, compared with the freedom and power of real and substantial action and suffering.[3]

We start off, then, from a radical pessimism about poetry's capacity for recording experience, and, as a corollary of this, a view of its ideal function as *photographic*, which is in complete contradiction to the creative view of the poetic imagination developed elsewhere by both Wordsworth and Coleridge. Helen Darbishire has pointed out the paradoxical character of this pessimism:

> Has any other poet at any time held this perverse belief that poetry has *less* freedom and power to express human feeling than the human actors and sufferers themselves whose experience the poet tries to render?[4]

Wordsworth continues:

> So that it will be the wish of the Poet to bring his feelings near to those of the persons whose feelings he describes, nay, for short spaces of time, perhaps, to let himself slip into an entire delusion, and even confound and identify his own feelings with theirs; modifying only the language which is thus suggested to him by a consideration that he describes for a particular purpose, that of giving pleasure ... he will feel that there is no necessity to trick out or to elevate nature: and, the more industriously he applies this principle, the deeper will be his faith that no words, which *his* fancy or imagination can suggest, will be to be compared with those which are the emanations of reality and truth.[5]

This belief in the dignity of the subject as it is in nature, before the poet begins to embellish it, is widespread in the aesthetic

[3] *Preface* to the 2nd edn., London, 1802. The Poetical Works, eds. de Selincourt and Helen Darbishire, Oxford, 1940–9, Vol. II, p. 394.
[4] *The Poet Wordsworth*, p. 52.   [5] *Preface* to the 2nd edn., p. 394.

E

thought of the romantic epoch. As the change in taste during the later eighteenth century shifted attention from the poem as artifact to the aesthetic experience, it became convenient to consider poetic experience alongside cognate psychological phenomena, the sublime feelings aroused by natural scenery, or the benevolent social instincts prized alike by poets and moralists. In other words, the centre of interest moved from the poem as literary creation to that "poetry" which may be found in nature or in sublime actions. This extension of the term can be found in Hazlitt and in Keats's early poems:

> Many people suppose that poetry is something to be found only in books, contained in lines of ten syllables, with like endings: but wherever there is a sense of beauty, or power, or harmony, as in the motion of a wave of the sea, in the growth of a flower that "spreads its sweet leaves to the air, and dedicates its beauty to the sun", – *there* is poetry, in its birth.[6]

> For what has made the sage or poet write
> But the fair paradise of Nature's light?[7]

Wordsworth's belief in the superiority of "real and substantial action and suffering" over its rendering in verse bears some relation to this psychological type of poetic theory: but his view is distinguished from it by a deep pessimism concerning the adequacy of language as a means of communication. The view of the "poetry of nature" found in Hazlitt and Keats is expansive and inspirational. The poet surveys a large realm of natural activity to which his sensitive responses hold the key. But Wordsworth's sense of the poetic richness of nature is balanced by a melancholy concern with the limitations of language. While the younger romantics write like visionaries, for whom there is no problem of expression, because the poetry of the word is a simple reflexion of the poetry of the world, he speaks as a man nearer to the neoclassical tradition, for whom poetry means making in words;[8] and,

---

[6] W. Hazlitt, *Lectures on the English Poets*, Lecture 1. London, 1818–19.

[7] John Keats, "I Stood Tip-Toe", 125–6.

[8] *Cf.* Rachel Trickett, *The Honest Muse: A Study in Augustan Verse*. Oxford, 1967, pp. 280–1: ". . . the same careful labouring for words which mean no more nor less than he can say with honesty . . . is present in Wordsworth's strange power of conveying elementary impressions, even abstract ideas".

as maker, he confronts a situation in which the tools crumble in his hands.

A pessimism so bleak about the possibilities of poetic language could not be sustained for long by any writer who was to go on writing. One might say that, though every imaginative writer is liable to such pessimism at some stage of the creative process, creation takes place just in proportion to his power to overcome it and break down those materials of experience which seem so impervious to literary catalysis. M. Maurice Blanchot has suggested that dissatisfaction with the linguistic means at his disposal – contempt for literature in the face of experience – is in fact always a prelude to the emergence of an individual style.[9]

Wordsworth was certainly not a consistent pessimist about language; he was highly productive, and even in the period immediately preceding the composition of *Lyrical Ballads* he was able to write a number of longish poems. Moreover, apart from this practical testimony, the *Preface* itself is not a consistent statement of the pessimistic view. That view is expressed with such assurance in the passage quoted above, and its implications are so devastating, that some of Wordsworth's departures from it in the course of his general argument may be considered as in the nature of evasions, expedients called up to temper the harsher consequences of his beliefs. However this may be, the statement about the validity of poetry as a mode of apprehending truth which occurs among the additions to the *Preface* in 1802 does not seem to be a mere evasion. It is very near to being a flat contradiction of the anti-literary argument, and it has an air of profound conviction about it that makes it one of the most eloquent passages in the *Preface*. It is introduced as an answer to those who would agree with him in perceiving a gap between human language and human passion, but who would do nothing to bridge it, preferring to accept a state of affairs in which the poet is always in the situation of a translator "who does not scruple to substitute excellencies of another kind for those which are unattainable by him". This "would be to encourage idleness and unmanly despair", for poetry is not a matter of artificial amusement:

Aristotle, I have been told, has said, that Poetry is the most

[9] Maurice Blanchot, *Faux Pas*. Paris (Gallimard) 1943, pp. 97–107.

philosophic of all writing: it is so: its object is truth, not individual and local, but general, and operative; not standing upon external testimony, but carried alive into the heart by passion; truth which is its own testimony, which gives competence and confidence to the tribunal to which it appeals, and receives them from the same tribunal. Poetry is the image of man and nature.[10]

The contradiction between this view and the other one is especially prominent in the last sentence; we may compare it with an earlier phrase, employing a similar metaphor, but with a different and pessimistic intention: "Those passions, certain shadows of which the Poet thus produces, or feels to be produced in himself." The contradiction may partly be explained as the result of an emotional recoil from the nihilism of the other viewpoint; I use nihilism advisedly, because it does not seem likely that anyone would entertain such a disbelief in the communicability of moral experience without implying a solipsistic view of that experience and a rejection of metaphysical or social patterns of any kind. But this is not the place to consider the post-Godwinian despair of the *Guilt and Sorrow* period, intimately related though it is to Wordsworth's linguistic crisis. It is sufficient to notice that the recoil is justified by an appeal to the traditional Aristotelian conception of the generalising power of poetry; the poet can combine general truth and its particular application, without being subject to the abstractions of the philosopher or the amoral particulars of the historian. (It is the argument of Sidney and Shelley.)

In the context of this passage, Wordsworth's despair over literature may be seen as a creative despair. Some such feeling precedes the long period of germination which an experience undergoes in the mind, and which is followed by that recollection and re-creation described in the most familiar part of the *Preface*. In *The Prelude* and *The Excursion* he discoursed more fully on the creative power of the imagination, and developed a view of it as a plastic faculty, intuitively ordering the raw material of experience, analogous to the Kantian position of Coleridge. This view is foreshadowed in the 1802 addition on the autonomy of poetry, but as Garrod has noted, the imagination is only mentioned twice in the

[10] *Preface* to the 2nd edn., pp. 394-5.

course of the *Preface*; and after this passage the *Preface* again becomes a document of anti-literary pessimism. The whole Wordsworthian theory of poetic diction is a concession to this despair: it represents an attempt to abolish any diction, any literary medium, in favour of the only words which can convey the object or experience as nakedly as possible, the words of the original participants in the action. "What has been thus far said applies to Poetry in general; but especially to those parts of composition where the Poet speaks through the mouths of his characters . . . the dramatic parts of composition are defective, in proportion as they deviate from the real language of nature." The qualification of the original battle-cry of 1798 ("the language of the lower and middle classes of society") which caused it to become in 1802 "a selection of the language really used by men", only emphasises his photographic (or phonographic) conception of the language proper to poetry. For the stress is upon the retention of speech, visual observations, or states of emotion, not their transmutation. It is now recognised that they may be retained only in part, and the selection is carried out by that "more lively sensibility" which alone distinguishes the poet from other men. We may say that this is again a way of admitting imagination by the back door: but it is to be suspected that Wordsworth thought of the selection as belonging more to nature and universal sympathy than to the skill of the poet: the emotions behind the significant words throw them into a high light, and the poet simply picks out these significant commonplaces.

The pessimistic, anti-literary argument is faithfully adhered to in the experiments in the first edition of *Lyrical Ballads*. In poems like "The Thorn", "The Last of the Flock", and "The Idiot Boy", the characters speak for themselves: their banalities are offered as the safest mode of interpreting "the great primary human affections", and "the poetry is in the pity". "The Thorn" is peculiarly interesting, because it is entirely dramatic. Wordsworth never wrote the introductory poem he intended for it, and the whole story of the abandoned woman is told, in character, by a market-town bore, the retired "Captain of a small trading vessel". If we remember this, we can agree with Thomas Hutchinson that the notorious lines

I've measured it from side to side:
'Tis three feet long, and two feet wide.[11]

are "perhaps the most dramatically fit and proper in the whole ballad". Wordsworth wanted, as he explains in the note to the poem added in 1800, "to exhibit some of the general laws by which superstition acts upon the mind", and he chose to do this through a psychological study of a person who is slow-witted, credulous, and talkative, but therefore *imaginative* (in the full Coleridgean sense: his unsophisticated repetitions "produce impressive effects out of simple elements"). But the real subject of the poem, of course, is the woman's tragedy, not the sea-captain's superstitious nature, though Wordsworth's interest in the dramatic vehicle he employs, both in the 1800 note and in the poem itself, has tended to obscure the emotional core of the work. "The Thorn" is a vision of desolation and alienation from human society which is similar to that of other poems about betrayed or unfortunate women written in the post-Godwinian period. But only rarely does this emotion of utter dereliction stand out from the dramatised narration:

> At all times of the day and night
> This wretched Woman thither goes;
> And she is known to every star,
> And every wind that blows;
> And there beside the Thorn she sits
> When the blue day-light's in the skies,
> And when the whirlwind's on the hill,
> Or frosty air is keen and still,
> And to herself she cries,
> "Oh misery! oh misery!
> Oh woe is me! oh misery!"[12]

Here there is nothing in the simple words which the Two Voices school could censure as bathos; the slight arbitrariness of some of the descriptive lines merely suggests the near-craziness of the woman's mind. But in other stanzas, except for the repetition of the stark refrain, the emotion and the language of the narrator fall out of focus; banality is predominant:

[11] "The Thorn", 32-3.   [12] *Op. cit.*, 67-77.

> You'd say that they were bent
> With plain and manifest intent
> To drag it to the ground.
>
> Oh me! ten thousand times I'd rather
> That he had died, that cruel father.
>
> Old farmer Simpson did maintain . . .
>
> And then the wind! in faith it was
> A wind full ten times over.[13]

But when Wordsworth wrote like this in "The Thorn" he was not turning to a secondary subject, the delineation of the sea-captain's psychology by means of his tricks of speech. The sea-captain with his banality and repetitions was chosen because they provide the most fitting medium for an experience which defies language by its tragic poignancy. To quote Wordsworth's note again: "The Reader cannot be too often reminded that Poetry is passion: it is the history or science of feelings: now every man must know that an attempt is rarely made to communicate impassioned feelings without something of an accompanying consciousness of the inadequacy of our powers, or the deficiencies of language." These banalities, which literary criticism must consider as uncongenial to the pathos of the subject, constitute an attempt to present the experience in its pure state without literary contamination. The verbosity of an unsophisticated but sensitive narrator affords a well-established method of presenting passion or emotion, and even intensifying it. A similar technique of clichés and repetitions is to be found in much American prose fiction of this century, and especially in Faulkner and Hemingway. When two characters in a novel by Faulkner (*Soldiers' Pay*) enter a drug-store and ask the girl behind the counter "How much is pie?" and she replies, "Pie is ten cents", the selected commonplaces have made a contribution towards the required impression of boredom and frustration more effective than any piece of literary evocation. In the case of Hemingway, the polished handling of apparently incoherent statements about sensations or mental states has been developed to a high pitch. But the technique of incoherent repetition is unsuited to the self-conscious and intellectual narrators; Wordsworth does

[13] *Op. cit.*, 18–20, 131–2, 138, 179–80.

better by choosing as narrators people like the sea-captain who would really think and talk in commonplaces.

Again, in "The Last of the Flock", though the shepherd's story contains lines like:

> Oft-times I thought to run away;
> For me it was a woeful day.[14]

the method of unvarnished statement bears fruit at the end in the moving simplicity of:

> Today I fetched it from the rock;
> It is the last of all my flock.[15]

In 1798 the last lines of "Old Man Travelling" were as follows:

> I asked him whither he was bound, and what
> The object of his journey; he replied
> That he was going many miles to take
> A last leave of his Son, a Mariner,
> Who from a Sea-fight had been brought to Falmouth,
> And there was dying in a hospital.[16]

These lines, which (as George Sampson says) "really spoil the piece", spoil it according to plan, and provide a striking example of this deliberately naïve, anti-literary manner. After 1798 Words-worth became less passionately convinced of the inadequacy of language, as the successive revisions of *Lyrical Ballads* show. In 1800 he took away the full force from this magnificent, defiant bathos by putting the lines into direct speech. In later editions he omitted them altogether.

"The Idiot Boy" and "Peter Bell" are further examples of the poem relying on verbose statements and commonplaces to achieve truth to nature. The trouble is that this bald realism often fails to communicate that particular emotional excitement which is the chief thing in the poems. Again there is psychological analysis: of the illness of Susan, which so quickly disappears when her curiosity is aroused, and of the superstitious fears of Peter. But this analysis is subordinate to the illustration of elemental human experiences, mother-love and the strange innocence of the mentally deranged in "The Idiot Boy", guilt and repentance in "Peter Bell". In the

---

[14] "The Last of the Flock", 79–80.   [15] *Op. cit.*, 99–100.
[16] "Old Man Travelling", 15–20.

former poem, of which Wordsworth said that he never wrote anything with so much glee, the rhapsodic babbling of the boy himself provides the emotional centre:

> The Cocks did crow to-whoo, to-whoo,
> And the Sun did shine so cold.[17]

These lines of fantastic joy, which might have come from a traditional mad-song, were the point of departure for Wordsworth's glee. But the lyrical impulse is directed into anecdote, and our glimpse into the fanciful world of the Boy's mind is contained in, and finally lost in, a narrative of external incident. The poem is written in the commonplace style prescribed by the canons of moral realism laid down in the *Preface*:

> She's in a sad *quandary* . . .
> The grass you almost hear it growing . . .
> If Betty fifty ponds should see . . .
> Your Pony's worth his weight in gold . . .[18]

The Idiot Boy's imaginative freedom with words has not been allowed to affect the diction of the poem as a whole; many poets dealing sympathetically with the theme of insanity would have made some use of this freedom, but for all its metrical gaiety and grotesque humour, Wordsworth has written what must be quite the most sober poem about insanity in the language. The grotesque element is intended, like the irrelevant banalities in "The Thorn", to reproduce a constituent of real life which cannot safely be omitted if the genuine experience is to be preserved. Only in certain stanzas describing the stillness of the night and the hooting of the owls is the joyous emotion clarified, and this is when the verse departs from photographic realism and reveals Wordsworth's individual sensibility:

> By this the stars were almost gone,
> The moon was setting on the hill,
> So pale you scarcely looked at her:
> The little birds began to stir,
> Though yet their tongues were still.[19]

[17] "The Idiot Boy", 450-1.
[18] *Op. cit.*, 171, 285, 309, 362.   [19] *Op. cit.*, 402-6.

Here there is creative observation: we look at the night landscape through the seeing eye. Elsewhere, obedient to the dictates of his theory, he dramatises, and deliberately cultivates the common-place sentiments of simple people; though the substance of "The Idiot Boy" is given in his own words, he is not so much the poet of nature as its Alfoxden correspondent with a kind of folk personality. He denies himself the liberty of the poet to transform experience by imposing a pattern on it. His only concession to literature, apart from these touches of description, is the metre, and certain repetitive devices proper to the ballad. We learn from the *Preface* that he regarded metre as something imposed on the poetic record in order to provide an additional pleasure, not as an integral part of the creative process.

"Peter Bell" is a Wordsworthian "Ancient Mariner". By surrendering himself to the supernatural in a way of which Wordsworth would never have approved, Coleridge was able to create a myth. Wordsworth writes a psychological essay on the same theme, guilt and purgation, and is at pains to provide a natural explanation for each of the mysterious phenomena which hasten the conversion of his hero. It is his most ambitious exercise in psychological realism. Because of its conscious rejection of Coleridgean imagination, it demonstrates better than any other poem the poet's obstinate insistence on the ultimate value of matter-of-fact.

These, then, and lesser poems like them, are to the Two Voices school Wordsworth's failures. In examining them afresh in the light of his view of poetry in 1798–1802, I do not wish to rehabilitate them, or even to qualify the usual judgment and call them magnificent failures. But I think that we may be wrong if we consider them failures *as poems*, and contrast them with such fine and unsectarian poems of Wordsworth's as "Michael" and "Tintern Abbey". They should be viewed rather as attempts to get behind poetry altogether and make a photograph (or a recording) of the raw data of human experience which might preserve the original emotion. They are in fact, without quibbling, absurdities rather than failures: they try to overcome in words the brutal limitations of language with its inexorable associations and ambiguities. As readers of poetry we recognise their absurdity and turn to "Tintern Abbey" or *The Prelude*, but there may be times when such a protest against the imperfections of human communication can be of value.

The ballads never fully communicate their inner excitement because the technique of commonplaces is unable to do justice to it. But Wordsworth is not consistent in his application of this technique, any more than his *Preface* is a consistent plea for extreme realism. In the additions made to the *Preface* in 1802 there are suggestions of a more optimistic view of the poet's ability to mould and modify his subject-matter. And in many early poems, notably in "The Ruined Cottage", we find examples of such imaginative modification. A narrative poet in the modern period, who has no mythology to draw on, can organise his experience into a pattern by selecting some object or element in it and making it a focus for all the other elements. It thus assumes, not a symbolic function, but a co-ordinating one. Wordsworth employs the device in "The Ruined Cottage" and in "Michael", though I think he was unconscious of its implications and possible repercussions on his anti-literary theory. The story of "Michael" is a rural tragedy similar to the "unsuccessful" ballads. Its superiority is partly due to the more dignified simplicity of his blank verse as compared with the slightly arch jog-trot of the ballads. But it is also more deeply moving because at two focal points the reader is shown what the story is about in terms of emotion. In the ballads, factual simplicity has defeated itself, and we never know what they are about till we read the *Preface* and the Fenwick notes: the photograph has faded and the emotion remains buried in brute experience. In "Michael" there is poetic structure. First, all the emotions connected with the thrifty couple and their hopes are gathered up in the description of the cottage lamp burning far into the night; oddly enough, without any intention of commenting on the aesthetic machinery of his poem, Wordsworth actually calls the light a symbol:

> The light was famous in its neighbourhood,
> And was a public symbol of the life
> The thrifty Pair had lived. For, as it chanced,
> Their cottage on a plot of rising ground
> Stood single, with large prospect, north and south,
> High into Easedale, up to Dunmail-Raise,

> And westward to the village near the lake;
> And from this constant light, so regular
> And so far seen, the House itself, by all
> Who dwelt within the limits of the vale,
> Both old and young, was named THE EVENING STAR.[20]

Later, when the story turns to tragedy, the focus of emotion is again provided by a tangible object, this time the heap of stones marking the unfinished sheep-fold:

> And to that hollow dell from time to time
> Did he repair, to build the Fold of which
> His flock had need. 'Tis not forgotten yet
> The pity which was then in every heart
> For the old Man – and 'tis believed by all
> That many and many a day he thither went,
> And never lifted up a single stone.[21]

The tragic austerity of these lines has been remarked, but not their organic relation to the earlier passage. Note, however, that both the light and the sheep-fold stand out as eminences: the former because it is on a height, the latter as a solitary pile of stones in a lonely valley. The apparently prosy phrase "'Tis believed by all" brings out the idea of a surrounding community – sympathising equally in the tragedy of Michael's loss as in the visible symbol of his prosperity.

Both before and after 1798 incidents and objects are used in this manner to give shape and dramatic intensity. In contrast, the experimental ballads sometimes contain abortive symbols which are never sufficiently clarified. Such are the Thorn itself, or the hooting owls in "The Idiot Boy". In the period when Wordsworth was working on *The Prelude* and examining the growth of his own poetic mind he came to recognise the active character of the imagination which can "build up greatest things From least suggestions". *The Prelude* is perhaps a better handbook of poetics than the *Preface* to *Lyrical Ballads*. Wordsworth ceased to struggle against the necessities of poetic structure as his interest in the cathartic effects of poverty and desolation gave way to an interest in man as a member of a community. But he remained "a cold,

[20] "Michael", 129–39.   [21] *Op. cit.*, 460–6.

hard, silent, practical man", with an unflinching respect for observed facts; he never took the step initiated by Coleridge, and adopted by the second generation of romantic poets, into a private poetic universe governed by its own laws. There may be a "visionary dreariness" about the Leechgatherer and the vast organic images which are applied to him, but they are circumscribed by the limits of an eighteenth-century moral poem on Resolution and Independence. The elemental figure, "like a huge Stone", is also a real person designed to inculcate a moral lesson. Wordsworth stands outside the main romantic line of development, because his personal vision never expressed itself in the creation of myth. But in one work, *The White Doe of Rylstone*, he does show a consciousness of the advantages to be gained from a bolder use of the imaginative correlative, in marked contrast to his earlier theoretical reliance on raw transcripts of experience. *The White Doe* returns to his earlier preoccupation with the ruined and desolate, and the peculiar bond with nature that their misery establishes. Emily has to look on at the destruction of her whole family in a cause in which she does not believe. The White Doe, which remains by her during her sorrow, and visits the churchyard after her death, is the symbol of her submission. The Doe gives a palpable form to the remote, stoical beauty of Emily's passive suffering, which would otherwise hardly emerge from the episodic structure of a verse tale in the manner of Scott:

> —When soft ! – the dusky trees between,
> And down the path through the open green,
> Where is no living thing to be seen;
> And through yon gateway, where is found
> Beneath the arch with ivy bound,
> Free entrance to the church-yard ground –
> Comes gliding in with lovely gleam,
> Comes gliding in serene and slow,
> Soft and silent as a dream,
> A solitary Doe!
> White she is as lily of June,
> And beauteous as the silver moon
> When out of sight the clouds are driven
> And she is left alone in heaven;

Or like a ship some gentle day
In sunshine sailing far away,
A glittering ship, that hath the plain
Of ocean for her own domain.[22]

Throughout the poem the Doe's presence embodies the consola-
tion which Emily has achieved through suffering; now she is

held above
The infirmities of mortal love;
Undaunted, lofty, calm, and stable,
And awfully impenetrable.[23]

Her experience is similar to that of the abandoned heroines of the
Lyrical Ballads, or of Margaret in "The Ruined Cottage", but it is
clearer and more satisfying because a poetic fiction does something
to create a bridge between its "awful impenetrability" and the
reader. That Wordsworth was fully conscious of the function
performed by the Doe is shown by his words to J. T. Coleridge in
1836:

The true action of the poem was spiritual – the subduing of
the will, and all inferior passions, to the perfect purifying and
spiritualizing of the intellectual nature; while the Doe, by
connection with Emily, is raised, as it were, from its mere
animal nature into something mysterious and saint-like.[24]

In a letter to Coleridge written immediately after the composition
of the poem, Wordsworth had said: "The principle of action in all
the characters . . . was throughout imaginative; . . . all action (save
the main traditionary tragedy) . . . was fine-spun and inobtrusive,
consonant in this to the principle from which it flowed . . . Emily
is intended to be honoured and loved for what she endures."[25]
The drama of the emotions had been advocated as an ideal by
Wordsworth when he distinguished the *Lyrical Ballads* from the
popular poetry of the day on the grounds that "the feeling therein
developed gives importance to the action and situation", and not
the other way about. But without some imaginative symbol or

---

[22] *The White Doe of Rylstone*, 49–66.   [23] *Op. cit.*, 1625–8.
[24] Christopher Wordsworth, *Memoirs of William Wordsworth*, II. London,
1851, p. 311.
[25] *Letters of the Middle Years*, ed. E. de Selincourt, I. Oxford, 1937, p. 197.

focus the feeling in the ballads remains too fine-spun to communicate its importance to the action.

Wordsworth's poetic practice in "Michael", "Resolution and Independence", and *The White Doe,* shows that, whether consciously or not, he could resolve the difficulty latent in his theory and demonstrated in the experimental ballads. The devastating psychological experience which he underwent between 1793 and 1796 left him in a frame of mind that was hostile to literary art and intent only on the contemplation of "real and substantial action and suffering". Literature might be, at its worst, mere embroidery, at its best a high-minded escape from the facts of the human situation. But he wished to share his contemplation with the widest possible audience; and his meditation on the problem of language led him to plan a poetry which should dispense with all social and literary associations, and present "the thing itself". Unfortunately, the significance of the situations he wished his readers to contemplate lay in complexes of emotion which the method of anti-literary realism was able to communicate only in fragments. In criticising the "unsuccessful" ballads one is often tempted to talk, not about the texts, but about the poems Wordsworth might have written had he given his imagination full play; as Mr J. C. Smith says, Legouis's account of "Peter Bell" is more interesting than the poem itself. When he returned from reportage and the dramatic ballad to a restrained handling of the imaginative symbol, the difficulty was removed. "Michael" and *The White Doe* are self-contained: the emotions they deploy are imaginatively realised within the poem, and there is no need to look to other poems for a commentary.

Wordsworth's statement about the spiritualising function of the White Doe is a far cry from his earlier realism. It adumbrates the symbolist aesthetic of the later nineteenth century, so much more clearly anticipated in "The Ancient Mariner". The poetic movement of the first half of the present century has carried the exploration of symbols a stage further. But this movement, like that of Wordsworth and Coleridge, began with a revolt against literature:

> Objectivity and again objectivity . . . nothing – nothing that you couldn't, in some circumstances, in the stress of some emotion, actually say. Every literaryism, every book-word,

fritters away a scrap of the reader's patience, a scrap of his sense of your sincerity. When one really thinks and feels one stammers with simple speech.[26]

The last sentence echoes Wordsworth's belief about his ideal rustics. But Pound had in mind his own thinking and feeling, and he wanted from the start to create poetry; he was, after all, optimistic about language. Wordsworth, with a northern obstinacy of purpose, turned his face away from the poetry to the pity, and relied for a time on the commonplaces by which most people give vent to their emotions. It seems almost grudgingly that he allowed his imagination to exercise its plastic power on the hallowed substance of ordinary lives.

[26] Ezra Pound to Harriet Monroe, January 1915. *The Letters of Ezra Pound*, ed. D. D. Paige. London, 1951, p. 91.

Edward E. Bostetter

WORDSWORTH'S DIM
AND PERILOUS WAY[1]

Few critics have ever been very happy with *The Excursion*. Even those who support or justify Wordsworth's turn to traditional attitudes have read it with no apparent enthusiasm or care. And for most modern readers who come to it after reading *The Prelude*, *The Excursion* can be no more than a painful anticlimax. It is hard for them not to suffer a sense of shock as they read its pious platitudes and realise that the poem was originally intended to embody and develop the fresh perceptions of the opening books of *The Prelude*. No wonder modern critics have been fascinated by the question: what happened to cause the narrowing and hardening of Wordsworth's attitudes? And there have been nearly as many suggestions as critics. Perhaps because they have too readily accepted the Fenwick notes and taken the poem for granted as reflecting only the results of a change in the poet's attitudes, they have tended to neglect or to misinterpret the record in the poem itself of the state of mind which helped cause the change.

This record is in the narrative of the Solitary in Books II and III. The doubts and questions of the Solitary are aimed at the faith of *The Prelude*, and they indicate clearly that Wordsworth modified his beliefs because for him the alternative was despair. If we listen closely to the long introverted monologues of the Solitary and the Wanderer, we become aware as we would not otherwise be of the extent to which Wordsworth was bound and limited by the eighteenth-century poetic tradition out of which the faith of *The Prelude* had evolved. We understand why it was psychologically

[1] Reprinted from *Publications of the Modern Language Association of America*, LXXI (June 1956), pp. 433–50.

impossible for him to transcend or break free from the limitations of the tradition, or even to hold to the faith of *The Prelude* for any length of time; and why once that faith had proved inadequate, the faith of *The Excursion* was inevitable.

By the tradition I mean that to which the long contemplative or "retirement" poem belongs. How pervasive and potent this tradition was may be seen by glancing at the line of descent from Thomson to Wordsworth. The eighteenth-century poems of major importance in shaping Wordsworth's poetry and thought, such as *The Seasons*, the *Night Thoughts*, *The Minstrel* and *The Task*, were "retirement" poems, in all of which the poets elevated the life of retirement from just an accompaniment or prelude to the life of action into the preferable alternative to it. They believed that through contemplation the ultimate purpose and design in the universe was revealed to them; they perceived through contemplation the evidence for the beneficence of God or God in Nature. Indeed, they took for granted that the act of contemplation was itself proof of divine purpose. The psychological attitude thus engendered was one of immense egoism in which the desire of the poet became the will of the universe. It was an attitude which provided little encouragement for, in fact made almost impossible, a patient objective observation of man and society, or the "negative capability" which Keats struggled to define. It led almost inevitably to a rationalised religion in which apparent evil was optimistically ignored or transformed into ultimate good.[2]

Both *The Prelude* and *The Excursion* are in the main current of this tradition. They have for their principal subject, as Wordsworth puts it in the preface to *The Excursion*, "the sensations and opinions of a poet living in retirement". In *The Prelude* Wordsworth extends the philosophical possibilities of the tradition almost as far as they will go through his bold autobiographical presentation of the interrelation of Nature and man. But in *The Excursion* he is writing what is, in general, a conventional "retirement" poem.[3] The Wanderer, the Poet, and the Pastor are typical

[2] For all the complex and diverse elements in the tradition see H. N. Fairchild, *Religious Trends in English Poetry*. New York, 1939–49, 3 vols., esp. I, 535 ff. (Ch. xii), and II, 365 ff. (Ch. xi.)

[3] For a detailed discussion of sources and analogues see Judson S. Lyon, *The Excursion: A Study*. New Haven, 1950, pp. 29–60.

characters. The Wanderer, in particular, is a stock figure, similar
to countless other wanderers, hermits, and recluses of eighteenth-
century poetry. It is true that as a pedlar he has been given an
artificial cosmopolitanism, and is presented as having travelled
widely. But we see him only as a wanderer in the countryside of
England who has never been an active participant in society. He is,
rather, a detached spectator and philosopher of rustic life. The
most significant new thing about him is that he is a self-educated
representative of the lower classes. Indeed, the fact that he was a
pedlar was so upsetting to Jeffrey, Coleridge, and other critics of
the day that they failed to notice his perfectly respectable literary
ancestry and conventional behaviour. The revolutionary implications were enormous, and Wordsworth had within his grasp the
means of breaking through the traditional limitations and establishing a new perspective for the poet. In the first book, most of
which was written before 1800, he seems to be aware of this, but
he never follows up the implications; and the Wanderer becomes
in the later books as much a member of the upper classes in attitude
and behaviour as the poet or pastor. As a matter of fact, as a
pedlar of the *status quo* he is almost unbearably complacent and
self-righteous, as if compensating for his lowly origins. He is also
compensating, of course, for the Solitary.

The Solitary is an intruder into the eighteenth-century garden of
optimism. His antecedents are not to be sought in literary proto-
types, although he is foreshadowed in the Lorenzo whom Young
belabours so fearfully in the *Night Thoughts*;[4] in the sorrow over the
death of his wife which causes the retirement of the Hermit in
Savage's *Wanderer*; in the disillusionment with society that the
Hermit in Beattie's *Minstrel* declaims. But the hermits of Savage
and Beattie are in their general philosophy more like the Wanderer. The Solitary is rather the materialisation of the melancholy
doubts and questionings that hover in the atmosphere and often
colour the texture of the most ostensibly confident eighteenth-
century poems. He is most vividly foreshadowed in the melancholy of the poets themselves – of, for example, Young, Gray,
Collins, and Cowper, who were victims of the psychological

---

[4] Though Lorenzo never gets a chance to speak for himself, his sceptical
arguments as paraphrased by Young are often similar to those of the Solitary.
See esp. Nights VI and VII, "The Infidel Reclaimed".

disease so prevalent that it was called the English malady. Undoubtedly he owes a great deal to the disillusionment of Wordsworth and his contemporaries with the French Revolution which, as the testing ground of ideas, inevitably released doubts and fears that had long been repressed or evaded. But in his old age Wordsworth disingenuously implied that disillusionment with the revolution was the sole cause of the Solitary's dejection, when he told Miss Fenwick that the chief prototype of the Solitary was Joseph Fawcett, a revolutionary preacher and Godwinian, who became "pretty much such a person as I have described; and early disappeared from the stage, having fallen into habits of intemperance, which I have heard . . . hastened his death".[5]

One may suspect that this false account of Fawcett, which the poet could certainly have checked if he had wanted to, was part of the elaborate structure of rationalisation by which he shut out from his memory his past crises and conflicts. For it is obvious that the chief prototype of the Solitary is Wordsworth himself. He is the product of a powerful characteristic of the poet, the "meddling intellect" that made him question and constantly examine his basic convictions, and finally wore him out through internal strife. It is the French Revolution, perhaps, which first released the "meddling intellect"; Wordsworth's most vivid description of it in action comes in Book x of *The Prelude* in connection with the moral crisis following his disillusionment with the Revolution:

> From the first
> Having two natures in me, joy the one
> The other melancholy, and withal
> A happy man, and therefore bold to look
> On painful things, slow, somewhat, too, and stern
> In temperament, I took the knife in hand
> And stopping not at parts less sensitive,
> Endeavoured with my best of skill to probe
> The living body of society

[5] *Poetical Works of William Wordsworth*, eds. Ernest de Selincourt and Helen Darbishire. Oxford, 1940–9, v. 375. All citations to Wordsworth's poetry with the exception of *The Prelude* will be from this edition. For the facts of Fawcett's life, see M. Ray Adams, "Joseph Fawcett and Wordsworth's Solitary", *P.M.L.A.*, XLVIII (1933), pp. 505–28.

Even to the heart; I push'd without remorse
My speculations forward; yea, set foot
On Nature's holiest places.[6]

The Solitary provides the evidence that the meddling intellect did not cease its probing, as some believe, with Wordsworth's acceptance of the faith of "Tintern Abbey", but continued ruthlessly to function through the period in which he wrote *The Prelude* and *The Excursion*. Undoubtedly Wordsworth tried to repress it, and the Solitary is perhaps best looked upon as the therapeutic vessel into which he more or less consciously poured his doubts. The colloquy of the Solitary and the Wanderer is in one sense a psychomachia, a soul-debate, in which the Solitary presents the questions which threatened to undermine Wordsworth's faith, and the Wanderer the only possible answers. Let us now test these introductory generalisations by examining in some detail the two books in which the Solitary is the dominant character.

2

The Wanderer's priggish description of the Solitary at the opening of Book II[7] indicates clearly enough that Wordsworth's initial intention was to make him a straw man for whom the reader would feel such contempt that his arguments would be immediately suspect. In Blakean terms, error was to be given form in order that it might be destroyed. Weak in character, lax in morals, plunged into despair by the sudden death of his wife and children, disillusioned by the failure of the French Revolution, the Solitary had "forfeited / All joy in human nature", says the Wanderer, and retreated into the remoteness of the Lake country where now he

wastes the sad remainder of his hours,
Steeped in a self-indulging spleen, that wants not
Its own voluptuousness . . .[8]

Obviously the arguments of such a sullen self-pitying pessimist

---

[6] *The Prelude*, ed. E. de Selincourt. Oxford, 1926, pp. 408, 410. x. 868–79 (1805). All further citations to *The Prelude* will be from this edition.
[7] *The Excursion*, II, 155–315.　　　　[8] *Op. cit.*, II, 310–12.

could be set up and knocked down at will. But the Solitary whom we meet does not fit this description at all. He is a true Wordsworthian, sensitive to the beauty of nature, tender towards children, passionately aware of the still, sad music of humanity. He is unable, however, to believe in a benevolent orderly nature and the goodness of man because such a belief conflicts with his experience. As a result he is tortured by questions concerning life, death and, immortality. It is clear that when Wordsworth turned from superficial preconception to actual delineation of the Solitary, he could not help presenting him as an honest man with honest doubts; the subject was too close to him to be handled lightly. And almost as soon as the Solitary opens his mouth we are aware that the poet has identified with his character, and that we are confronted by that "species of ventriloquism" of which Coleridge complains, "where two are represented as talking, while in truth one man only speaks".[9]

When the Wanderer and the Poet came upon the Solitary in the second book of *The Excursion*, he tells them the story of an old man whose funeral has just taken place, a story designed to show

> What stuff the Dwellers in a solitude,
> That seems by Nature hollowed out to be
> The seat and bosom of pure innocence,
> Are made of . . .[10]

The old man, feeble-minded and dependent upon public charity, had been taken in by a heartless housewife who exploited him as "her vassal of all labour". Sent into the mountains to gather fuel he had been caught in a storm. A searching party, including the Solitary, found him in the ruins of an old chapel the next day and brought him home to die. The story presents a bleak counterargument to the thesis of the "Old Cumberland Beggar" in which the Beggar aroused in all who met him only goodness and kindness, and the housewife though pressed by her own wants gave unsparingly and "with exhilarated heart" built "her hope in

---

[9] S. T. Coleridge, *Biographia Literaria*, ed. J. Shawcross. Oxford, 1907, II, p. 109. *Cf.* Hazlitt's remark, "The recluse, the pastor, and the pedlar are three persons in one poet", in "Observations on the *Excursion*", *The Round Table*, London, 1817.

[10] *The Excursion*, II, 622–5.

heaven". The story also questions by implication the benevolence of nature. In the earlier poem Wordsworth is moved to cry out:

> And, long as he can wander, let him breathe
> The freshness of the valleys; let his blood
> Struggle with frosty air and winter snows;
> And let the chartered wind that sweeps the heath
> Beat his grey locks against his withered face . . .
> As in the eye of Nature he has lived,
> So in the eye of Nature let him die![11]

In the Solitary's story the raging storm is as much a cause of the old man's death as the housewife. What is emphasised in the story is not evil, but indifference – the thoughtless greed of the house-wife, the indifferent violence of nature, the indifferent kindness of the searchers and mourners. We are made aware of the complete insignificance of the old man. Only the Solitary and the little boy will mourn him.

Descending the mountain in the mist after finding the old man, the Solitary had a strange and wonderful experience. Suddenly there was opened to his view a glorious spectacle of a "mighty city" wrought by "earthly nature"

> Upon the dark materials of the storm
> Now pacified . . .
> That which I *saw* was the revealed abode
> Of Spirits in beatitude: my heart
> Swelled in my breast. – 'I have been dead,' I cried,
> 'And now I live! Oh! wherefore *do* I live?'
> And with that pang I prayed to be no more![12]

Now the Solitary's experience is similar to experiences recounted in "Tintern Abbey" and *The Prelude* as revelations of the divinity in nature, when Wordsworth saw "into the life of things". But the very passage which in *The Prelude* could have been used like the experience on Mt Snowden as an affirmation of ultimate truth becomes when given to the Solitary a cause of despair. For the Solitary, much as he wishes for a mystical experience, remains acutely aware that the vision is an apparition wrought by earthly

[11] "The Old Cumberland Beggar", 172–6, 196–7.
[12] *The Excursion*, II, 847–8, 873–7.

nature. And though he says in recounting the experience, "I forget our Charge, as utterly / I then forgot him", back of his despair lies the ironic implications of the conjunction of the heavenly vision and the painful story of the insignificant old man. If he forgets the old man, it is because he has taken his place. He cannot believe that the apparition is meaningful, or at least that it gives any meaning to his life. He cannot ultimately reconcile vision and human experience.[13]

It is interesting that the Wanderer never attempts any direct answer to the Solitary's story. In Book IV when he is apostrophising the benignity and bounty of nature – "he shall find / Who seeks not" – he refers suddenly to the Vision. Three weeks ago, he says, addressing the Solitary, you climbed these heights "on a service bent / Of mere humanity":

> And what a marvellous and heavenly show
> Was suddenly revealed! – the swains moved on,
> And heeded not: you lingered, you perceived
> And felt, deeply as living man could feel.[14]

He launches, then, into a great exhortation to the Solitary to stop burning the midnight taper, to rise with the lark, and to be so vigorously active during the day that he will fall asleep of ex-

---

[13] Two recent critics have assumed that Wordsworth was presenting a personal experience to be interpreted quite literally like those in *The Prelude*. Professor Abbie Potts, assuming that the original version of the vision is to be found in MS. x, which contains passages later to become part of Book VII of *The Prelude*, believes that the Solitary was first conceived of in the spirit of Bunyan's pilgrim on the Delectable Mountains coming out of the valley of the shadow of death and looking towards the Celestial City (*Wordsworth's Prelude*, Cornell, 1953, pp. 11, 238). But the textual note in *P.W.*, v, 415, indicates that the vision passage was not part of MS. x. Furthermore, both the story of the old man and the vision are based upon an experience related to Wordsworth in November, 1805. See *P.W.*, v, 417–18.

John Jones sees the Solitary's experience as Wordsworth's own vision of Paradise "in an exact Christian and literary sense. . . . We must believe that Wordsworth was in the spirit when he beheld this vision" (*The Egotistical Sublime*, London, 1954, pp. 170–2). But both Potts and Jones overlook the fact that, whatever the circumstances under which he first wrote the passage, Wordsworth has quite deliberately given it to one who wants to but cannot believe in such a vision.

[14] *The Excursion*, IV, 471–4.

haustion at night – in other words, to keep so busy that he won't
have time to think. This may be excellent therapy, but it is an
evasion of the questions raised by the Solitary. And the implication that the "heavenly show" should be looked upon as Nature's
unexpected bonus or reward for a service of "mere humanity" is
a sad mockery of Wordsworth's earlier belief. Finally, the Wanderer draws an invidious distinction between the sensitive Solitary
and the insensitive swains – a piece of gratuitous sophistry which
simply obfuscates the argument, and shows how confused Wordsworth's retreat from his former belief has been. The whole
passage is an excellent example of what has gone wrong between
The Prelude and *The Excursion*. The refusal or inability to answer
the questions of the Solitary inevitably makes the Wanderer's
arguments seem shallow and inadequate, and his transports
hollow.

3

The setting for Book III[15] is heavily symbolic.[16] The Wanderer
suggests to his friends that they follow a rill to the spot where it
probably issues "like human life from darkness". But the rill
leads to a hidden nook into which it falls "disembodied and
diffused" over the smooth surface of a lofty crag. At the foot of
the precipice lies a mass of rock resembling a stranded ship, with
keel upturned, that rests "fearless of winds and waves". The
similarity of the image to the circumstances of the sinking of John
Wordsworth's ship in 1805 is striking. Nearby stand three smaller
stones, not unlike "monumental pillars"; and further on two stones
supporting a flat smooth fragment like an altar. Out of a chink in
the altar grows "a tall and shining holly":

> As if inserted by some human hand
> In mockery, to wither in the sun,
> Or lay its beauty flat before a breeze. . . .[17]

But at the moment there is no breeze, no motion except the water

[15] *Op. cit.*, III, 50–73.
[16] For dates of composition for Book III, see *P.W.*, v, 418–19. The first
draft was probably written in 1806.
[17] *The Excursion*, III, 64–6.

"softly creeping" down the barrier of rock. The hidden rock, the falling water, the stranded ship, the pillars and the altar, the shining holly – these are all symbols in a tableau of the riddle of human life. What is the meaning of the riddle: design or chance?

The Wanderer is ecstatically certain that the rocks bear "a semblance strange of power intelligent". He is haunted by "shadowy intimations" that they are a record

> Of purposes akin to those of Man,
> But wrought with mightier arm than now prevails.[18]

Though he never makes clear just what he has in mind, Druids or some pre-Adamic race such as Cuvier postulated, he does make clear that he finds this the perfect place for contemplation of design in the universe. Gazing upward from the "calm centre" towards the abyss "in which the everlasting stars abide" one may penetrate "wherever truth shall lead".[19]

On the other hand, the Solitary can see these rocks only as

> The sport of Nature, aided by blind Chance
> Rudely to mock the works of toiling Man.[20]

His fancy has amused itself by naming one rock Pompey's pillar, and another a Theban obelisk, and the altar a Druid cromlech.

> But if the spirit be oppressed by sense
> Of instability, revolt, decay,
> And change, and emptiness . . .[21]

then these freaks feed and aggravate "pity and scorn, and melancholy pride" just as do Stonehenge, the Pyramids, or Syria's ruins. The setting that has raised the Wanderer's mind to an exalted pitch is for the Solitary "fraught rather with depression", because it emphasises the meaningless of human existence.[22] Happier even than the Wanderer, he thinks, is the botanist or geologist who never bothers about the riddle. And he agrees with

---

[18] *Op. cit.*, 90–1.
[20] *Op. cit.*, 126–7.
[22] *Op. cit.*, 116–58.

[19] *Op. cit.*, 74–112.
[21] *Op. cit.*, 137–9.

the Poet that happiest of all is the thoughtless cottage boy who
mends the dam that runs his toy mill.

> Ah! what avails imagination high
> Or question deep?
> . . . if nowhere
> A habitation, for consummate good,
> Or for progressive virtue, by the search
> Can be attained, – a better sanctuary
> From doubt and sorrow, than the senseless grave?[23]

He cries out in the same agony of mind that led Wordsworth to
ask in a letter to Beaumont following the death of his brother:
"Would it not be blasphemy to say that, upon the supposition of
the thinking principle being destroyed by death, however inferior
we may be to the great Cause and Ruler of things, we have *more of
love* in our nature than He has? The thought is monstrous; and yet
how to get rid of it, except upon the supposition of *another* and a
better world, I do not see."[24] It is significant that after extolling his
brother's virtues he goes on to quote from Young's *Night Thoughts*
a passage which raises the question more ruthlessly than does the
Solitary:

> When to the grave we follow the renown'd
> For valour, virtue, science, all we love. . . .
> Dream we, that lustre of the moral world
> Goes out in stench, and rottenness the close?[25]

The question is the most painful, perhaps the most crucial,
raised by eighteenth-century science. Newtonian theory offered a
universe of order, but an impersonal one. It undermined the old
grounds for personal immortality, and provided no new place for
it in the tight logic of its own frame. To accept "a universe of
death" with equanimity was emotionally impossible for most
eighteenth-century men. The matter is nowhere more bluntly or
crudely stated than in Young's preface to Night VI of his *Night
Thoughts*. The dispute about religion "may be reduced to this single
question; Is man immortal, or is he not? If he is not, all our

[23] *Op. cit.*, 209–10, 220–4.

[24] 12 Mar. 1805. *Early Letters of William and Dorothy Wordsworth*, ed. E. de
Selincourt. Oxford, 1935, p. 460.

[25] *Op. cit.*, p. 461. Night VI. 205–6, 210–11.

disputes are mere amusements, or trials of skill . . ."[26] James Beattie, attacking Hume, believed that a chief source of melancholy in his age was "metaphysical controversy": "To a man educated in Christian principles, and not corrupted by affectation or debauchery, nothing can give keener anguish, or overwhelm the mind with a deeper gloom than to be perplexed with doubts concerning that futurity which is the foundation of his dearest hopes."[27] This sentence could stand as a summary of the emotional heritage behind Wordsworth's letter and the Solitary's question.

The eighteenth-century poets had tried in varying degrees to combine an acceptance of the Newtonian universe with a belief in personal immortality. But Wordsworth when he began *The Prelude* apparently had conceived of man's participation in a "bright and breathing world" as sufficient compensation for personal immortality, and was satisfied to think of death as absorption back into a living nature. He had carried over from his eighteenth-century heritage a belief in a moral universe, specifically a nature friendly to man, and he made this the cornerstone of his philosophy. Man was important to nature; and in the high flush of youthful enthusiasm he cried, "Nature never did betray the heart that loved her." But he could not long conceal from himself that the individual, at least, was not important to nature; and the death of his brother shocked him so violently because it brought him face to face with the fact, forced him to a decision. Nature had wantonly betrayed one heart that loved her. That it is the destruction of his own youthful faith that he is mourning in the death of his brother is shown by the letters he wrote Beaumont and Losh.[28] John is almost hysterically described as the perfect man. "But alas! what avails it?" he asks Beaumont. We are back to the Solitary's question. The Solitary, unable to believe in anything beyond Nature and finding her indifferent or capricious, faces the comfortless thought of the river of life sinking engulfed "like Niger, in impenetrable sands / and utter darkness". His

26 *Night Thoughts on Life, Death and Immortality.* New York, 1854, p. 249.

27 *Dissertations Moral and Critical: On Memory and Imagination.* London, 1783, p. 201.

28 To Beaumont, 20 Feb. 1805 (*Early Letters*, pp. 449 ff. and 452); to James Losh, 16 Mar. 1805 (pp. 463 ff.).

bitterness and hopelessness are so great that he longs for death with an almost Keatsian passion. Night is better than day, sleep than waking, death than sleep:

> Feelingly sweet is stillness after storm,
> Though under covert of the wormy ground.[29]

After his expression of despair the Solitary turns to trace the steps that led to it. Once, he says, "in more genial times" the shades of death never hindered his power "to enjoy the vital beams of present sunshine". He even found pleasure in the storms of autumn, and believed the change of seasons "from mild to angry, and from sad to gay" benign and beautiful, and far preferable to the fanciful pictures of the unchanging paradise of a golden age. Here an interruption by the Poet, presumably Wordsworth *in propria persona*, leads to a passage which reveals how completely and consciously Wordsworth identified himself with the problem of the Solitary. The Poet agrees with the Solitary and goes on to attack the Epicureans for preferring "tranquillity to all things". Most of the Solitary's reply was first written as part of a long unfinished personal poem, "The Tuft of Primroses", in 1807–8.[30] It could be considered as variations for the central theme of the "Ode to Duty":

> My hopes no more must change their name,
> I long for a repose that ever is the same.[31]

Slight if you must the means, cries the Solitary, but not the end of those who ranked "As the prime object of a wise man's aim",

> Security from shock of accident,
> Release from fear . . .[32]

What drove the hermit to his cell in the forest? It was a craving for peace,

> Not as a refuge from distress or pain,
> A breathing-time, vacation, or a truce,

---

[29] *The Excursion*, III, 280–1.
[30] "The Tuft of Primroses" is printed in Appendix C in *P.W.*, v, 348–62. Lines 265–96 are identical with *The Excursion*, III, 367–405.
[31] 39–40.
[32] *The Excursion*, III, 363–4. Not in "The Tuft of Primroses".

> But for its absolute self; a life of peace,
> Stability without regret or fear;
> That hath been, is, and shall be evermore![33]

And a little later he speaks of "the life where hope and memory are as one", "the immortal Soul / Consistent in self-rule".

Following the passage drawn from "The Tuft of Primroses", he returns to the admission that in his youth he would have been disdainful of such a goal. Youth tries to solve doubts and determine questions by the rules of "inexperienced judgment":

> is inflamed,
> By courage, to demand from real life
> The test of act and suffering, to provoke
> Hostility – how dreadful when it comes,
> Whether affliction be the foe, or guilt![34]

Living as a "child of earth" upon earth's native energies, the Solitary forgot that his was then a condition which required neither energy nor fortitude – it was "a calm without vicissitude". And so he lived thoughtlessly in love and joy "without the aid of hope", assuming that the future would be like the present. But as he discovered, "Mutability is Nature's bane; / And slighted Hope *will* be avenged." When one needs her favours he will find instead "fear – doubt – and agony".[35]

The Solitary's "bitter language of the heart" parallels strikingly Wordsworth's description of himself in "Resolution and Independence". Like the Solitary, Wordsworth had been "a happy child of earth".

> My whole life I have lived in pleasant thought,
> As if life's business were a summer mood;
> As if all needful things would come unsought
> To genial faith, still rich in genial good . . .[36]

But he knows that there may come another day – "Solitude, pain

---

[33] *Op. cit.*, 383–7; "Tuft", 276–80. Apparently originally intended for the Poet in Book v, further evidence that Wordsworth saw the Solitary's desires as his own. See *P.W.*, v, 153, 421.

[34] *Op. cit.*, 416–20.

[35] *Op. cit.*, 458–61.

[36] "Resolution and Independence", 36–9.

of heart, distress, and poverty." Similarly in the "Ode to Duty" he refers wistfully to those "who in love and truth . . . rely / Upon the genial sense of youth." Such was he, but he can live so no longer. Implicit in all these passages, by the way, is a Puritan fear that one will be punished *because* one has been too happy and carefree. This fear has its roots deep in Wordsworth's childhood memories of the death of his father, if we may trust the conclusion of Book XI (1805 version) of *The Prelude*. He tells there of the happy expectation with which he awaited the Christmas holidays, the feverish impatience with which he watched, in a setting as bleakly symbolic as the hidden recess, for the horses that would take him home. Within ten days his father was dead:

> The event
> With all the sorrow which it brought appear'd
> A chastisement. . . .
> With trite reflections of morality,
> Yet in the deepest passion, I bow'd low
> To God, who thus corrected my desires . . .[37]

Logically, the Solitary, unable to believe in God, should be free from this particular sense of guilt. But he simply substitutes the idea of a Nature or Fate actively hostile to man. "Tremble, ye," he says, "to whom hath been assigned" a period of happiness. "Mutability is Nature's bane"; and he uses the word "bane" with the force of carefully calculated, deliberately planned retribution, for the next line is "And slighted Hope *will* be avenged". What does the Solitary mean by "hope"? We are never told; but we know what the word meant for Wordsworth. Actually the Solitary can believe only in a merciless fate, which cannot be appeased no matter what we do or how we live. Commenting later on the Pastor's stories, he speaks of

> the dread strife
> Of poor humanity's afflicted will
> Struggling in vain with ruthless destiny.[38]

The Solitary's superstitious awe of a vengeful Nature, looking

[37] *The Prelude*, XI, 368–70, 373–5.
[38] *The Excursion*, VI, 555–7.

back to the Greeks and forward to Hardy, reveals the naked, primitive fear that lay behind the poems of 1802–4. The genial face of Nature had become for Wordsworth a mask behind which a malevolent fate might lie in wait to catch the unwary.

The story of his life which the Solitary now tells us is, in part, a curious jumbling of Wordsworth's own life. His idyllic life in Devon following his marriage is markedly like Wordsworth's at Alfoxden in 1797–8. His description of the birth of the children, the seven years of domestic happiness, and the death of the children and his wife is apparently a very late insertion, after the deaths of Wordsworth's own children in 1812.[39] One would like very much to know what catastrophe Wordsworth had originally planned as the basic cause of the Solitary's dejection; but there is no reason to doubt from the passage in which the Solitary describes his despair that it was a personal loss, or perhaps, if we think of Oswald in *The Borderers*, some moral crisis:

> Then my soul
> Turned inward, – to examine of what stuff
> Time's fetters are composed; and life was put
> To inquisition, long and profitless!
> By pain of heart – now checked – and now impelled —
> The intellectual power, through words and things,
> Went sounding on, a dim and perilous way![40]

It is after this that the Solitary becomes a convert to the French Revolution. In rapid succession there follows disillusionment with the Revolution, with Godwinism, with democracy in America, and, last of all, with "Primeval Nature's child", the Indian, whom he finds to be "a creature squalid, vengeful, and impure". He concludes on a note of stoical despair. He has found neither in man nor in nature the evidence for belief which he seeks. Yet "I exist, / Within myself, not comfortless". He compares his life at the moment to a still passage in the swift course of a mountain stream and can only hope

[39] See note, *P.W.*, v, 421, 418–19.

[40] III. 695–701. The last 2 lines are an echo of 1774–5 of *The Borderers* (*P.W.*, I, 198) in which Oswald describes his state of mind upon learning that the Captain he has marooned is innocent.

That my particular current soon will reach
The unfathomable gulf, where all is still![41]

4

The dejection of the Solitary, it must be emphasised, is grounded
first and foremost in his loss of wife and children, and the con-
sequent loss of faith in a benevolent nature. His disillusionment
with the French Revolution, democracy, and natural man follows
upon these, and is at most merely contributory. In brief, his story
has been moulded by crises in Wordsworth's life more recent and
more potentially destructive than the French Revolution. We
can be sure that as Wordsworth wrote, his meddling intellect
went every step of the "dim and perilous way" with the Solitary.
For when we turn to Book IV we find that the Wanderer accepts
the basic assumption of the Solitary – that this is a world of un-
avoidable suffering and evil in which man can do little to help
himself or to improve his lot. He does not try to refute the
Solitary or to provide an alternative view – he simply builds his
faith upon the foundation of the Solitary's disillusionment. Like
a magician he transforms pessimism into the optimism of "Whatever is, is right" in the opening lines of Book IV:

> One adequate support
> For the calamities of mortal life
> Exists – one only; an assured belief
> That the procession of our fate, howe'er
> Sad or disturbed, is ordered by a Being
> Of infinite benevolence and power;
> Whose everlasting purposes embrace
> All accidents, converting them to good.[42]

Wordsworth could imagine the fortitude of the Solitary, but he
did not have that kind of fortitude himself. From the "unfathomable gulf" he drew back in horror. Furthermore, all his cultural
conditioning – his education, his reading, and now the social
structure represented by the Beaumonts, of which he was increasingly a part – assured him that such fortitude was needless.

[41] *Op. cit.*, III, 990–1.   [42] *Op. cit.*, IV, 10–17.

In the last book of *The Prelude* (1805) he says proudly that he shrank back with jealousy from anything that might aid the tendency to

> substitute a universe of death,
> The falsest of all worlds, in place of that
> Which is divine and true.[43]

He is referring here primarily to his avoidance of "private aims" and "selfish passions" in the quest for right and wrong, and perhaps to materialist or sensational philosophies; but the larger religious and psychological implications are undoubtedly present. The possibility that man might live usefully without despair in an indifferent universe was inconceivable to him. When therefore he found that his naturalism threatened to substitute a universe of death for the "divine and true", he fell back almost automatically upon the supernatural. The rhapsodies of the Wanderer reveal that Wordsworth rationalised the change in his beliefs, in so far as he recognised it at all, simply as an expansion and strengthening through intuitive knowledge of the scope of his philosophy, by which he retained the essence of his earlier beliefs. The patchwork of crucial portions of *The Excursion*, like Books I and IV, in which passages from before 1800 and after 1806 are crudely stitched together, is proof that he had anaesthetised himself against the violence he had inflicted on his earlier attitudes.

The most striking illustration of the way in which Wordsworth blurred the shift in his beliefs is in the character of the Wanderer. The story of the Wanderer's life in the first book differs in no essential respect from the way it was originally told in 1798. The description of his childhood relationship with nature is almost identical with Wordsworth's account of his own in the early books of *The Prelude*: in fact, one of the most important passages in Book II of *The Prelude* was first written for the Wanderer.[44] Set within this context, the exuberance and spontaneous joy of the Wanderer is as believable and acceptable as is Wordsworth's in "Tintern Abbey". Nature had never betrayed him; he had never suffered. Under the benign influence of nature he kept

---

[43] *The Prelude*, XIII, 141–3.
[44] See *P.W.*, v, 385. *The Ruined Cottage*, MS. B (1796–98), 238–56, becomes *The Prelude*, II, 416–34.

> In solitude and solitary thought
> His mind in a just equipoise of love.
> Serene it was, unclouded by the cares
> Of ordinary life; unvexed, unwarped
> By partial bondage. In his steady course,
> No piteous revolutions had he felt,
> No wild varieties of joy and grief.
> Unoccupied by sorrow of its own,
> His heart lay open . . .
> > He could *afford* to suffer
> With those whom he saw suffer.[45]

But this becomes preposterous as the qualification of one who is to cure the despondency of the Solitary who also has loved nature and yet has suffered terribly; and to cure it by expounding a doctrine based on the necessity of suffering is even more fantastic. As a result the Wanderer is a pompous old prig, who at times is perilously close to moral dishonesty. It seems incredible that Wordsworth would not recognise how unnecessarily he had weakened his protagonist, and therefore the intellectual and artistic integrity of his poem. But he did not; and therein is a clue to why he could at one and the same time delineate so clearly the changes in his attitudes, and be blind to them. The Wanderer represents Wordsworth's unchanging ideal; the way of life and state of mind which is the end to which all his beliefs were means; he symbolises the person Wordsworth wanted to be and hoped to be, first through nature, and then through Christian faith – serene, cheerful, confident, unsuffering. At the end of his life, in the Fenwick note, Wordsworth says wistfully, "I am here called upon freely to acknowledge that the character I have represented in his person is chiefly an idea of what I fancied my own character might have become in his circumstances."[46]

The Excursion, Harper suggests, "marks the third phase of a great literary duel between optimism and a doubting mood which at least bore some semblance of pessimism".[47] The first phase, he says, was represented by Pope's *Essay on Man* and the second by Voltaire's *Candide*. Harper's comment indicates the historical

---

[45] *The Excursion*, I, 354–62, 370–1.   [46] *P.W.*, V, 373.
[47] George MacLean Harper, *William Wordsworth*. London, 1929, p. 517.

perspective from which we can best see what happens to the doctrine of "the best of all possible worlds" when Wordsworth falls back upon it after the intrusion of the Solitary, who was a reader, we should remember, of that "dull product of a scoffer's pen", *Candide*. As Pope and other poets of the eighteenth century used it, the doctrine conveyed a genuine if superficial optimism. Stimulated by scientific discoveries, it implied further investigations would uncover further evidence to confirm it. It encouraged the hope that laws of human nature would be found by which society could be brought to conform to universal law. It contained within itself the possibility of progress and perfectibility.

When Wordsworth returns to the doctrine in *The Excursion*, it is with the disillusionment and sophistication of the Solitary. He returns to it in weakness, as to a place of refuge, in a desperate search for the "central peace, subsisting at the heart / Of endless agitation".[48] It becomes for him a justification not merely for accepting the world as it is but for doing everything he could to preserve and reinforce traditional culture. And by traditional culture Wordsworth means what Fairchild calls "the ideal commonwealth of the Lakes",[49] its unchanging continuity symbolised by the stories of those buried in the churchyard. As the doctrine is developed by the Wanderer and Pastor, it implies that any attempt by man to pry into the secrets of nature, or to change the structure of society, is to tamper with God's will and is likely to lead to far worse conditions than prevail at present. Even when the Wanderer advocates what seems to be a programme for social change, like the religious education of the poor, he does it as a means of inculcating "the discipline of virtue", so that they will acquiesce cheerfully in their lot.[50] The third phase of the literary duel has ended in a hollow victory for reaction and timidity. In retrospect, at any rate, the despair of the Solitary seems far more courageous and admirable than the easy faith of the Wanderer. Perhaps one reason why Wordsworth was unable to work any more on *The Recluse* is that it meant opening his mind again to the Solitary and renewing the conflict.[51] In the long run, it was simpler to sit in the

[48] *The Excursion*, IV, 1146–7.   [49] H. N. Fairchild, Vol. III, p. 218.

[50] *The Excursion*, IX, 293–362.

[51] For comments and letters from 1815 to 1845 on the unfinished *Recluse*, see *P.W.*, V, 367–8. The psychological implications of Wordsworth's com-

shelter of his self-convictions, secured against the endless agitation that swirled without. The last five books of *The Excursion* almost justify Shelley's bitter joke in *Peter Bell The Third*:

> But from the first 'twas Peter's drift
> To be a kind of moral eunuch,
> He touched the hem of Nature's shift,
> Felt faint – and never dared uplift
> The closest, all-concealing tunic.[52]

Few of Wordsworth's contemporaries would have agreed with Shelley. A great many of them complained because *The Excursion* was not orthodox enough. Probably most of them were bored and vaguely irritated, like Jeffrey, by what they considered "a tissue of moral and devotional ravings, in which innumerable changes are rung upon a very few simple and familiar ideas". Interestingly enough, Jeffrey finds the Solitary's narrative at the end of Book III "the most spirited and interesting part of the poem", although he seems completely to miss the point of the rest of the book which he calls "exceedingly dull and mystical" and "insufferably diffuse".[53] But even if contemporaries were bored, they were impressed, particularly the poets. Keats's extravagant praise, though it may have been based upon one passage only, is indicative.[54] And during the next thirty-five years, while Wordsworth's reputation as poet-philosopher grew, the reputation of *The Excursion* grew also. It is probably impossible to say to what extent the poem is a major influence in moulding attitudes of Victorian poets and to

[52] 313–17. *Shelley's Poetical Works*, ed. Thomas Hutchinson. Oxford, 1935, p. 349.

[53] Review of *The Excursion* in *Edinburgh Review*, Nov. 1814; reprinted in *Contemporary Reviews of Romantic Poetry*, ed. John Wain. New York, 1953, pp. 71 ff.

[54] In a note to Haydon, 10 Jan. 1818, Keats wrote that "there are three things to rejoice at in this Age – The Excursion Your Pictures and Hazlitt's depth of Taste" (*The Letters of John Keats*, ed. Maurice Buxton Forman, Oxford, 1935, p. 79). The passage to which Keats was especially attracted was that on the origins of Greek mythology, IV, 718–62, 847–87. See *P.W.*, v, 427.

---

ment in a letter to Landor on 20 Apr. 1822 are obvious: "The *Recluse* has had a long sleep, save in my thoughts; my MSS. are so ill-penned and blurred that they are useless to all but myself; and at present I cannot face them".

what extent it merely anticipates them. But one can say with Graham Hough that "anyone who wishes to understand the nineteenth century must read it", for in it one can see clearly at work the forces which determine and limit the direction of nineteenth-century poetry.[55] Wordsworth's conflict foreshadows the conflict of most Victorian poets, who shuttle back and forth between the dead ends of the Solitary's despair and the Wanderer's faith. The factors that we have examined which prevented Wordsworth from developing a new and meaningful philosophy prevailed throughout the century. Indeed so immense was Wordsworth's reputation that his failure to find a way out must have had a great deal to do with the failure of poets during the rest of the century. The compromise between orthodoxy and naturalism which he fell back upon can without exaggeration be called the official faith of Victorian England. But it is a faith more and more uneasily held, and the sombre spirit of the Solitary, subdued at the Picnic which concludes *The Excursion*, is an increasingly unwelcome intruder at the Victorian Picnic, as new causes for pessimism arise. Ironically the harmless botanist and geologist are the most destructive of all.

[55] *The Romantic Poets.* London, 1953, p. 90. It is only fair to say that Hough sees the influence of *The Excursion* as entirely beneficial: "It is one of the great reassertions of traditional values against the unhistorical rationalist optimism of the enlightenment".

E. A. Horsman

THE DESIGN OF
WORDSWORTH'S *PRELUDE*[1]

When we are criticising a long poem like Wordsworth's *Prelude*, we need to consider not only the quality of its language but also the disposition of its materials. I believe that this poem is organised so as to compare certain crucial experiences, and that we need to understand the pointers to this which Wordsworth gives in the argument of the poem.

Dr Leavis spoke years ago as if the alternatives were either to treat the argument as "philosophic", as "explaining" the experiences the poem embodies, or to regard it as a mere sleight of hand, commanding a certain kind of attention but yielding no paraphrasable content at all.[2] Now while I think Wordsworth has a paraphrasable argument, I do not think it is there to "explain" in any "philosophic" sense, except in a very few cases. What Wordsworth is doing is not philosophising about God or Nature (though he may be presupposing a number of philosophies about both) but trying to understand his own experience by relating to each other what he takes to be the significant examples and setting upon each of them a comparative value. He has already used this comparative procedure in the Tintern Abbey lines. To read them, it is more important to understand the difference Wordsworth presents between experience dominated by the senses and experience in which something further is supplied by intellect and feeling, than to press the poem for a theology. So, in reading *The*

---

[1] Reprinted from the *Proceedings and Papers* of the Tenth Congress of the Australasian Universities Language and Literature Association, ed. Peter Dane, Auckland (University of Auckland), 1966.

[2] F. R. Leavis, *Revaluation.* London, 1936.

Prelude, we need to grasp, not a set of ideas about God or Nature which may be taken out of the poem, but rather a set of ideas which are there in it and must be taken into our reading of it, if the relations amongst its parts are to be understood. These ideas involve a terminology which is rudimentary and quite uncriticised, the very uncertainties of which, as William Empson and Colin Clarke have shown, enrich the poem;[3] terms like sense, feeling, intellect, reason, are sufficient to support and emphasise the contrasts embodied in the major passages.

Readers of Proust will remember the comical disgust of Marcel that he should be exalted "not by an important idea but by a mouldy smell".[4] All the same, the gift of the "impressions" which he values above everything else must be followed, he says in *Le temps retrouvé*, by the work of the intelligence:[5] the impressions must be "penetrated" to see not only what are their contents but also what are their associations. I defer in this to those who know Proust properly, but it does seem possible to see as the ground-work of his novel an activity of comparison, comparison to find out which experiences had been more precious for Marcel's spiritual renewal,[6] which had left the profoundest part of his mind inert and which had activated it. Wordsworth's effort in *The Prelude* seems to me a similar one. He does not go as far as Proust in finding that "everything is in the mind", but he does agree that "only crude and erroneous perception places everything in the object".[7] As a user of images, he agrees with Proust on the very figure of a flash or a gleam, to characterise the crucial experiences. As the architect of a whole work, he agrees upon a similar structure which "recomposes" the materials furnished by life "around verities apprehended within".[8] And because the crucial experiences are too rare to make up a work of art on their own, he enshrines

---

[3] William Empson, *The Structure of Complex Words*. London, 1951. Colin Clarke, *Romantic Paradox*. London, 1962.

[4] Marcel Proust, *A la recherche du temps perdu*, Bibliothèque de la Pléiade, Paris, 1954, I. 496. Tr. C. K. Scott Moncrieff, London, 1922–31, III. 93.

[5] *Op. cit.*, iii. 880; tr. xii. 227.   [6] *Op. cit.*, iii. 882; tr. xii. 230.

[7] *Op. cit.*, iii. 912; tr. xii. 270–1.

[8] Scott Moncrieff (xii. 249) offers suggestive criticism, rather than translation, at this point; compare Proust, iii. 898, with iii. 880, n. 2. The note contains almost the same passage, of which a more accurate translation is offered in Scott Moncrieff, xii. 227.

them, as Proust does,[9] in matter less pure, in truths which the intellect extracts directly from more ordinary experiences – love, politics, social relations, even from the sort of experience which fails to lead to the "flash" or "gleam", the sort which lays "the inner faculties asleep".

Wordsworth makes a design out of all this, because he has an artist's eye for similarity and dissimilarity. This controls the material, even though the poem seems to grow by mere accretion. We know a great deal about its actual evolution. We can watch him, for instance, in the early part (written first in Germany in 1798–9), rearranging the experiences he presents so as to bring out more clearly the subject of the poem and make it progress. In the earliest version there is first the account of bird-nesting, which seems purely a matter of the senses; then his robbing of some woodcock snares, after which the mind contributes an awareness of "Low breathings coming after me, and sounds Of undistinguishable motion"; then there is an incongruous passage about "hallow'd and pure motions of the sense" which seem to have "an intellectual charm". These lines are not at all appropriate to the experiences embodied just before and still less to the one which follows – the stealing of a boat, which results in "a dim and undetermin'd sense Of unknown modes of being". These passages he subsequently rearranges so that, with the addition of the ice-skating lines, the experiences in which the mind's contribution is explicit (in relation to the robbed snares and the stolen boat) alternate with those in which it is only implied; while the lines, incongruous in their first position, about a "calm delight" and "intellectual charm" follow them all so as to make the transition to Book II which emphasises "quiet" as the mark of the greater contemplative power of the mind. Already he is establishing a pattern of experiences which are apparently similar in that each leads to some kind of illumination: but, on the other hand, each differs from the others in some crucial respect which advances the poem – which marks an advance in awareness for the hero, the writer, and the reader. This is one principal feature of the whole design – repetition with progressively increasing awareness.

Herbert Lindenberger, who can find "no real progression in *The Prelude*, but only restatements of the poet's efforts to transcend the

[9] *Op. cit.*, iii. 898; tr. xii. 250.

confines of the temporal order", sees the similarities amongst the experiences Wordsworth values, but overlooks the dissimilarities to which the design gives as great an emphasis.[10] The pattern of repetition with increased awareness emerges out of Wordsworth's method of handling experience in Book I, when he is presenting an unbroken unity of being in childhood – making us subtly aware of what was going on, but without superimposing the categories of a later, adult experience of division.

What the somewhat inflated passages of blank verse commentary do, between these episodes, is less to account for the experiences he selects than to offer thanks for them from the point of view of the regenerated hero of the conclusion to the whole poem. It is because he has been renewed that he gives the credit to a personified Wisdom of the Universe or speaks of his pain and fear as having been sanctified. It is not quite such nonsense as the intelligent critic in the *Pelican Guide to English Literature* thinks it,[11] but it makes sense in relation to the completed poem rather than to the detail of this part of it.

Repeatedly, it seems to me, we must interpret the parts in the light of our reading of the whole. In Book II, for instance, the experiences included are less boisterous, and the emphasis falls on the recognition of "an auxiliar light" from the mind, a "visionary" and "plastic" power which turns organic pleasure into a profounder joy. At times this power conquers the senses themselves, so that "bodily eyes" are forgotten;[12] as an inward power, it is characterised by a union of thought and feeling.[13] So we begin to be aware of possible division – sense, thought, feeling. Each of these is to become dominant at later points in the poem, as the hero – who could well be called Albion – "fall[s] into divison"; they are to rejoin as he is "resurrect[ed] into unity" (compare Blake, *Vala* I. 18–20). The passage about the child at the breast (which Dr Leavis took as one of his examples, though hardly a fair one, as Wordsworth is constructing, not reconstructing, the

[10] Herbert S. Lindenberger, *On Wordsworth's Prelude*, Princeton, 1963, p. 188.

[11] *Pelican Guide to English Literature*, ed. Boris Ford, 7 vols. Harmondsworth 1959–61, v. 155–6.

[12] *The Prelude*, II, 368–9, eds. E. de. Selincourt and Helen Darbishire, Oxford, 1959 edition of the 1805 text.

[13] *Op. cit.*, 417–18.

experience) is offered by Wordsworth as a case of sensation inter-penetrated with feelings of affection. Because of the close human relation, he says, feeling gives inner power, which, working through the faculties of sense, "Creates, creator and receiver both".[14] Whether this is true of the child is less important than the value which is being set – in language which Dr Leavis and Professor Donald Davie both find moving – upon internal unity of being (the co-operation of sense and feeling), and, through the mother, upon a relation of close kinship with the world outside.[15] Dr Leavis was quite right to make a connexion between the passage and how Wordsworth "comes to have the kind of experience he describes in "Tintern Abbey"": but it would have been more to the point to relate the passage to the rest of the poem in which it occurs. For the passage follows lines in which Coleridge has been praised as one to whom the unity of all has been revealed, and the creative power of the mind, with which even the child at the breast is credited, is placed in contrast to what Wordsworth calls the "false secondary power", which confuses distinctions the mind has made with things which we perceive.[16] The point about the false secondary power is that it places a barrier of its own making between the mind and the rest of the world. At this point a rejected draft shows very clearly Wordsworth's habit of comparison: this secondary activity of the mind

> Not only is not worthy to be deemed
> Our being, to be prized as what we are
> But is the very littleness of life.[17]

The activity of discovering what is to be prized in our being: here is the life of the poem. It is continued even in the garrulous book which follows, on his life at Cambridge. For here the point is that, in the absence of the natural forms which had at first nourished his powers, the mind becomes "busier in itself than heretofore", "[turned] in upon itself".[18] The phrase "I . . . spread my thoughts"[19] recalls directly the one used of the child at the

[14] *Op. cit.*, 269–73.
[15] F. R. Leavis, *Revaluation*; Donald Davie, *Articulate Energy*, London, 1955.
[16] *The Prelude*, II, 221–4.   [17] *Op. cit.*, 434–5 n.
[18] *Op. cit.*, III, 104, 112.   [19] *Op. cit.*, 113.

breast: "his mind spreads".[20] The result of this, in Book III, is an experience in which external forms are endowed with a life explicitly communicated by the active mind: "I gave [them] a moral life", he says.[21] Does he mean a life related to human good and evil? This is less important than the emphasis, which is characteristic of Book III, upon the power of the mind to give such a life, upon the mind, like Newton's, voyaging alone (the lines, 62–3 (1850), added in MS. D, one of the latest versions, are an excellent example of great poetry generated by the inner concerns of the whole book) – all this in contrast to the plastic power of Book II which is

> for the most
> Subservient strictly to the external things
> With which it commun'd.[22]

Wordsworth uses passages of secondary intensity like this one in order, as Eliot puts it, "to elicit . . . the significance of other parts and to unite them into a unity greater than all the parts".[23] Wordsworth uses them, that is, to throw emphasis upon the varied kinds of commerce possible between a man's mind and the rest of the universe.

Book III contrasts with Books I and II, also, in that the hero's "outward life", though to all appearance as trivial as the sports of his boyhood, fails to move him to anything more momentous. It sends imagination to sleep, unlike his earlier pleasures which had awakened it. Later he will speak of Bartholomew Fair as something which "lays . . . the whole creative powers of man asleep",[24] or of the power of the senses "to lay the inner faculties asleep".[25] One thinks of such phrases of Blake's as "Newton's sleep" or "the sleep of Ulro".

Book IV returns to the equally trivial occupations (and this is stressed) which, at home, do stimulate his mind. (He uses a similar overt contrast between Book VII – man in London – and Book VIII – man in the Lake District.) The variables which thus receive emphasis are the presence of the hills, and the sense the hero com-

---

[20] *Op. cit.*, II, 253.   [21] *Op. cit.*, III, 126.

[22] *Op. cit.*, II, 385–7.

[23] T. S. Eliot, *To Criticize the Critic*. London, 1965, p. 34.

[24] *The Prelude*, VII, 652–4.   [25] *Op. cit.*, XI, 195.

municates of being where he belongs. The connection is both back to Book II, in which the child at the breast was seen as achieving a sense of being at home (with its earthy and social metaphors, "the gravitation and the filial bond"), and forward to Book v with its contrast between wilful education of the mind alone and the sort of education which, if we are at home in our environment, is always going on, "Even in what seem our most unfruitful hours."[26]

Each of the two main episodes of Book IV arises out of an unpromising mood of quiescence; one recalls Proust's hero saying, of the extra-temporal sense which he most values, "that being had never manifested itself except when I was inactive".[27] In Wordsworth's case, not only is his mind stirred when apparently listless, but emphasis falls upon the way in which the senses and the social affections co-operate: in the books concerned with the French Revolution, these separate parts of the whole man are to act independently, to tug different ways and are eventually to be defeated by "independent intellect".[28] Book v gives a foretaste of this by singling out the work of the "independent intellect", "commerce of [man's] nature with itself", and contrasting it with the commerce of man's nature with the Nature outside himself. At every turn the crucial experiences, while conveyed with moving particularity, yet point beyond themselves. It is their arrangement within the poem which enables them to do this. By such means, Wordsworth moves from the particular to the general without throwing too great a strain on the slacker verse in which he tries to elicit part of the significance of the more concentrated passages.

In Book VI is the point of balance of the whole. Here, the "independent intellect" emphasised in Book v becomes the "mind beset With images, and haunted by itself",[29] conscious of "paramount endowment" as it engages in mathematics, but stultified if "compell'd to be a life unto itself"; here the example is Coleridge, giving himself to "subtle speculations" and to "Platonic forms", "Debarr'd from Nature's living images". This latter line[30] shows how, despite the mode of wandering meditation characteristic of the poem, its subject is in fact firmly under control. For Book VI

[26] *Op. cit.*, v, 388.
[27] Proust, *A la recherche du temps perdu*, iii, 871; tr. xii, 216.
[28] *The Prelude*, x, 830.   [29] *Op. cit.*, VI, 179–80.
[30] *Op. cit.*, VI, 313.

is to show the extreme importance and the extreme oddity of the relationship between the images in the mind and Nature's images outside it. To this end, three crucial incidents are presented: the visit to the Grande Chartreuse (added after 1805), the contrast between Mont Blanc and the Vale of Chamouny, and the crossing of the Alps.

In the first of these, the convent of Chartreuse is praised for the relief it brings, in two almost contradictory ways, to the mind haunted by itself. On the one hand, monastery life is "this embodied dream This substance by which mortal men have clothed, Humanly clothed, the ghostliness of things"[31]; and this happens in a setting of cliff and forest to which man, "lost within himself In trepidation", may look with "bodily eyes", away from the "abyss" of the mind, "and be consoled".[32] One thinks, of course, of II. 368-9: "I forgot That I had bodily eyes", or of the Fenwick note to the Immortality *Ode*: "Many times . . . have I grasped at a wall or tree to recall myself from this abyss of idealism to the reality". What the senses supply is something to be grasped as consoling, just as real as the terrifying life of the inner mind. But, on the other hand, there is equal danger in the dominance of the senses over the mind, reducing it to the status of a "mean pensioner On outward forms".[33] So the "convent" of Chartreuse is praised for its "conquest over sense",[34] which means not merely, as Empson thinks, sensuality, but all the senses which may reduce the mind to subjection.[35] I want to come back to this later.

When he first sees Mont Blanc (to take the second episode), he grieves

> To have a soulless image on the eye
> Which had usurp'd upon a living thought
> That never more could be.[36]

For some reason, sense fails to co-operate with the mind, the image on the eye is soulless, dead by comparison with the living thought, which it obliterates. (The parallel with the repeated disappointment of Proust's Marcel is very close here.) Wordsworth

[31] *Op. cit.*, VI, p. 198, 27-9.   [32] *Op. cit.* (1850), VI, 469-71.
[33] *Op. cit.* (1805), VI, 667-8.   [34] *Op. cit.* (1850), VI, 458.
[35] William Empson, *The Structure of Complex Words*, p. 293.
[36] *The Prelude*, VI, 454-6.

goes on to make a contrast between Mont Blanc and the pleasant pastoral vale beneath: the contrast is carried by the language as much as anything, the generalised image of the conventional pastoral:

> There doth the Reaper bind the yellow sheaf,
> The Maiden spread the haycock in the sun[37]

instead of his own stark and strange idiom of soulless images and living thoughts. And the pastoral scene, he says, "reconcil'd us to realities" – the very carelessness of the phrase carrying the doubt as to where "reality" is to be found. This doubt he makes clear as he returns to his own language – to "something of stern mood, an under-thirst Of vigour, never utterly asleep".[38] The reference, as with all these "under-" compounds of Wordsworth's ("under-presence", "under-consciousness', in XIII, 71 and variants, or "under-soul" in III, 540) is to a part of his being which is only rarely kindled to life, but which, when it is, gives him the touch-stone for all other experience – a touchstone which it is the business of *The Prelude* as a whole to apply.

Here the under-thirst is satisfied by the Simplon Pass; and Wordsworth recognises that the experience he values most is made possible only when an "awful Power" rises "from the mind's abyss",[39] when the light of sense

> Goes out in flashes that have shewn to us
> The invisible world . . .[40]

As is clear from Dorothy Wordsworth's *Journal* (23 Aug., 9 Sep. 1820, when they revisited the place), the high hopes he had had of triumphantly crossing the Alps were suddenly extinguished when he found he had done so without knowing it. As he writes *The Prelude*, the loss of the physical triumph brings to the fore that power of the mind which is at home "with infinitude . . . with hope . . . and something evermore about to be".

Geoffrey Hartman distorts this episode, the crucial one in the poem.[41] He fails to see Wordsworth's contrast, very plain in

---

[37] *Op. cit.*, 464–5.   [38] *Op. cit.*, 489–90.
[39] *Op. cit.* (1850), VI, 594.   [40] *Op. cit.* (1805), VI, 535–6.
[41] Geoffrey H. Hartman, *Wordsworth's Poetry 1787–1814*. New Haven and London, 1964, pp. 40 ff.

Book VI, between the sterile activity of the mind haunted by itself
and the creative activity of the mind in contact with the external
world. The Simplon episode is not completed until the description of the chasm which follows the lines about the light of sense
going out: it is because the power of the mind had been suddenly
revealed (when its hopes were defeated by the facts) that the chasm
assumed its magnificence, its winds, torrents, and crags becoming
themselves like characters of an Apocalypse. Professor Hartman
even claims that Wordsworth actively avoids "apocalyptic self-
consciousness": that is, that he avoids confronting his own inner
mind.[42] But Wordsworth has shown himself constantly aware of
"the might of Souls, And what they do within themselves"[43]; he
has not been afraid to turn "the mind in upon itself"[44]; he has
emphasised the forgetting of bodily eyes in Book II, and has referred directly to the light of sense going out:

> One song . . .
> Most audible then when the fleshly ear . . .
> Forgot its functions, and slept undisturb'd.[45]

Our being's heart and home may be finally "with infinitude", but
it is plain, from the experience embodied in the rest of Book VI
and from the poem as a whole, that, constituted as we are, we shall
be lost, Wordsworth believes, in "the abyss of idealism", unless
infinitude clothe itself in finiteness. The whole experience is both
similar to that of III, 124 ff. in which he claims to give a moral life
to natural forms, and dissimilar (and richer) because of the inter-
action between inner and outer worlds – what he calls later, in
summing up, "an ennobling interchange Of action from within
and from without". The episode in Book VI can be radically misunderstood unless it is seen in the context of the book and of the
whole poem.

To take another, and final, example from recent criticism: when
Lindenberger makes his extraordinary statement that Wordsworth's "visionary experiences . . . are ultimately not very different
from one another", he makes this passage one of his examples:
"For the sake of Wordsworth's more fundamental purposes the
ascent of Mt Snowdon in the last book might just as well have

[42] Op. cit., p. 63.
[44] Op. cit., 112.
[43] The Prelude, III, 178–9.
[45] Op. cit., II, 431–4.

is curiously similar to the conflict Blake mobilises between states of being to which he gives mythological names. The actual states which Blake finds crucial do not, of course, correspond to Wordsworth's, but both poets use the basic notion of a unity of being which, after disruption, is reconstituted; both use the language of religion in describing and evaluating this process. Sometimes the resemblances, indeed, seem even closer: when, for instance, in *Jerusalem*, Blake displays, on a stage of universal history, the way in which men repeatedly refuse the divine vision and have to be brought back to it by the imaginative artist, he sees the successive stages in this process as stages in the growth of a man:

> the wonders Divine
> Of Human Imagination throughout all the Three Regions
> immense
> Of Childhood, Manhood & Old Age . . .[68]

In a way which seems to me comparable, Wordsworth has selected stages of his own growth to maturity and arranged them so that they function as images for the stages in the commerce between inner and outer worlds, in the "interchange Of Action from within and from without", which he sees as the foundation of man's dignity. He shows the reverse of what Keats saw in Byron who, he said, "cuts a figure but is not figurative". Wordsworth cuts no sort of figure; he is even willing to make himself appear quite ludicrous: but he does succeed in making his own life figurative to a startling degree, by using it to show the diversity of relations that are possible between the mind of man and the rest of the universe. The selection and ordering of instances of this diversity is the key to the design of the whole poem.

To examine this design may take one too far away from consideration of the quality of the language; but this quality is only part of what makes the work a poem (even though, if the quality is predominantly bad, we will not be justified in considering it at all). The question is, can we, without examining the design, the interrelation of the parts for both the writer and the reader, claim to have read the poem at all? Must we not, at the very least, be sure we can discern its face value before we go on to see what other value it may have?

[68] Plate 98, Nonesuch Edition, p. 566.

Donald Davie

DIONYSUS IN *LYRICAL BALLADS*

I

"I am myself," said Wordsworth, "one of the happiest of men; and no man who does not partake of that happiness, who lives a life of constant bustle, and whose felicity depends on the opinions of others, can possibly comprehend the best of my poems." It was thus that he delivered himself on 8 May, 1812, to Henry Crabb Robinson: and it is a good example of the frightening and repellent self-assurance with which Wordsworth contemplated the fact and the nature of his own genius, and communicated his sense of these to others. But this need not mean that Wordsworth was self-deluded, that there was nothing to contemplate, or that what was there was something different from what Wordsworth saw. It will be the contention of this essay that Wordsworth knew the facts of his own genius better than anyone.

It is remarkable, to begin with, how readily Wordsworth proceeds to oppose his happiness, or his own sense of it, to "a life of constant bustle". Did it not occur to him that many men experience a quite genuine happiness precisely in "bustle", in a sense of purposeful activity around them, in the changing spectacles of energetic life? Apparently not; and this from the first tells us something about Wordsworth's sort of happiness. It expressed itself in stillness and silence:

> I was glad to accompany the Wordsworths to the British Museum. I had to wait for them in the ante-room, and we had at last but a hurried survey of the antiquities. I did not perceive that Wordsworth much enjoyed the Elgin Marbles;

but he is a still man when he does enjoy himself, and by no means ready to talk of his pleasure, except to his sister.[1]

"He is a still man when he does enjoy himself." And so are the people in his poems, like the Idiot Boy, who was "idle all for very joy". We shall go some way towards understanding how Words-worth's personal happiness goes into his poems, as he asserted it did, if we begin by noticing, as many have done already, how often silence and immobility are the distinguishing features of the per-sonages he introduces into his poems. This connection is forced upon the attentive reader with particular vividness by what is the profoundest response to this aspect of Wordsworth the man as he was known to his contemporaries. This is Benjamin Robert Haydon's account of how he took a cast of Wordsworth's face:

> I had a cast made yesterday of Wordsworth's face. He bore it like a philosopher. John Scott was to meet him at breakfast, and just as he came in the plaster was put on. Wordsworth was sitting in the other room in my dressing-gown, with his hands folded, sedate, solemn and still. I stepped in to Scott and told him as a curiosity to take a peep, that he might say the first sight he ever had of so great a poet was in this stage towards immortality.
>
> I opened the door slowly, and there he sat innocent and unconscious of our plot, in mysterious stillness and silence.[2]

"Solemn and still . . .", "mysterious stillness and silence . . .": these are the very terms in which Wordsworth himself charac-teristically offers for contemplation his own most important human figures, such as the Idiot Boy, Michael, the Leech-Gatherer. And Haydon's prose, here bringing out the symbolic reverberations of a commonplace and accidental situation, is already half-way to poetry.

---

[1] Crabb Robinson, *Diary* (20 Nov. 1820). Compare Robinson's description (5 Apr. 1823) of Wordsworth at a musical party: "(he) declared himself perfectly delighted and satisfied, but he sat alone, silent, and with his face covered, and was generally supposed to be asleep".

[2] Haydon's *Autobiography*, ed. M. Elwin. London, 1950, p. 245. Journal entry for 13 Apr. 1825.

But Haydon goes on:

> When he was relieved he came in to breakfast with his usual
> cheerfulness and delighted us with his bursts of inspiration.
> At one time he shook us both in explaining the principles of
> his system, his views of man, and his object in writing.
>   Wordsworth's faculty is in describing those far-reaching
> and intense feelings and glimmerings and doubts and fears
> and hopes of man, as referring to what he might be before he
> was born or what he may be hereafter.
>   He is a great being and will hereafter be ranked as one who
> had a portion of the spirit of the mighty ones, especially
> Milton, but who did not possess the power of using that
> spirit otherwise than with reference to himself and so as to
> excite a reflex action only: this is, in my opinion, his great
> characteristic.

Haydon's testimony is uniquely valuable in thus proceeding,
though by an associative rather than logical link, from the stillness
of Wordsworth the man to the stillness of his poetry. For that is
what it amounts to, this "reflex action only": the conspicuous
lack in Wordsworth of any dramatic feeling, the way his insights
never express themselves in terms of energetic action or of steadily
suspenseful events developing out of an initial situation. It is
clear that this feature of Wordsworth's work, whether we interpret
it as a limitation or merely a distinguishing characteristic, was
a commonplace in the circles which Haydon and Robinson and
(less constantly) Wordsworth himself frequented. It is what lies
behind Keats's famous judgment about "the egotistical sublime",[3]
and there is obviously a close relationship between this and
Hazlitt's remarks in *The Spirit of the Age*:

> Those persons who look upon Mr Wordsworth as a merely
> puerile writer, must be rather at a loss to account for his
> strong predilection for such geniuses as Dante and Michel-

---

[3] Keats, *Letters*, ed. Forman (3rd edn.), p. 227, Oct. 1818, to Richard
Woodhouse: "As to the poetical Character itself (I mean that sort of which, if
I am any thing, I am a Member; that sort distinguished from the Wordsworthian or egotistical sublime; which is a thing *per se* and stands alone) it is
not itself – it has no self – it is everything and nothing – It has no character –
it enjoys light and shade; . . ."

angelo. We do not think our author has any very cordial sympathy with Shakespear. How should he? Shakespear was the least of an egotist of any body in the world.[4]

Plainly, in this curiously left-handed compliment, the word "egotist" is meant to convey a sense of Wordsworth's incapacity for the dramatist's feat of sinking his own personality in those of his creations. And this is one of the places where the relationship is clearest between Hazlitt and Keats, who in his letters expatiated on the judgments here passed by implication on both Wordsworth and Shakespeare. Similarly, the whole Keatsian doctrine of "negative capability", as exemplified especially by Shakespeare, must be related to what Hazlitt says of the latter in his *Lectures on the English Poets*.

Less obviously related but more arresting is a Shelleyan judgment which puts him in the same camp. This is expressed in four acute and crucial stanzas from *Peter Bell the Third* (Part the Fourth):

> He had a mind which was somehow
>   At once circumference and centre
> Of all he might or feel or know;
> Nothing went ever out, although
>   Something did ever enter.
>
> He had as much imagination
>   As a pint-pot; – he never could
> Fancy another situation,
> From which to dart his contemplation,
>   Than that wherein he stood.
>
> Yet his was individual mind,
>   And new-created all he saw
> In a new manner, and refined
> Those new creations, and combined
>   Them, by a master-spirit's law.
>
> Thus – though unimaginative –
>   An apprehension clear, intense,

[4] Hazlitt, *The Spirit of the Age*, ed. A. R. Waller. London, 1910 (Everyman Edition), p. 258.

> Of his mind's work, had made alive
> The things it wrought on; I believe
> Wakening a sort of thought in sense.[5]

The imagination which Shelley here denies to Wordsworth is specifically the dramatic imagination. "Nothing went ever out although / Something did ever enter" – this limiting judgment is as just as the wonderful compliment, "wakening a sort of thought in sense". And it is worth pondering. It is not just that *The Borderers*, while it has an interesting and important theme and contains distinguished writing, is yet, by common consent, an unsuccessful drama. Whenever Wordsworth essays the dramatic monologue, writing in character, as in the notorious case of "The Thorn", the effect, as Coleridge pointed out, is disastrous. And to go further again, to that loose sense of "dramatic" which covers the contrivance of tense situations and logical development of plot in narrative, it will be generally allowed that here too Wordsworth is deficient. The plot of "The Idiot Boy", for instance, is illogical and arbitrary – unforgivably so, were it not that Wordsworth, humorously and arrogantly, makes it clear that his perfunctory handling of it is deliberate. For Wordsworth was aware of this peculiarity in himself, and as usual stood over it without apology. Admitting the absence from his poetry of the interest, for the reader or spectator, of dramatic conflict and crisis, he throws down the gauntlet:

> then let him see if there are no victories in the world of spirit, no changes, no commotions, no revolutions there, no fluxes and refluxes of the thoughts which may be made interesting by modest combination with the stiller actions of the bodily frame.[6]

Let Wordsworth's own word "stiller", applied with characteristic arrogance to the eventful world of dramatic action, stand as one more proof that the peculiarity of Wordsworth's imagination, the way it resists dramatic embodiment, is related to his being "a still

---

[5] *The Complete Poetical Works*, ed. Thomas Hutchinson. London, 1945, 293–312.

[6] *The Letters of William and Dorothy Wordsworth: The Middle Years*, ed. E. de Selincourt, 2 vols. Oxford, 1937, p. 198.

man when he does enjoy himself". And it is a real peculiarity, for of no earlier poet of comparable stature by common consent (Chaucer, Dante, Milton, not to speak of Shakespeare) is it true to anything the same extent. Presumably it does not seem so odd to later generations of Wordsworthians as to the first one, simply because we have ceased since then to expect the great poetic imagination to express itself dramatically, and hence objectively. Perhaps one way to define the Romantic movement would be to call it that change in artistic sensibility which substituted the reflective or the ruminative for the dramatic imagination.

2

De Quincey shows one way of getting into Wordsworth's poems by way of the avenue he himself indicated: his happiness, his capacity for joy. De Quincey says finely:

Whoever looks searchingly into the characteristic genius of Wordsworth, will see that he does not willingly deal with a passion in its direct aspect, or presenting an unmodified contour, but in forms more complex and oblique, and when passing under the shadow of some secondary passion. Joy, for instance, that wells up from constitutional sources, joy that is ebullient from youth to age, and cannot cease to sparkle, he yet exhibits in the person of Matthew, the village schoolmaster, as touched and overgloomed by memories of sorrow. In the poem of *We are Seven*, which brings into day for the first time a profound fact in the abysses of human nature – viz. that the mind of an infant cannot admit the idea of death, cannot comprehend it, any more than the fountain of light can comprehend the aboriginal darkness . . . – the little mountaineer, who furnishes the text for this lovely strain, she whose fullness of life could not brook the gloomy faith in a grave, is yet (for the effect upon the reader) brought into connexion with the reflex shadows of the grave; and if she herself has *not*, the reader *has*, and through this very child, the gloom of that contemplation obliquely irradiated, as raised in relief upon his imagination, even by *her*. That same infant, which subjectively could not tolerate death, being by the reader contemplated objectively, flashes upon us the tenderest images of death. Death and its sunny antipole are forced into connexion.[7]

This account of "We are Seven" is just, and central to my argument. But as De Quincey says, it is only a particular instance of something that is generally true of Wordsworth's Lyrical Ballads, in which "joy that is ebullient" is constantly being "overgloomed by memories of sorrow". The necessity of this for Wordsworth, and its attraction for him, is well but teasingly expressed (to take a further instance) in a stanza from his "Anecdote for Fathers":

> A day it was when I could bear
> Some fond regrets to entertain;
> With so much happiness to spare,
> I could not feel a pain.[8]

The poem tells how Wordsworth walked out with a five-year-old boy at Liswyn farm, and found himself, while relishing to the full the attractions of that place, regretting that it had not also the beauties of a seaside-place which he calls "Kilve".[9] It is most important to take the force of Wordsworth's explanation of this. It is not the trite observation that joy unalloyed is no part of man's lot. Nor is it that man necessarily manipulates his emotions to bring about a more piquant taste, as for instance the enervated enthusiasts of the sensibility cult would roll their feelings on the tongue, to produce "grateful tears, delicious sorrow". No; it is, as De Quincey saw, the very "ebullience" of natural joy which brims over into regret. The phenomenon is of superabundant feeling, not enervation; as the quoted stanza says.

And this, too, is what the poem says. The poet presses the boy to admit that he shares the same sort of ambiguous feeling; and, when he admits it, he badgers him to know how he explains it. The boy resists, until at last:

[7] *De Quincey's Literary Criticism*, ed. H. Darbishire. London, 1909, pp. 227–8.
[8] 13–16.
[9] The poem was written at Alfoxden, and the names, though the names of real places, were chosen for euphony; the boy was Wordsworth's ward, son of his friend Basil Montagu.

> His head he raised – there was in sight,
> It caught his eye, he saw it plain —
> Upon the house-top, glittering bright,
> A broad and gilded vane.
>
> Then did the boy his tongue unlock,
> And eased his mind with this reply:
> "At Kilve there was no weather-cock;
> And that's the reason why."[10]

If we have not taken the point of the earlier stanza, we shall miss the poignancy in the boy's artlessness. The point is not the child's inability to see things in adult perspective, so that to him the presence or absence of a weather-vane over-rides all other considerations. Wordsworth precludes this by making the boy say he preferred the other place because it hadn't a weather-vane, not because it had. Wordsworth does not invite us to adult condescension. We are not to say, "Oh, how sweet!" On the contrary, we have to see that the adult and the child are at one; that the boy, like the man, is enjoying himself so much that he can afford, and deliberately seeks out, some regret for which there is no objective reason. Pressed by the grown-up to find a reason, he fobs him off with a weather-vane: but he does not deceive himself, and as it happens he does not deceive the poet, though he deceives some readers. The pathos in the close derives from our compassionate realisation that the child feels the same complex emotion as the man, and is even less able to explain it to himself. And yet that's not right either; for, left to himself, the boy would feel no need to account for it. Hence:

> O dearest, dearest boy! my heart
> For better lore would seldom yearn,
> Could I but teach the hundredth part
> Of what from thee I learn.[11]

What the poet has learned is not to badger other people, and still more not to badger himself, to find reasons for feeling as he does; what he has to do is to feel thus and thus, and trust the feeling.

On no other reading is there justification for those lines which seem at first so deplorable:

[10] "Anecdote for Fathers", 49–56.   [11] *Op. cit.*, 57–60.

> His head he raised – there was in sight,
> It caught his eye, he saw it plain —

This is not inexcusable padding-out, saying one simple thing three ways; it is daring. Pressed and fussed by the probing elder, the boy's eyes have a hunted look; and casting about in desperation, his eye lights upon the weather-cock. The lines convey brilliantly how his eye flits across the weather-cock, returns to it, and then, seeing it will do for a pretext, focuses on it.

Even so, Wordsworth had more in hand than the evoking of a pathos, however poignant. De Quincey in another fine passage emphasises that the best of the Lyrical Ballads are genuine *discoveries* about human sentiment. Wordsworth was exploring unmapped territories, and coming home with treasure-trove. The realisation that in the child's mind, as in the man's, abundant elation could express itself in illogical regret – this was such a discovery. Its importance, for Wordsworth as perhaps for us, can be brought home if we see it in the context of the cult of sensibility in the late eighteenth century, and the special sort of sentimentality it produced. One most marked feature of that cult, perhaps the central motive behind it, was a consuming interest in ambiguous emotional states. Sterne and Richardson, who had more important matters on hand, nevertheless could be (and were) excerpted and bowdlerised in order to nourish this appetite. One finds it everywhere in the minor poetry of Wordsworth's time and a little earlier. It is for instance the point of Samuel Rogers' verses "On a Tear". It is in the very title of James Montgomery's appallingly vulgar poem, "The Joy of Grief":

> 'Tis the solemn feast of feeling,
> 'Tis the Sabbath of the soul.

Or else we recognise it very readily in the elegiac form, as with John Logan:

> Nor will I court Lethean streams,
> The sorrowing sense to steep;
> Nor drink oblivion of the themes
> On which I love to weep.

We are accustomed to regard this sort of thing as vicious, and there can be little doubt that Wordsworth would have agreed. The ambiguous feeling that concerns him in "Anecdote for Fathers" is something different, though it looks the same. As De Quincey noticed, Wordsworth himself defined the difference, insisting that the one sort of ambiguity is the effect of ebullience, the other, of enervation. The same distinction had to be made, in the same situation, by a writer concerned with ancient Greek literature:

> Is pessimism inevitably a sign of decadence, warp, weakened instincts, as it was once with the ancient Hindus, as it is now with us modern Europeans? Or is there such a thing as a *strong* pessimism? . . . Could it be, perhaps, that the very feeling of superabundance created its own kind of suffering: a temerity of penetration, hankering for the enemy . . . so as to prove its strength . . .?[12]

The same strange attitude is defined, with equal precision, in the "Lines written in Early Spring":

> I heard a thousand blended notes,
> While in a grove I sate reclined,
> In that sweet mood when pleasant thoughts
> Bring sad thoughts to the mind.[13]

Again we misread if we think that the joy and peace of "nature" remind the poet by contrast of the turbulence of man. This is not a scene, "Where every prospect pleases and only man is vile." For both "pleasant thoughts" and "sad thoughts" are comprised in "that sweet mood". It is a case, once again, of joy brimming over from its first motive into thoughts which, to the reason, are joyless. This is not, I think, forced quite home in this poem, but we need it to explain the jaunty movement, which seems so much at odds with the poet's assertion that he has "reason to lament / What man has made of man." This jaunty movement is characteristic of the Lyrical Ballads and, more than any peculiarities in the diction, is what unsettles the reader in "Simon Lee" and "The Last of the Flock". It is in any case easy to point out the faults in both diction

[12] Nietzsche, *A Critical Backward Glance* (1886) to *The Birth of Tragedy* (1871). *The Birth of Tragedy* and *The Genealogy of Morals*, tr. Francis Golffing. Garden City, N.Y., 1956, p. 4.
[13] 1–4.

and metre which ruin these poems (though both, incidentally, have fine moments). And when we seek to generalise these failures, we usually do so by reference to Wordsworth's theory of diction. But that, it may be, is a red herring which Wordsworth drew across Coleridge's path and ours. And in any case to lay the blame there is not to generalise far enough. These failures among the Lyrical Ballads could be explained by supposing that in these poems Wordsworth tried for, and failed to achieve, this same tone of almost lunatic elation in which "pleasant thoughts / Bring sad thoughts to the mind". Wordsworth's word for this state, or one of his words, is "glee"; and it is possible to regard all the Lyrical Ballads as experiments in expressing glee and/or investigations of that state.

Wordsworth said of "The Idiot Boy", "I never wrote anything with so much glee". And in fact, for the effect of this splendid poem, "glee" is the exact word. The poet writes with glee, and the principal figure is the incarnation of glee:

> But when the Pony moved his legs,
> Oh! then for the poor Idiot Boy!
> For joy he cannot hold the bridle,
> For joy his head and heels are idle,
> He's idle all for very joy.
>
> And, while the Pony moves his legs,
> In Johnny's left hand you may see
> The green bough motionless and dead:
> The Moon that shines above his head
> Is not more still and mute than he.
>
> His heart it was so full of glee
> That, till full fifty yards were gone,
> He quite forgot his holly whip,
> And all his skill in horsemanship:
> Oh! happy, happy, happy John.[14]

And yet the subject is one that is, or ought to be, extremely painful – an idiot boy is not normally a pleasant or reassuring spectacle. What redeems the image, for the poet and for the reader, is the stillness, the muteness, the idleness.

[14] "The Idiot Boy", 72–86.

The idleness should send us back to "Expostulation and Reply" and "The Tables Turned", where the poet is accused of idleness by the old schoolmaster, Matthew. He replies:

> The eye – it cannot choose but see;
> We cannot bid the ear be still;
> Our bodies feel, where'er they be,
> Against or with our will.

DONALD DAVEY

> Nor less I deem that there are Powers
> Which of themselves our minds impress;
> That we can feed this mind of ours
> In a wise passiveness. . . .;[15]

and in the second poem:

> One impulse from a vernal wood
> May teach you more of man,
> Of moral evil and of good,
> Than all the sages can.[16]

MAN DISTINGUISHED FOR WISDOM

These are famous lines which we try to read with due solemnity, however their doctrine may outrage us. But perhaps we give them more solemnity than is due. For put them back in their contexts, and willy-nilly they read jauntily, trippingly. It will not do to decide that these stanzas are saying in another way what is said in "Tintern Abbey". It is the other way of saying that is important. The bearing and sense of these lines, when abstracted from them, may be identical with the bearing of some lines in "Tintern Abbey", but these differ from those in being informed with glee, carried on the back of that lunatic elation which Wordsworth was at some pains to define, if only by rhythm – and never better than by the helter-skelter stumbling rhythms of "The Idiot Boy".

Wordsworth *was* the Idiot Boy. Consider these lines given to the idiot, lines from which, so Wordsworth says, the whole poem evolved:

> The cocks did crow to-whoo, to-whoo,
> And the sun did shine so cold![17]

This piercing shrillness can be described only by repeating what

---

[15] "Expostulation and Reply", 17–24.
[16] "The Tables Turned", 21–4.   [17] "The Idiot Boy", 450–1.

Matthew, in "Expostulation and Reply", is made to say to Wordsworth:

> You look round on your Mother Earth,
> As if she for no purpose bore you;
> As if you were her first-born birth,
> And none had lived before you![18]

The idiot, seeing the moon and hearing the owls, is Adam on the
first night after Creation.

It is the same with the other lunatic of the Lyrical Ballads, the
mad mother of "Her Eyes are Wild":

> "Sweet babe! they say that I am mad,
> But nay, my heart is far too glad;
> And I am happy when I sing
> Full many a sad and doleful thing; . . ."[19]

What sort of sad things could thus be sung in high glee? What,
but "The Idiot Boy" or "Goody Blake and Harry Gill"? Except
for the Tintern Abbey lines, all Wordsworth's Lyrical Ballads are
either analyses of the state of glee (as are "Expostulation and
Reply" and "Anecdote for Fathers") or else expressions of that
glee (as are "Goody Blake and Harry Gill" and "The Idiot Boy").

To be sure, it should now be clear that the sort of enjoyment
called glee, no less the "happiness" to which Wordsworth laid
prescriptive claim, are something different from what normally
goes under those names. If a definition is required beyond that
furnished by Wordsworth's poems, one may go to S. T. Coleridge
as recorded by E. H. Coleridge:

> He (Coleridge) called it joy, meaning thereby not mirth or
> high spirits, or even happiness, but a consciousness of entire
> and therefore well being when the emotional and intellectual
> faculties are in equipoise.

This carries special weight as the contribution of a poet, who, in
Dejection: An Ode, showed himself ready to put as high a price on
this state as Wordsworth did. It was because Coleridge thought it
impossible he would ever experience this state anew, that he seems
to have thought that his career as a poet was over.

[18] 9–12.   [19] "Her Eyes are Wild", 11–14.

The ass, the idiot, the moon, the owls – these motifs from "The Idiot Boy" recur in Wordsworth's poems of 1799. There is the ass in *Peter Bell*; there are owls in the lines beginning, "There was a Boy; ye knew him well, ye cliffs"; the moon figures with appalling effect in the "Lucy" poem, "Strange fits of passion have I known"; and Ruth, deserted by her lover, becomes a harmless lunatic. What is more, it is clear that all these images retain, for Wordsworth, the symbolic force he gave them in "The Idiot Boy". Wordsworth says comically that he studied the habits of asses before he wrote *Peter Bell*; but it was a sort of study which strove to learn what was the *meaning* of the ass, not what it looked like or how it behaved. In the same way, the owls:

> And they would shout
> Across the watery vale, and shout again,
> Responsive to his call, – with quivering peals,
> And long halloos, and screams, and echoes loud
> Redoubled and redoubled; concourse wild
> Of jocund din![20]

This "jocund din" is what no one else, no previous poet and surely no reader, has ever heard in the calling of owls. It is not one of Wordsworth's discoveries, which we can corroborate, once the fact has been pointed out. The owls have a symbolic force, or none. Surely, then, the "jocund din" is another version of that lunatic glee with which, stock-still in silence, the Idiot Boy heard the owls, and with which Wordsworth conceived him doing so.

In the "Lucy" poem, the symbolic function of the moon is insisted on:

> My horse moved on; hoof after hoof
> He raised, and never stopped:
> When down behind the cottage roof,
> At once, the bright moon dropped.
>
> What fond and wayward thoughts will slide
> Into a Lover's head!
> "O mercy!" to myself I cried,
> "If Lucy should be dead!"[21]

[20] "There was a Boy", 11–16.
[21] "Strange fits of passion have I known", 21–8.

The connexion between the obscuring of the moon and the death of a girl remains mysterious. The irrationality of it is pressed upon our attention.

But it can be rationalised without much trouble. Coleridge, in Germany with the Wordsworths at the time this poem was written, wrote to Thomas Poole:

> There are moments in which I have such power of life in me, such a *conceit* of it, I mean, that I lay the blame of my child's death on my absence.[22]

Coleridge was just emerging from his Berkeleyan phase, and the brilliant Berkeleyan paradox, *esse est percipi*, had led him to wonder how we could know that anything existed except in those moments when the mind perceived it. In his letter he takes the further step of speculating why, if the movements of the mind can thus annihilate whatever is out of mind, the movements of the body (from England to Germany, for instance) should not have the same power. Similarly, in Wordsworth's marvellous poem, the movements of the poet's body astride his horse make the moon drop out of sight and therefore (by Berkeleyan logic) out of existence; and if the movements of the body are thus capable of snuffing out the moon, why should they not snuff out a life, or, if the body has this power, must we not suppose the mind has equal power, such that, if you cease to think of a person, that person dies? We know from the famous note which Wordsworth dictated to the Immortality *Ode*, that he was capable of such an "abyss of idealism". Moreover, if we recall Coleridge's definition of joy ("a consciousness of entire and therefore well being"), or Wordsworth's definition of the poet ("a man pleased with his own passions and volitions, and who rejoices more than other men in the spirit of life that is in him"), we realise that when Coleridge writes of "such power of life in me, such a *conceit* of it", he is talking of joy or glee. And thus, Wordsworth's poem about Lucy turns once again upon the central theme of joy, and expresses in fact one of those "fond regrets" which, "with so much happiness to spare", the mind can bear, and delights, to entertain.

Common to all the treatments of glee is the silence and im-

22 Coleridge, *Letters*, ed. E. H. Coleridge. London, 1895, p. 295 (6 May 1799).

mobility of the chief actor. The Idiot Boy goes "Burr-burr" and
the teeth of Harry Gill "chatter-chatter", but these sounds seem
even further from human speech than silence would be. They only
define the inhuman silence into which erupt, with piercing effect,
the hooting of owls and the braying of donkeys. As for immobility, Charles Williams noticed long ago its mysterious attraction for Wordsworth in such later poems as "Resolution and
Independence" and "Michael". It is already present, as a potent
force, in 1798; the Idiot Boy throughout, and Peter Bell after his
criminal fury with the ass, and the horseman of the "Lucy" poem,
are immobile without being statuesque. None of them ride their
mounts, for they do not guide them: they sit idle and immobile
upon the animal's back, rapt in glee. "Idle" is one of Wordsworth's words in this period, and he seems to see it, not as in
reality it most commonly appears, as an aimless toying and fussing,
but as a state of relaxed immobility.

3

The reader who has noticed this, though subconsciously, will not
be surprised at a new feature of the poems of 1799, a recurrent
concern with the fact of death. A corpse is silent and motionless,
as Peter Bell was, and the Idiot Boy. What more natural than for
Wordsworth to start wondering where the difference was, between this life and this death? It is as if Wordsworth, having
repeatedly demanded a specially high value for rapt and silent
immobility, should have a voice protest: "Why, this that you value
so highly – what is it but being half-dead?" "Half-dead" is
precise; for idiots are only half-alive. And Wordsworth turns to
deal with the heckler. In the passive absorption of glee, a man is
rapt out of time as the dead are out of time.

Wordsworth answers his heckler in two ways. On the one hand
he seems to say: "Yes, death is a state of permanent glee. And
death is therefore good." And he says the same thing, but subjectively, when he seems to say: "Yes, my glee is so abundant that
I can regard even death with joy." The joy that spills over and
transforms sad thoughts can now transform even thoughts of
death. When Wordsworth's expression is at its most concentrated
and masterly, he says both these things together:

A slumber did my spirit seal;
I had no human fears:
She seemed a thing that could not feel
The touch of earthly years.

No motion has she now, no force;
She neither hears nor sees;
Rolled round in earth's diurnal course,
With rocks, and stones, and trees.[23]

The boy who called to the owls died young, but there is no implication that this was cause for sorrow, any more than the death of Lucy:

Thus Nature spake – The work was done –
How soon my Lucy's race was run!
She died, and left to me
The memory of what has been,
And never more will be.[24]

This is much truer to the experience (to judge from the appropriately trance-like melody, as from the logic of the situation) than is that other version of Lucy's death:

But she is in her grave, and, oh,
The difference to me![25]

It is possible to hear the rhythm in these lines as gleeful, tripping. If we hear it in this way, we can hardly believe what the verses say. And we shall prefer to believe other, more honest poems, which seem to say that it makes next to no difference at all. Wordsworth is indifferent, since death and life can be equally gleeful, as in "The Danish Boy":

For calm and gentle is his mien;
Like a dead Boy he is serene.[26]

Wordsworth does not care whether the Danish Boy is a live boy or a dead ghost; in either case, he is *"glee"*. Nor does he care about "Lucy Gray":

---

[23] "A slumber did my spirit seal".
[24] "Three years she grew", 37–42.
[25] "She dwelt among the untrodden ways", 11–12.   [26] 54–5.

> Yet some maintain that to this day
> She is a living child;
> That you may see sweet Lucy Gray
> Upon the lonesome wild.
>
> O'er rough and smooth she trips along,
> And never looks behind;
> And sings a solitary song
> That whistles in the wind.[27]

Are the boy and girl both ghosts? The possibility is not brought in as a piece of fabulous machinery. It is to that suggestion Words- worth conducts us, just to emphasise how little the possibility disturbs him. Alive or dead, their existence is joy. They represent a mode of being to which the question of life or death as normally conceived is irrelevant.

At the same time as Wordsworth probes this new vein, of the connexion between glee, or natural joy, and death, he probes and extends an old vein, trying to define what this "glee" is, to establish the conditions most favourable for it, and to distinguish it from perversions or vicious imitations.

Wordsworth repeats the definition he gave in "Anecdote for Fathers"; glee is a state in which abundant joy spills over and transforms trains of feeling normally not joyful at all. In the fragment "Nutting", the objects on to which joy spills over are merely "indifferent":

> In that sweet mood when pleasure loves to pay
> Tribute to ease; and, of its joy secure,
> The heart luxuriates with indifferent things,
> Wasting its kindliness on stocks and stones,
> And on the vacant air.[28]

But the old ambiguity re-appears in its original form, with "The Danish Boy":

> The lovely Danish Boy is blest
> And happy in his flowery cove:
> From bloody deeds his thoughts are far;
> And yet he warbles songs of war,

[27] 57–64.   [28] 39–43.

> That seem like songs of love,
> For calm and gentle is his mien;
> Like a dead Boy he is serene.[29]

If we ask why, when "from bloody deeds his thoughts are far", the boy none the less "warbles songs of war", and why, when warbled, they "seem like songs of love", the only answer is the one we gave when the mad mother unaccountably found happiness singing "many a sad and doleful thing". Their consciousness of the richness of their own being is such that they deliberately seek out what is inimical to it, so as to transform it out of their own resources.

On the other hand, Wordsworth greatly extends his conception of "glee", for it now seems elastic enough to include the state of mind of the Old Cumberland Beggar, or that defined in the related fragment, "Animal Tranquillity and Decay". The connexion is in the term "tranquillity", but it is brought home in a stanza of "Three years she grew in sun and shower":

> She shall be sportive as the fawn
> That wild with glee across the lawn,
> Or up the mountain springs;
> And her's shall be the breathing balm,
> And her's the silence and the calm
> Of mute insensate things.[30]

The wildly sportive and the mutely insensate are alike manifestations of a glee which expresses itself as readily in a breathing silence as in wild activity. Or again, the connexion is made in the fine poems on Matthew, "The grey-haired man of glee". For if glee is a state in which joy spills over into thoughts of sadness, we observe from Matthew's case that old age is naturally gleeful; for the joy of animal tranquillity in Matthew turns to sad thoughts of those near to him whom he has out-lived. To survive contemporaries and juniors is sad, and yet few will consider it a matter of regret to have that evidence of the power of life in one's self. (It is a fine stroke, incidentally, to make Matthew rebuff the poet's offer to take the place of his dead sons; for he is in a state of *animal* tranquillity, in which there can be no substitute for the animal passions of the blood-tie.)

---

[29] 49–55.   [30] "Three years she grew", 13–18.

Of course the state of mind of the principal figure is not the centre of interest in "The Old Cumberland Beggar". This is the first of the poems which asks, in respect of glee, what are the conditions in which glee can flourish; and the conditions in question are social conditions. This poem, therefore, like the other long narratives ("The Brothers" and, in its way, "Michael"), expresses Wordsworth's view of the good society, the right social philosophy. In fact, it was occasioned by specific enactments for the relief of the indigent, and was sent to Charles James Fox, with a very bold and reasoned letter on the state of the poor laws.

Wordsworth's originality is not in choosing a subject such as a country beggar, but in making the light fall on him from an unforeseen angle. For he is concerned with acts and habits of charity not as they affect the recipient of alms, but as they affect the alms giver – a concern foreshadowed in the last stanza of "Simon Lee".[31] The "moral" of "The Old Cumberland Beggar" (our squeamishness demands the quotation-marks round "moral", though Wordsworth would have seen no need for them) is that the old beggar was invaluable for cementing together in a common responsibility a community otherwise loosely knit. As Martin Buber has said, "A community is where community happens." And Wordsworth's poem has the effect of stressing that proper use of the word as denoting a spiritual fellowship, bound together in habitual disciplines of usage and unwritten law. This Burkean view of society as bound together by unwritten law and not by paper constitutions, coming so early in Wordsworth and so plainly in keeping with the whole tenor of his thought, serves to show how, despite his generous fellow-feeling with the French revolutionaries, his political outlook was innately conservative; and accordingly the charge that he was a political renegade loses most of its point. These habitual disciplines of custom and unformulated precedent are part of what Wordsworth was later to praise and examine as "natural piety".

Both "The Brothers" and "Michael" look rather different from

[31] "I've heard of hearts unkind, kind deeds
With coldness still returning;
Alas! the gratitude of men
Hath oftener left me mourning".

this point of view. In the former poem, the younger brother, James, personifies glee:

And many, many happy days were his . . .[32]

(The line as it stands is commonplace, but in the context, not just of this poem but of others, the "happiness" carries weight.) Glee is possible to James Ewbank because, no less than the Cumberland Beggar, he is the responsibility of the whole rural community:

He was the child of all the dale – he lived
Three months with one, and six months with another,
And wanted neither food, nor clothes, nor love; . . .[33]

The poem revolves around the uncertainty of Leonard, the elder brother, whether James is alive or dead. With him, as with the other personifications of glee, it is hard to tell. And it is magnificently appropriate that in the end it should appear that James died while sleep-walking, for this narrows still further the gap between life and death in the case of existences so fortunate as his. Equally ingenious and masterly is the device by which Leonard's uncertainty is made plausible, that is, the habit in the dale-village community of burying the dead without headstones or other means of identification. The whole community partakes of the idyllic life of glee, and the community's refusal to identify their dead exemplifies this people's difficulty in separating the dead from the living, and their indifference about it. (It is "We are Seven" all over again.) The wandering brother, outside the community and *déraciné*, cannot share this indifference. He is shut out from glee and its concomitant, animal tranquillity. So in the end, oppressed and sorrowful, he leaves the dale for a second and final time. Those who regard Wordsworth as a proto-Victorian figure would do well to ponder this figure of Leonard Ewbank, and the doom that Wordsworth reserves for him. He has all the virtues of Smiles's self-help: independence, pride, resourcefulness, energy, courage. Not for him the solution that his weaker brother embraces – of living on charity. Yet it is the weak who inherit Wordsworth's earth. And indeed the praise of idleness, of idleness as a

---

[32] "The Brothers", 346.   [33] *Op. cit.*, 342–5.

duty, should have prepared us: if the early Wordsworth is a Tory, he is a Tory anarchist. But all this was changed after the "Ode to Duty".

Wordsworth's blank-verse in "The Brothers" is quite undistinguished, and barely adequate: but the poem is a great one because of the invention, the masterly conduct and disposition of the fable.[34] If this is bitter medicine to swallow in an age which believes that poetry exists in diction and nowhere else, this is not Wordsworth's fault.

The same is true of "Michael", even though the verse as such is a little better, and in particular gets off to a better start. (At this period, Wordsworth's attempts to "lead in" to his subject are lamentable, and the first lines of "The Brothers" are especially disastrous; this is a particular case of Wordsworth's lack of dramatic imagination in even the loosest sense.) "The Brothers" and "Michael" are really very similar. In the first poem, one brother stays in the dale and benefits from the communal discipline of glee, while the other leaves the dale and the community, thereafter unable to return; in the second poem, a father stays in the dale and within the community, exhibiting the animal tranquillity which is glee's counterpart or other aspect, while his son leaves never to return. If in these broad terms the poems treat of an identical situation, within this frame occur other situations which are identical:

> They had an uncle; – he was at that time
> A thriving man, and trafficked on the seas:
> And, but for that same uncle, to this hour
> Leonard had never handled rope or shroud;
> For the boy loved the life which we lead here;
> And though of unripe years, a stripling only,
> His soul was knit to this his native soil . . .[35]

[34] *Cf.* Wordsworth's definition of "invention" (as one of five "powers requisite for the production of poetry") in the Preface of 1815: "Invention, – by which characters are composed out of materials supplied by observation; whether of the Poet's own heart and mind, or of external life and nature; and such incidents produced as are most impressive to the imagination and most fitted to do justice to the characters, sentiments and passions, which the poet undertakes to illustrate".

[35] "The Brothers", 292–8.

> . . . We have, thou know'st,
> Another kinsman – he will be our friend
> In this distress. He is a prosperous man,
> Thriving in trade – and Luke to him shall go,
> And with his kinsman's help and his own thrift
> He quickly will repair this loss, and then
> He may return to us. If here he stay,
> What can be done?. . . .[36]

To be sure, in an age of agricultural depression and industrial expansion, this situation – of the beggared agriculturalist sending one or more of his family to be set up by an urban and mercantile relative – was being repeated in villages all over England (though incidentally Cumberland and Westmorland constituted rather a special case).[37] And of course Wordsworth was cognizant of this, and had something to say about it, more obviously in "Michael" than in "The Brothers". But all the same, once we detect the identical situation in the two poems, the fact that Luke, Michael's son, turns out to be a bad lot, is hardly important. His bad behaviour, after leaving the dale, seems at first to be the pivot on which everything turns: but when we compare "Michael" with "The Brothers", we see that the crux of the story is Luke's departure in the first place. In the same way, Michael's inability to complete his sheepfold is often taken to mean that he has no will to continue, once his son has failed him. Undoubtedly this implication is present and throws a beam of pathos on the famous line,

> And never lifted up a single stone.[38]

But once again, the attainment of pathos is not the end of Wordsworth's intention; and this is not the last line of the poem.

Michael, as has been pointed out, belongs with the other great figures which loom, in Wordsworth's poems, immobile through the mist upon the fells. He belongs with the Leech-gatherer, and with that other who is

---

[36] "Michael", 247–54.
[37] See Kenneth Maclean, *Agrarian Age. A Background for Wordsworth*. New Haven, 1950.
[38] "Michael", 466.

insensibly subdued
To settled quiet; he is one by whom
All effort seems forgotten; one to whom
Long patience hath such mild composure given,
That patience now doth seem a thing of which
He hath no need.[39]

Michael at the unfinished sheepfold is, in fact, another instance of animal tranquillity. Tranquillity may seem out of the question in respect of one so grievously wounded in the one relationship that was his life; and if we remember the close connexion between this tranquillity and "glee", we may seem to make of Wordsworth a monster of inhumanity. But in the quite special senses of tranquillity and of glee which Wordsworth's other poems have established, the idea becomes more acceptable. For instance, he has insisted from the first that *his* tranquillity and *his* glee in no way exclude sorrow and regret. If he still seems inhuman, this is because any insight carried relentlessly through to its conclusion looks what it is, relentless. And Wordsworth is inhuman only as the fact and presence of genius is inhuman.

4

If Wordsworth's central interests in *Lyrical Ballads* are such as I have expounded, if the connexions he makes are indeed such as I have seen, the first response of the humane and intelligent reader must be to exclaim at his originality. And this is just. But in a period like ours when originality does not command such respect in and for itself as it did in the age succeeding Young's *Con-iectures on Original Composition*, this perception can be made into a limitation; we are often asked to see Wordsworth, on whatever terms we present him, as a special case, and to dismiss him from our minds accordingly whenever we think of poetry in general and of poetry at the present time in particular. In these circumstances, at a time when (thanks to Eliot) we never use the concept of originality without at once passing nervously to the supposedly complementary notion of tradition, it is worth pointing out that Wordsworth's concerns, and his attitudes, were not

[39] "Animal Tranquillity and Decay", 7–12.

unprecedented; that he had a tradition, and an ancient one, to
which he could have appealed if he had chosen. It is characteristic
of him that he didn't choose, and for the most part disdained to
invoke the [authority of Aristotle and Longinus. Nevertheless,
such authority is available.

Wordsworth's emphasis on the poet's pleasure in perception as
the central and distinguishing feature of poetry – a pleasure even
in perception of what is painful, indeed especially in such perceptions[40] – goes back to the classical and originally Aristotelian
commonplace, *admiratio*, which was, in classical and again in
scholastic and Renaissance times, particularly of moment in
respect of the painful subjects of tragedy. *Admiratio* in these contexts is normally translated as "wonder"; and this does not help
matters, since Watts-Dunton's definition of the Romantic movement as "The renascence of wonder" is now a very unfashionable
idea. At the risk of rehabilitating a much-disliked Victorian, the
point must be made; and we find the root of the tradition of poetic
wonder in Aristotle's *Metaphysics*:

> For it is owing to their wonder that men both now
> begin and at first began to philosophize. . . .

St Albert the Great, commenting on this passage, remarks,
"Wonder is something like fear in its effect on the heart." And
this may serve to show the connexion between Aristotle on this
point and Longinus, whose treatise on the elevated style, *On the
Sublime*, is centrally concerned with the rhetorical concept of
admiratio. For most readers will be aware of how eighteenth-
century commentators on Longinus, such as Burke, spent a great
deal of time with the apparently nonsensical proposition, which
was however validated by experience as well as by Longinus'
authority, that the pleasurable effect of sublime art was hardly
distinguishable from the usually very unpleasurable emotion of
fear. While Burke and others revived and explored this ancient

[40] Henry Crabb Robinson, *Diary* (9 May 1815): "Wordsworth, in answer to
the common reproach that his sensibility is excited by objects which produce
no effect on others, admits the fact, and is proud of it. . . . The poet himself,
as Hazlitt has well observed, has a pride in deriving no aid from his subject.
It is the mere power which he is conscious of exerting in which he delights,
not the production of a work in which men rejoice on account of the sym-
pathies and sensibilities it excites in them".

connexion between wonder (*admiratio*) and fear, Wordsworth can
be seen in Lyrical Ballads to be exploring its connection with joy.
This too was a traditional connexion, though it was always secondary to the connexion with fear. J. V. Cunningham, for instance
(to whom I am indebted for all these citations) defines *admiratio* as
"the shocked limit of feeling", and, summing up the implications
for an understanding of Shakespeare of his use of the marvellous
in his latest plays, decides:

> Wonder, then, is associated not only with extreme fear but
> also with extreme joy, and is marked by silence and im-
> mobility.[41]

As has been seen, states of silence and immobility occur in nearly
every one of the Lyrical Ballads, and these features are explained
in the poems as the effects of joy.

It is with deliberation that I describe what these poems do by
the homely word, "explaining"; for it is characteristic both of
Wordsworth's practice in his poems and of his theory in his
Preface, that he is quite unembarrassed by any wish to distinguish
between knowing the human mind through poetry and knowing
it in other ways, through the case-book of the field researcher or
the rationally controlled introspection of the philosophical
psychologist. It is therefore not only appropriate but necessary to
point out, as J. V. Cunningham does for his purposes, that for
Aristotle "wonder" is a concept which straddles the gap between
logic and rhetoric, or, as we might say, between conceptual and
aesthetic experience. This is the point of citing Aristotle's reference in the *Metaphysics*, and it is taken up in the *Rhetoric*:

> Again, since learning and wondering are pleasant, it follows
> that such things as acts of imitation must be pleasant – for
> instance, painting, sculpture, poetry – and every product of
> skilful imitation: this latter, even if the object imitated is not
> in itself pleasant; for it is not the object itself which here
> gives delight; the spectator draws inferences ("That is a so-
> and-so") and thus learns something fresh.

Cunningham comments on this passage very justly,[42] "What we

[41] J. V. Cunningham, *Woe or Wonder*. Denver, Colo., 1951, p. 92.
[42] *Op. cit.*, p. 65.

call aesthetic experience is for Aristotle substantially the experience of inferring." This is true of Wordsworth also, and this is the pleasurable experience he gave to a reader such as De Quincey. Poetry for Wordsworth is a means of knowing the world, not a means of self-expression or self-adjustment.

Again, on the point that "it is natural for all to delight in works of imitation", Aristotle writes in the *Poetics*:

> The truth of this second point is shown by experience: though the objects themselves may be painful to see, we delight to view the most realistic representations of them in art, the forms for example of the lowest animals and of dead bodies. The explanation is to be found in a further fact: to be learning something is the greatest of pleasures not only to the philosopher but also the rest of mankind, however small their capacity for it; the reason of the delight in seeing the picture is that one is at the same time learning – gathering the meaning of things, e.g. that the man there is a so-and-so; . . ."

St Thomas makes the same connexion. "Wonder," he says, "is a kind of desire for knowledge"; and he goes on:

> For this reason, everything wonderful is pleasurable: for example, anything that is infrequent, as well as any representation of things, even of those that are not in themselves pleasant. For the soul delights in comparing one thing with another, since this is a proper and connatural activity of reason, as Aristotle says in his *Poetics*.

If we can rid ourselves of the notion that Wordsworth's *Preface* is exclusively or even chiefly the expression of an extreme and unbalanced theory of poetic diction, and read it again looking for other things, it will appear that what chiefly interests Wordsworth about poetry is that which interested Aristotle, Longinus, Aquinas and Albertus Magnus, and that in speculating about it Wordsworth follows, whether he knows it or not, in paths trodden by those great predecessors. Moreover, all this element in the *Preface* is far more immediately and fruitfully relevant to the poems thus introduced, than is the theory of diction.

Wordsworth's theory of metre, for instance, is, as expounded in the *Preface*, generally and rightly thought to be inadequate –

chiefly for the reason that Wordsworth lights upon an adequate rationale for metre only after he has already advanced several inadequate justifications, which he was then too careless or too idle to expunge. And so, when Elisabeth Schneider decides, "The conclusion is inescapable . . . that in theory at least, he did not get beyond the conception of metre as something 'superadded' to poetry, not an organic part of it,"[43] we can hardly blame her, for Wordsworth appears to have lit upon such a conception without realising it or else without caring for what he had come upon. Nevertheless, the passage exists to prove that at least the discovery was made, even if nothing was to be made of it; and the conception of metre there expressed is superior to either Hazlitt's or Coleridge's (those with which Miss Schneider compares it), superior because it sees metre as far more organic to poetry than on either Coleridge's or Hazlitt's showing. Metre in this conception is more organic to poetry because it is derived immediately from the principle which Wordsworth saw as central to all poetry whatever – the principle of delight, of the mind taking pleasure in the exercise of its own powers:

> If I had undertaken a SYSTEMATIC defence of the theory here maintained, it would have been my duty to develope the various causes upon which the pleasure received from metrical language depends. Among the chief of these causes is to be reckoned a principle which must be well known to those who have made any of the Arts the object of accurate reflection; namely, the pleasure which the mind derives from the perception of similitude in dissimilitude.

It is easy to see Aquinas ("For the soul delights in comparing one thing with another") in this pleasurable "perception of similitude in dissimilitude," which is, as Wordsworth goes on to say, "the great spring of the activity of our minds, and their chief feeder". Moreover, this view of what metre does locks in with the rest of Wordsworth's thought as do none of his alternative cases for metre, which he develops earlier and at greater length. For just as St Thomas's perception of the pleasure of comparing is based on a perception of how knowing is pleasure and pleasure is in

[43] Elisabeth Schneider, *The Aesthetics of William Hazlitt*. Philadelphia, 1933.

K

knowing, so Wordsworth's recognition that the pleasure in metre consists in the perception of similitude in dissimilitude is based upon the same realisation: knowing is pleasure, and pleasure is in knowing.

> We have no sympathy but what is propagated by pleasure: I would not be misunderstood; but wherever we sympathise with pain, it will be found that the sympathy is produced and carried on by subtle combinations with pleasure. We have no knowledge, that is, no general principles drawn from the contemplation of particular facts, but what has been built up by pleasure, and exists in us by pleasure alone.

And if it is still required to be proved that this pleasure without which "we have no knowledge" is the pleasure which Aristotle perceived when he wrote how "learning and wondering are pleasant", the proof is in the poems themselves, which concern themselves continually with those features of immobility and silence which are, as we have seen, traditionally connected with the rapt delight of the state of wonder.

5

It may still be unclear where the connexion is between the central concern of Wordsworth's poetry and the forms that poetry took. In particular, why were those forms, as Wordsworth's contemporaries noticed, so consistently undramatic? What is the connexion, if any, between this habit of Wordsworth's imagination and the central importance, for that imagination, of the fact of happiness, of joy? I can only venture a reply, and that reply in such general terms as perhaps to be useless. But Nietzsche has been cited already as one who was struck, as Wordsworth was, by the way in which health seeks out morbidity, by (to use Nietzsche's own terms) "A penchant of the mind for what is hard, terrible, evil, dubious in existence, arising from a plethora of health, plenitude of being." And this "penchant of the mind" Nietzsche identifies with the Dionysiac temper or the Dionysiac principle. Now, in some exceptionally close and difficult passages of *The Birth of Tragedy*, Nietzsche explains how the Dionysiac dithyramb evolved into dramatic presentation, by the necessity for the

Dionysiac to relate itself to (and in part assuage itself by) the sunny objective images of the Apollonian. Thus it becomes possible to conceive that in Wordsworth his contemporaries were struck by the Dionysiac spirit operating without any Apollonian admixture or complement; and if so, Wordsworth's Romanticism manifests itself very exactly as the rejection of the classical and neo-classical tradition, as the rejection of the supposedly necessary harmony between these two principles – a harmony continuously maintained or aimed at from ancient Greece through Rome to Augustan England. And is this, after all, to say any more than that Wordsworth witnesses to the conquering by the subjective of the objective world, of a reality bodied over against the perceiver? This after all is no new diagnosis of Romanticism. All that we gain, perhaps, from putting it in Nietzschean terms, is the realisation that in pre-history men had lived in those "abysses of idealism" into which Wordsworth plunges anew, with all the excitement and assurance of a man who treads where none have trod for centuries.

W. J. B. Owen

WORDSWORTH, THE PROBLEM OF COMMUNICATION, AND JOHN DENNIS[1]

I

I wish to explore two polarities in Wordsworth's thinking about poetry, his own more especially; his drift towards one rather than the other; and his search for a justification of this drift. The one is that poetry is, or can be, or should be, universally intelligible; that communication should proceed from poet to reader, if not without effort, then without the need for special qualifications in the reader; that the poet, some superior intellectual qualities granted, has essentially normal human characteristics. The other is that the understanding of poetry is in the nature of a laborious task, albeit a labour of love; that in some instances the poet cannot hope to communicate with some readers at all, and that in others he can communicate only by a kind of analogical understanding on the part of the sympathetic reader; that the poet is a seer, akin to Blake's Bard "Who present, past, and future, sees". The first of these polarities is early and is associated mainly with *Lyrical Ballads*; the second is late, not in Wordsworth's lifetime or career as a poet, but in the development of his critical theorising, and is associated with the critical writings and letters of about 1815.[2]

[1] Read at the annual meeting of the Association of Canadian University Teachers of English, Carleton University, June 1967.

[2] Almost all the documents cited are conveniently collected in *Literary Criticism of William Wordsworth*, ed. Paul M. Zall, Lincoln, Neb., 1966. Page references are given below. Where this edition is deficient I cite W. Knight's edition of the *Prose Works*, London, 1896. The quotations from Dennis are taken from *The Critical Works of John Dennis*, ed. E. N. Hooker, Baltimore, 1939, 1943, cited as "Dennis".

In a sense, both polarities are always present. It is true that the Advertisement to *Lyrical Ballads*, 1798, finds the materials of poetry "in every subject which can interest the human mind"[3] and therefore implies the universal appeal of poetry: but it also talks of "Readers of superior judgment" and of the acquisition of "An accurate taste in poetry . . . by severe thought, and a long continued intercourse with the best models of composition".[4] The claims made in the Preface of 1800 for "the primary laws of our nature", epitomised in "Low and rustic life", as the proper subject-matter for *Lyrical Ballads*, and for the language of rustics, "more permanent and . . . far more philosophical" than poetic diction,[5] are, as I have shown elsewhere,[6] claims for the universal and permanent appeal of the poetry Wordsworth hoped he had written. "Many hundreds of people" had added to their store of truth by reading "Goody Blake and Harry Gill"[7]. But the Preface[8] also retains the deference to Sir Joshua Reynolds which called forth the passage last quoted above from the Advertisement, and, more significant, it adds the concession that "my associations must have sometimes been particular instead of general, and . . . , consequently, giving to things a false importance, sometimes from diseased impulses I may have written upon unworthy subjects".[9] The contemporary note to "The Thorn", while it does not admit that the poem is on an "unworthy subject", nevertheless concedes the existence of "Readers who are not accustomed to sympathize with men feeling in that manner or using such language" as Wordsworth proposed to use in the interest of dramatic realism.[10]

The revised Preface of 1802 retains, of course, the opposed emphases of 1800, but it adds, in the major insertion near the middle of the text, considerable weight in favour of ease of communication. To the fundamental questions: "What is a Poet? To whom does he address himself?" this Preface offers the now classic reply: "He is a man speaking to men".[11] Concessions towards the

---

[3] Advertisement to *Lyrical Ballads* (1798), p. 10.

[4] *Op. cit.*, pp. 10–11.

[5] Preface to *Lyrical Ballads*, (1800), p. 18.

[6] *Wordsworth's Preface to Lyrical Ballads*, Copenhagen, 1957, Chap. I.

[7] Preface to *Lyrical Ballads* (1800), p. 28.   [8] *Op. cit.*, p. 31.

[9] *Op. cit.*, p. 29.

[10] Note to "The Thorn" (1800), p. 13.

[11] Preface to *Lyrical Ballads* (1802), p. 48.

bard-like image of the poet which is more in evidence in 1815 are offered ("more lively sensibility, more enthusiasm and tenderness, . . . a greater knowledge of human nature, and a more comprehensive soul, than are supposed to be common among mankind"); but these are modified with as much emphasis as possible: "nothing differing in kind from other men, but only in degree"; the Poet shares "the general passions and thoughts and feelings of men"; he "thinks and feels in the spirit of the passions of men"; moreover, "Poets do not write for Poets alone, but for men . . . [the Poet] must express himself as other men express themselves".[12] As to the audience, it is involved in the first definition of the Poet cited above: "a man speaking to men". The reader envisaged is "a human Being possessed of that information which may be expected from him, not as a lawyer, a physician, a mariner, an astronomer or a natural philosopher, but as a Man". To such a reader, furthermore, the Poet aims to give *"immediate pleasure"*.[13]

The Appendix to *Lyrical Ballads* (1802) contributes little to our discussion except one image of the poet as seer: "the Poet spake to [the audience] in the character of a man to be looked up to, a man of genius and authority".[14] This viewpoint is also that of another utterance of 1802, Wordsworth's letter to John Wilson, which concedes, first, a multiplicity of tastes such as no version of the Preface envisages and such as effectively precludes universality of appeal; and, secondly, the possibility of a divided response to such a poem as "The Idiot Boy": "This poem has, I know, frequently produced the same effect as it did upon you and your friends; but there are many also to whom it affords exquisite delight, and who, indeed, prefer it to any other of my poems".[15] The letter postulates, moreover, that the assent of a part, perhaps of a minority (though Wordsworth does not say so), of the audience justifies the approach of the *avant-garde* seer; it proceeds immediately: "This proves that the feelings there delineated are such as men *may* sympathise with. This is enough for my purpose. It is not enough for me as a Poet, to delineate merely such feelings as all men *do* sympathise with; but it is also highly desirable to add to these

---

[12] *Op. cit.*, pp. 48, 54.   [13] *Op. cit.*, p. 50. (My italics.)
[14] Appendix to the Preface (1802), pp. 63–4.
[15] Letter to John Wilson (1802), p. 74.

others, such as all men *may* sympathise with, and such as there is reason to believe they would be better and more moral beings if they did sympathise with".[16]

By 1807 Wordsworth was even more convinced that his audience was divided into two races of men, which he was shortly to call the People and the Public. The Public failed to accept the *Poems* of 1807, as he recognised in his letter to Lady Beaumont of 21 May of that year. The Public (he does not yet mention the complementary group, the People)[17] are "worldlings of every rank and situation . . . enveloped" in "pure absolute honest ignorance"; they are those "who live, or wish to live, in the broad light of the world – among those who either are, or are striving to make themselves, people of consideration in society"[18] – "Gentlemen, persons of fortune, professional men, ladies, persons who can afford to buy, or can easily procure, books of half-a-guinea price, hot-pressed, and printed upon superfine paper", he had called them in 1802.[19] Nineteen-twentieths of this class are illiterate with respect to poetry, he now thinks.[20] And even "grave, kindly-natured, worthy persons, who would be pleased if they could", do not respond; for "their imagination has slept; and the voice which is the voice of my Poetry without Imagination cannot be heard".[21] Yet there is some hope of an educational process: as Coleridge had put it,

> every great and original writer, in proportion as he is great or original, must himself create the taste by which he is to be relished; he must teach the art by which he is to be seen; this, in a certain degree, even to all persons, however wise and pure may be their lives, and however unvitiated their taste; but for those who dip into books in order to give an opinion of them, or talk about them to take up an opinion – for this multitude of unhappy, and misguided, and misguiding beings,

---

[16] *Op. cit.*, pp. 74–5.

[17] See *Letters of William and Dorothy Wordsworth: The Middle Years*, ed. E. de Selincourt. Oxford, 1937, p. 169 (early 1808). For a discussion of the antithesis, see Patrick Cruttwell, "Wordsworth, the Public, and the People", *Sewanee Review*, LXIV (1956), pp. 71–80.

[18] Letter to Lady Beaumont (1807), pp. 76–7.

[19] Letter to John Wilson (1802), p. 72.

[20] Letter to Lady Beaumont (1807), p. 77.   [21] *Op. cit.*, p. 79.

an entire regeneration must be produced; and if this be possible, it must be a work of *time*.[22]

This is an argument which reached publication in the *Essay, Supplementary to the Preface* of 1815.[23]

The epitaph, as Wordsworth discussed it in the three essays of 1810, suggested to him, as *Lyrical Ballads* had, the possibility of direct communication between poet and reader: "The first requisite, then, in an Epitaph is, that it should speak, in a tone which shall sink into the heart, the general language of humanity as connected with the subject of Death".[24] The appeal of its subject-matter is inevitably universal, since "To be born and to die are the two points in which all men feel themselves to be in absolute coincidence".[25] And because its audience will be more or less universal, its style should be, appropriately, universally intelligible:

> an Epitaph is not a proud Writing shut up for the studious; it is exposed to all, to the wise and the most ignorant; it is condescending, perspicuous, and lovingly solicits regard; it's story and admonitions are brief, that the thoughtless, the busy and indolent, may not be deterred, nor the impatient tired; the stooping Old Man cons the engraven record like a second horn-book; – the Child is proud that he can read it – and the Stranger is introduced by it's mediation to the company of a Friend: it is concerning all, and for all: – in the Church-yard it is open to the day; the sun looks down upon the stone, and the rains of Heaven beat against it . . . the inscription which [the monument] bears is intended to be permanent and for universal perusal.[26]

The existence of "the witling and the worldling" is still recognised, as it was in 1807,[27] but the emphasis is different: in 1807 these were part of the insensitive Public who despised Wordsworth's *Poems, in Two Volumes*; in 1810 they are, rather, Pope and

[22] *Op. cit.*, p. 83.
[23] See p. 182. The operative part of the Essay begins with a view of poetry, not as a source of pleasure, but *"as a study"* (p. 159).
[24] *Essay upon Epitaphs*, I (1810), p. 100.
[25] *Op. cit.*, pp. 100–1.   [26] *Op. cit.*, p. 103.
[27] *Essay upon Epitaphs*, II (1810), p. 107. *Cf.* the Letter to Lady Beaumont, pp. 76, 79.

his followers in the genre of the epitaph, whose dealing is with "the adversary of Nature (call that adversary Art or by what name you will)".[28] The right-minded reader is here thought of as a man of naturally unsophisticated taste whose judgment can be readily invoked: "Every Reader will be able to supply from his own observations instances . . . an instance where no one can be at a loss . . . who can doubt that the writer was transported to the height of the occasion? . . . the difference [between two epitaphs] will flash upon the Reader at once . . . The Reader will perceive at once . . . who does not here feel a superior truth and sanctity . . .? . . . If those primary sensations upon which I have dwelt so much be not stifled in the heart of the Reader [some simple epitaphs] will be read with pleasure".[29] And the universality of the subject-matter of the epitaph is emphasised in one of Wordsworth's most eloquent pieces of critical prose: the epitaph

> is grounded upon the universal intellectual property of man, – sensations which all men have felt and feel in some degree daily and hourly; truths whose very interest and importance have caused them to be unattended to, as things which could take care of themselves. But it is required that these truths should be instinctively ejaculated or should rise irresistibly from circumstances; in a word that they should be uttered in such connection as shall make it felt that they are not adopted, not spoken by rote, but perceived in their whole compass with the freshness and clearness of an original intuition. The Writer must introduce the truth with such accompaniment as shall imply that he has mounted to the sources of things, penetrated the dark cavern from which the river that murmurs in every one's ear has flowed from generation to generation.[30]

And "all men, at some time or other", have had their souls "thoroughly stricken" by death.[31]

In the documents so far examined, we see our two polarities

---

[28] *Essay upon Epitaphs*, III (1810), p. 124.

[29] *Essay upon Epitaphs*, II (1810), Knight, ii, 150; *Essay upon Epitaphs*, II (1810), pp. 107, 108, 110, 112; *Essay upon Epitaphs*, III (1810), Knight, ii, 178, 186.

[30] *Essay upon Epitaphs*, II (1810), pp. 117–18.

[31] *Essay upon Epitaphs*, III (1810), p. 124.

presented with varying emphases and with appropriate corollaries: the Preface to *Lyrical Ballads* and the *Essays upon Epitaphs* on the whole emphasise the possibility of communication; the letters to John Wilson and to Lady Beaumont emphasise its difficulty, and on the whole they attribute the difficulty to the insensitivity of the contemporary audience.

2

By 1814–15 Wordsworth had reached a wider understanding of the problem, which retains all these elements – that poetry can communicate; that the intellectual stance of the audience may offer a difficulty in the way of communication – but which adds a new element: stated crudely, that some poetry makes its appeal with greater difficulty than some other poetry. The same poet may produce, and the same poem may contain, samples of "difficult" and "easy" poetry. The defects of the audience remain, and the insensitive may fail to grasp what ought to be easy; but even the sympathetic audience may find it difficult to grasp what the poet admits is difficult poetry. This is a major concession on Wordsworth's part; for hitherto, with the single exception in 1800, when he admits to the possibility of "unworthy subjects",[32] Wordsworth has blamed his failure to communicate upon the shortcomings of his audience.

Deficiencies in the audience are still recognised in the first major statement of the new point of view, but the deficiencies are not presented as blameworthy. Wordsworth, writing to Catherine Clarkson in early 1815,[33] admits that she may meet with "im-

[32] Preface to *Lyrical Ballads* (1800), p. 29.

[33] Zall dates this letter January 1815, de Selincourt December 1814. There is no date on the MS. It may be, however, that de Selincourt's Letter 512, firmly dated "New Year's Eve ([1814])" (*Middle Years*, p. 621), is earlier than Letter 511, now under discussion: in 512 (for instance) Dorothy Wordsworth mildly rebukes Mrs Clarkson "for leaving the Excursion with William Smith" (p. 624), whereas 511 gives Wordsworth's angry reaction to the criticism of *The Excursion* reported from William Smith's daughter; as if by the date of 511 Patty Smith had had time to read the poem and give her views to Mrs Clarkson. In that case Letter 511 must be dated January 1815 (as by Professor Zall) at earliest. – I am indebted to Professor G. H. Healey of Cornell for information about the MS of Letter 511 and for the suggestion that 511 may be later than 512.

pediments" in the way of her understanding of *The Excursion*. They will be

> of two kinds, such as exist in the ode [*Intimations of Immortality*] which concludes my 2d volume of poems. This poem rests entirely upon two recollections of childhood, one that of a splendour in the objects of sense which is passed away, and the other an indisposition to bend to the law of death as applying to our own particular case. A Reader who has not a vivid recollection of these feelings having existed in his mind in childhood cannot understand that poem. So also with regard to some of those elements of the human soul whose importance is insisted upon in the Excursion. And some of those images of sense which are dwelt upon as holding that relation to immortality and infinity which I have before alluded to; if a person has not been in the way of receiving these images, it is not likely that he can form such an adequate conception of them as will bring him into lively sympathy with the Poet. For instance one who has never heard the echoes of the flying Raven's voice in a mountainous Country, as described at the close of the 4th Book will not perhaps be able to relish that illustration; yet every one must have been in the way of perceiving similar effects from different causes.[34]

To define more precisely what I have called above "easy" and "difficult" poetry, Wordsworth, in the letter cited and in the two critical essays published in 1815, draws on the ideas of John Dennis. I do not know when he first became acquainted with the works of Dennis: there are ideas in the Preface to *Lyrical Ballads* which he could have borrowed from them, but verbal resemblances are not close enough for certainty.[35] In the letter cited above, however,

---

[34] Letter to Catherine Clarkson (1815), pp. 135–6. It is not clear whether Wordsworth thinks he has explained the "two kinds" of impediment or whether he merely omits the second. Both kinds are said to be present in the *Ode*, but he appears to instance only one (unless the "two kinds" correspond to the "two recollections"), and the explanations he gives of the difficulty of the *Ode* and of the image of the raven (*Exc.*, IV, 1175 ff.) seem essentially the same: the reader lacks the appropriate experience.

[35] See the references in my edition of the Preface, *passim*; and the imprecise account from De Quincey, cited in Dennis, ii, lxxiii.

his debt to Dennis is made explicit: "Poetic Passion (Dennis has well observed) is of two kinds imaginative and enthusiastic; and merely human & ordinary".[36] Wordsworth is drawing on concepts which Dennis repeats almost *ad nauseam* in his larger critical essays, *The Advancement and Reformation of Modern Poetry* and *The Grounds of Criticism in Poetry*:

> It is plain . . . that Passion in Poetry must be every where, for where there is no Passion, there can be no Poetry; but that which we commonly call Passion, cannot be every where in any Poem. There must be Passion then, that must be distinct from ordinary Passion, and that must be Enthusiasm. I call that ordinary Passion, whose Cause is clearly comprehended by him who feels it, whether it be Admiration, Terror or Joy; and I call the very same Passions Enthusiasms, when their Cause is not clearly comprehended by him who feels them. And those Enthusiastick Passions, are sometimes simple, and sometimes complicated . . . the Reason why we know not the Causes of Enthusiastick, as well as of ordinary Passions, is, because we are not so us'd to them, and because they proceed from Thoughts, that latently, and unobserv'd by us, carry Passion along with them.[37]
>
> . . . there must be two sorts of Passion: *First*, That which we call Vulgar Passion; and *Secondly*, Enthusiasm . . . Vulgar Passion, or that which we commonly call Passion, is that which is moved by the Objects themselves, or by the Ideas in the ordinary Course of Life . . . Enthusiastick Passion, or Enthusiasm, is a Passion which is moved by the Ideas in Contemplation, or the Meditation of things that belong not to common Life.[38]

In the *Essay, Supplementary to the Preface* of 1815 (written, probably, at about the same time as the letter to Mrs Clarkson), Wordsworth draws on these concepts again. The reader of poetry must be "invigorated and inspirited by his Leader [the Poet], in order that he may exert himself, for he cannot proceed in quiescence, he cannot be carried like a dead weight".[39] The next paragraph pro-

---

[36] Letter to Catherine Clarkson (1815), p. 133.
[37] Dennis, i, 216–17.   [38] Dennis, i, 338.
[39] *Essay, Supplementary to the Preface* (1815), p. 184.

ceeds to insist upon the need for the reader to "exert himself"
especially when he is faced with the second of two kinds of poetry:

> As the pathetic participates of an *animal* sensation, it might
> seem – that, if the springs of this emotion were genuine, all
> men, possessed of competent knowledge of the facts and cir-
> cumstances, would be instantaneously affected. And,
> doubtless, in the works of every true Poet will be found
> passages of that species of excellence, which is proved by
> effects immediate and universal. But there are emotions of
> the pathetic that are simple and direct, and others – that are
> complex and revolutionary; some – to which the heart yields
> with gentleness, others, – against which it struggles with
> pride: these varieties are infinite as the combinations of
> circumstance and the constitutions of character . . . There is
> also a meditative, as well as a human, pathos; an enthusiastic,
> as well as an ordinary, sorrow; a sadness that has its seat in the
> depths of reason, to which the mind cannot sink gently of
> itself – but to which it must descend by treading the steps of
> thought.[40]

In the opening sentence, "pathetic", contrasted with "the sublime"
in the last sentence of the paragraph (not quoted above), is used in
a common eighteenth-century antithesis and means "producing an
effect upon the emotions" (*O.E.D.*, sense I), not necessarily
"exciting pity, sympathy, or sadness" (*O.E.D.*, sense I.b).[41] When
we recall that "pathetic" is Dennis's adjective corresponding to
the noun "passion",[42] we recognise that Wordsworth is developing Dennis's concepts of "ordinary" or "vulgar" passion in contrast to "enthusiasm" or "enthusiastic passion". To clarify still
further, we need to notice that, in developing, Wordsworth also
simplifies: whereas Dennis says that "Enthusiastick Passions are
sometimes simple, and sometimes complicated", Wordsworth's
"simple and direct", "human", "ordinary",[43] or "human &

[40] *Op. cit.*, p. 185.
[41] But "pathos", later in the paragraph, linked with "sorrow" and "sadness", appears to have its modern sense.
[42] See, for instance, Dennis, i, 215; "Passion then, is the Characteristical
Mark of Poetry, and, consequently, must be every where: For where-ever a
Discourse is not Pathetick, there it is Prosaick."
[43] *Essay, Supplementary to the Preface* (1815), p. 185.

ordinary",[44] or "ordinary or popular",[45] correspond to Dennis's "ordinary" or "vulgar"; and Wordsworth's "complex and revolutionary", "meditative", or "enthusiastic",[46] or "imaginative and enthusiastic",[47] or "meditative",[48] correspond to Dennis's "enthusiastic" – though Dennis's division of "enthusiasms" into "simple" and "complicated" is the *verbal* source of Wordsworth's broader distinction. A diagram will illustrate:

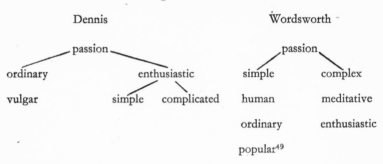

Dennis

Wordsworth

	passion		passion	
ordinary		enthusiastic	simple	complex
vulgar	simple	complicated	human	meditative
			ordinary	enthusiastic
			popular[49]	

Thus what was tentatively called "easy" poetry above is now defined in terms of Dennis's "ordinary" or "vulgar" passion, and what was called "difficult" poetry, in terms of Dennis's "enthusiastic" passion.

To name an abstraction is to give oneself a chance of talking about it, as Wordsworth seems to be doing in the paragraph cited from the Essay. In fact the paragraph remains abstract and obscure, especially the discussion of "enthusiastic" passion; and illustration becomes imperative if we are to understand. For this there are two main sources. The letter to Mrs Clarkson gives as instances of "ordinary or popular passion" the following passages from *The Excursion*: "the description of Robert, and the fluctuations of hope and fear in Margaret's mind, and the gradual decay of herself and her dwelling"; "the distress of the Solitary after the loss of his Family and the picture of his quarrel with his own con-

---

[44] Letter to Catherine Clarkson (1815), p. 133.   [45] *Op. cit.*, p. 136.
[46] *Essay, Supplementary to the Preface* (1815), p. 185.
[47] Letter to Catherine Clarkson (1815), p. 133.   [48] *Op. cit.*, p. 136.
[49] Probably "popular", and possibly "human", are Wordsworth's modernisations of Dennis's "vulgar"; for "meditative", *cf.* Dennis, i, 338: "Enthusiasm, is a Passion . . . moved by . . . the Meditation of things that belong not to common Life."

science (though this tends more to meditative passion)"; and "the anger of Ellen".[50] In the Preface of 1815, Wordsworth again draws on Dennis's distinction:

> The grand store-house of enthusiastic and meditative Imagination, of poetical, as contradistinguished from human and dramatic Imagination, is[51] the prophetic and lyrical parts of the holy Scriptures, and the works of Milton, to which I cannot forbear to add those of Spenser.[52]

As well as the passages in Dennis already noted, this sentence draws on Dennis's observation[53] that, in the narrative parts of epic, "the Enthusiastick Passions are to prevail", but that "the Vulgar Passions are to prevail in those parts of an Epick and Dramatick Poem, where the Poet introduces Persons holding Conversation together" (hence Wordsworth's "human and dramatic Imagination"); and, probably, it draws also on Dennis's view that a Christian poet is better equipped for his art than a pagan:[54] there is mention of Milton, of "the Prophet *Habbakuk*", and of Psalm 18; and Dennis claims that "The most important Parts of the Old Testament to us, are the Prophecies", and that "one of the Prophetick Functions" was "Praising God with Songs of the Prophets composing, accompany'd with the Harp and other Instrumental Musick".[55]

The nature of the episodes in *The Excursion* characterised by "ordinary or popular passion" is clear: they are episodes in which the protagonist currently feels emotion "whose Cause is clearly comprehended by him who feels it", as Dennis puts it. There is a kind of situation, Wordsworth is saying, in which the emotional elements are the factual data, which need only to be stated for the audience to grasp them. The episode last cited from *The Excursion* is a particularly clear instance. Ellen with difficulty attends the funeral of her illegitimate child, whom she has been permitted to see only once in its last illness:

[50] *The Excursion*, I, 469 ff; III, 680–705, 778–991; VI, 976–8. Letter to Catherine Clarkson (1815), p. 136. The story of "the little Infant, who was unexpectedly given, and suddenly taken away" (*Exc.*, VII, 632–94) is probably another such instance, but Wordsworth does not actually say so.

[51] In texts later than 1815, "storehouses . . . are".

[52] Preface to *Poems* (1815), p. 150.   [53] Dennis, i, 339.

[54] *Op. cit.*, i, 366 ff.   [55] *Op. cit.*, i, 370.

> She reached the house, last of the funeral train;
> And some one, as she entered, having chanced
> To urge unthinkingly their prompt departure,
> 'Nay,' said she, with commanding look, a spirit
> Of anger never seen in her before,
> 'Nay, ye must wait my time!' and down she sate,
> And by the unclosed coffin kept her seat
> Weeping and looking, looking on and weeping,
> Upon the last sweet slumber of her Child,
> Until at length her soul was satisfied.[56]

This situation speaks for itself emotionally from its mere factual content. As Dennis puts it, describing "Vulgar Passion": "Anger is moved by an Affront that is offer'd us in our presence, or by the Relation of one";[57] the affront offered to Ellen calls forth her anger accordingly. The poet's task, in such an instance, is merely to put his readers in possession of "competent knowledge of the facts and circumstances"; they will then be "instantaneously affected".[58] Dennis confirms: "Vulgar [passion] is preferable [in poetry], because all Men are capable of being moved by the Vulgar, and a Poet writes to all".[59] In a much earlier instance, Wordsworth reproaches Sara Hutchinson for failing to be "instantaneously affected" by the pathetic spectacle of the leech-gatherer in an early version of "Resolution and Independence", even though, he is convinced, he has provided for her the data for "competent knowledge of the facts and circumstances".[60] He

---

[56] *The Excursion*, VI, 973–82.   [57] Dennis, i, 338.

[58] *Essay, Supplementary to the Preface* (1815), p. 185.   [59] Dennis, i, 339.

[60] See *Early Letters of William and Dorothy Wordsworth*, ed. E. de Selincourt, pp. 305–7 (14 Jun. 1802). Note especially: "the figure presented in the most naked simplicity possible . . . I cannot conceive a figure more impressive than that of an old Man like this, the survivor of a Wife and ten children, . . . carrying with him his own fortitude, and the necessities which an unjust state of society has entailed upon him . . . It is in the character of the old man to tell his story in a manner which an *impatient* reader must necessarily feel as tedious . . . it may be comparatively [indifferent], whether you are pleased or not with *this Poem*: but it is of the utmost importance that you should have had pleasure from contemplating the fortitude, independence, persevering spirit, and the general moral dignity of this old man's character." Wordsworth is much less concerned with Sara's aesthetic response to the poem than with her emotional and moral reaction to reported fact.

expected the facts and circumstances to speak for themselves, and when Sara found them emotionally unremarkable, Wordsworth was puzzled, as he was puzzled and annoyed at the insensibility of Miss Patty Smith towards *The Excursion* in 1815.

It is harder to be sure of the kind of episode that Wordsworth had in mind when he drew on Dennis's jargon about "enthusiastic" or "meditative" passions, "complex and revolutionary" emotions, on which the critical essays of 1815 spend more space and emphasis. Milton and Spenser and the outpourings of the Hebrew prophets, Habbakuk and others, fit in a general way with Dennis's definition of "Enthusiasm . . . moved by . . . the Meditation of things that belong not to common Life",[61] but Wordsworth, on the whole, does not write in this way. He cites the Solitary's "quarrel with his own conscience" as an episode that "tends more to meditative passion"; and of this we may observe that the Solitary indulges in this quarrel over events and feelings connected with revolutionary France with which he has no direct personal experience or concern. He is no Frenchman and he takes no direct part in revolutionary activity: his involvement and subsequent disillusionment, though not dishonest, are remote and second-hand, though real enough to induce the rejection of "natural" feelings[62] and hence the moral despair which presumably reflects Wordsworth's own in the middle nineties. Such a situation is, no doubt, one that "belongs not to common Life" and that is emotionally more complex than the others listed from *The Excursion* in the letter to Mrs Clarkson; it might even be said that it proceeds "from Thoughts, that latently, and unobserv'd by us, carry Passion along with them";[63] "the Enthusiastick", says Dennis, "are more subtle, and thousands

[61] Dennis, i, 338.
[62] *Exc.*, III, 736–9:
> From the depths
> Of natural passion, seemingly escaped,
> My soul diffused herself in wide embrace
> Of institutions, and the forms of things;

808–12:
> thee,
> O fostering Nature! I rejected – smiled
> At others' tears in pity; and in scorn
> At those, which thy soft influence sometimes drew
> From my unguarded heart.

[63] Dennis, i, 217.

L

have no feeling and no notion of them".[64] Whether it can also be said that the feeling involved lacks a "Cause . . . clearly comprehended by him who feels it" is less obvious. But it is tolerably clear that the *reader*, if he understands it at all, understands such a situation (unless he happens to have been involved in one such himself) less directly than he understands, say, "the anger of Ellen", and rather by a process of "treading the steps of thought". [65] He understands the anger of Ellen because, at some time or other, he has suffered (or observed) a comparable affront and has been comparably angered (or has observed such anger); and upon the generality of this situation the poet can rely with some confidence. He cannot have this confidence in the reader's reaction to the story of the Solitary, which makes complete sense only in a particular historical context. Indeed, in some similar instances, Wordsworth insists that, lacking a particular experience, the reader will not understand at all: "A Reader who has not a vivid recollection of these feelings having existed in his mind in childhood cannot understand that poem".[66] So he writes of the Immortality *Ode*; as if this were fact, bald and regrettable, but implying no blame, either to himself for choosing a subject which, if not "unworthy", is at least "particular instead of general",[67] or to the reader for suffering from "pure absolute honest ignorance"[68] of some childhood feelings which Wordsworth happens to have had and to have remembered. The nearby instance of the "flying Raven's voice", however, offers a kind of escape from the difficulty, even though, "if a person has not been in the way of receiving these images, it is not likely that he can form such an adequate conception of them as will bring him into lively sympathy with the Poet". For "every one must have been in the way of perceiving similar effects from different causes":[69] from analogy, from the sense of a comparable though not identical experience, the reader, by an effort of imagination without which "the voice which is the voice of my Poetry . . . cannot be heard", may begin to bridge the gap of non-communication.

---

[64] *Op. cit.*, i, 339.   [65] *Essay, Supplementary to the Preface* (1815), p. 185.
[66] Letter to Catherine Clarkson (1815), p. 135.
[67] Preface to *Lyrical Ballads* (1800), p. 29.
[68] Letter to Lady Beaumont (1807), p. 76.
[69] Letter to Catherine Clarkson (1815), pp. 135–6.

After seventeen years of theorising, the largely increasing un-popularity of his poetry forced Wordsworth to admit that some at least of his writing presented difficulty to some at least (perhaps a majority) of his potential audience. To account for this failure to communicate, he built up several images or myths during the period, and especially in the years 1807–15: the dual image of People and Public; the historical myth which is the main theme of the *Essay, Supplementary to the Preface*, that great poets (including himself) are unpopular in their own time; the Coleridgean dogma, related to both these, that the poet must educate the taste of the audience. Dennis's vocabulary enabled Wordsworth to express a more realistic viewpoint: that the difficulty lay primarily in the poetry itself. This was especially useful because it expressed the viewpoint, not by criticising the poetry and so damaging the poet's own image, but, rather, by presenting the dual nature of the art as one of the facts of aesthetic life: there are two sorts of poetry, and one sort, by its very nature, communicates less readily than the other. Neither, according to this view, is a less valid form of art than the other, and therefore, even though the one may spring from "particular instead of general" associations, the question of "unworthy subjects" does not arise.[70]

The two polarities with which this discussion began are thus exposed side by side, though Wordsworth's emphasis is now on the need to recognise the nature and the difficulty of "enthusiastic" passions in poetry; Dennis's emphasis, which Wordsworth omits, is that "Vulgar [passion] is preferable [in poetry], because all Men are capable of being moved by the Vulgar, and a Poet writes to all".[71] If we were to translate these notions out of Dennis's language, we might reach the position that there is a poetry which communicates immediately because it deals with what both Aristotle and Wordsworth called general truth;[72] but that there is also a poetry of myth (Milton's, for instance), allegory or other oblique statement (Spenser's, for instance), or of private ex-perience and private imagery (Wordsworth's, for instance),[73] which is inevitably more difficult to the audience. These latter

---

[70] Preface to *Lyrical Ballads* (1800), p. 29.   [71] Dennis, i, 339.

[72] Preface to *Lyrical Ballads* (1802), p. 50.

[73] Milton and Spenser are examples cited by Wordsworth. Preface to *Poems* (1815), p. 150.

kinds may be subdivided or, in some instances, combined: as, for
instance, the traditional myth of Milton, generally intelligible to
Western minds, contrasted with the private myth, allegory, and
images of Blake's Prophetic Books, the obscurity of which remains largely unresolved. It is so with some at least of the
personal experiences of *The Prelude* and *The Excursion*, not difficult
to follow in factual terms, but so remote from general experience
that an understanding of the emotional significance is hard or
impossible to come by. I think of passages such as the two "spots
of time" described at the end of Book xii of *The Prelude*, as well as
of the *Ode* and the image of the raven in *The Excursion* which
Wordsworth himself points out. Indeed, of one of the "spots of
time" Wordsworth confesses that, though the natural scene presented "An ordinary sight", he cannot "paint" the emotional
tone with which he remembers it to have been suffused; which is
tantamount to saying that he does not understand the experience
himself, only (as he says of a comparable experience in London)
remembers it as "a thing divine".[74] To passages difficult for such
reasons, the critical vocabulary of Dennis, crude though its psychological basis may be, enabled Wordsworth to give a description, and hence a kind of authority by which he could defend
their validity as poetry, while he honestly admitted their only
partial success in communication.

[74] *The Prelude*, xii, 253–61; viii, 559.

Anthony Conran

THE GOSLAR LYRICS

Wordsworth and Coleridge set out for Germany on 15 Sep. 1798, in order to learn the language and become acquainted with German literature and philosophy. The previous year spent at Alfoxden had seen the writing of *The Ancient Mariner* and the other *Lyrical Ballads*. Wordsworth had composed over three thousand lines in six months, and had planned the long poem he called *The Recluse*. In Germany, the two friends separated. Coleridge made himself very much at home in German university circles, devouring metaphysics. For him the stay was a success. Wordsworth and his sister, on the other hand, settled in the provincial town of Goslar, where they found themselves social outcasts condemned to intellectual stagnation. They did not even succeed in learning German. They were cold, lonely, and miserable. When the two poets met again in the spring of 1799, Coleridge was alarmed by the change in Wordsworth. He himself had enjoyed the hard work and lively society of his stay; he looked forward to resuming his comfortable existence at Stowey, with the prospect of devoting his maturity to a major philosophical work. He was missing his family, and had not long since heard of the death of his second son. He was filled with husbandly solicitude towards his wife. Into this "wedding-guest" situation, like an Ancient Mariner for a second time Wordsworth erupted. In 1797, however, Wordsworth had been a god, an excitement, a new dimension of solitude. Now he was moody and almost hysterical with the panic and the loneliness of nearly eight months' exile. Coleridge was both baffled and exasperated by Wordsworth's tearful insistence that he should forsake his Bristol friends and settle within reach of the

Lakes – a move that, foreseeably, would cost him his health, endanger his marriage to breaking point, waste a career full of promise, and, finally, even embitter his friendship with Wordsworth himself.

The letters that Wordsworth wrote from Goslar are full of complaints: about the German inhospitality to strangers, the cold weather, his own and his sister's ill health. Again and again, however, he recurs to the difficulty he was having in writing poetry. After the miraculous output of Alfoxden and the high hopes he had of coming into his own as a great poet, this must have been particularly galling. It was probably the worst feature of his stay in Germany that it made him distrust, agonisingly, his creative powers as a poet. He did in fact write a fair amount: sixteen or so short poems in rhyme, and the tangled mass of blank-verse fragments that were eventually to be found (most of them) in Book One of *The Prelude*. The two groups are perfectly distinct, in theme as in technique; but underlying them both is the recurrent question that summoned from the depths of his memory the electing silences of his childhood, the presences that were his ultimate guarantee of his own creative powers. Through the early drafts of what was to become Book One of *The Prelude* this question – "Was it for this?" – tolls like a bell, conjuring up the spirits of the past, a bastion against an unmentionable chaos that must never, never be allowed to come again; a huge bulwark of sanity, that in Grasmere was left high and dry, like a Great Wall of China in a respectable market-town. In the context of the finished *Prelude*, "Was it for this?" is as rhetorical as a ruin or an eighteenth-century folly: but in the loneliness and self-questioning of Goslar, the question was as urgent as death itself.

2

When we examine the sixteen or so short ballads and lyrics of the German period, the first thing that must strike us is a quite clear disintegration of one style – that of *Lyrical Ballads* and *Peter Bell* – and the gradual reaching of perfection in another – what J. F. Danby[1] calls the "gnomic" style of the Matthew poems. The articulating medium of 1798 had been a style founded on the

[1] J. F. Danby, *The Simple Wordsworth*. London, 1960, p. 82.

popular ballad of the broadsheets. Coarse-grained, lively, tending towards a long stanza, mixing eights and sixes, couplets and quatrains, able to embrace many different attitudes and viewpoints, and to switch suddenly from one emotion to another: it had been a style as dramatic as anything in English verse since the seventeenth century. But of the Goslar poems, only "Ruth" is more than seventy-five lines long – and "Ruth" was written, not strictly at Goslar, but wandering in the Hartz forest the following spring; only two, "To a Sexton" and "The Danish Boy", have stanzas over seven lines apiece – and neither is a success. "The Danish Boy" is confessedly a fragment of a ballad that was never finished; from internal evidence I should say the same thing about "To a Sexton" – its ending is the sort of perfunctory job poets do when they patch up for publication a poem that isn't getting anywhere. "Ruth" and "Lucy Gray" are ballads, it is true: but they are quite different from those of 1798. They are not articulated with anything like the same exuberance of gesture or dramatic presence: they are narrative *genre*-pieces, rather than embodiments of lived-through humanity.

But if the primary impulse behind *Lyrical Ballads* has lost itself in futility, the poems of that winter in Goslar certainly attain their own triumphs of articulation and poise. The biographical inquisitiveness about Lucy – who she was, and why she died – has put an altogether disproportionate emphasis on the four short poems that concern her (the fifth, "I travelled among unknown men", was written in 1801). Critics who speculate on her death would surely see the problem in better perspective did they observe that in the Goslar poems almost everyone is as dead as she. The Matthew cycle takes its point of departure from an elegy for the dead schoolmaster; and even in "The Two April Mornings" (with its companion, "The Fountain", surely two of the finest short poems in the language) the fact of his death is insisted upon:

> Matthew is in his grave, yet now,
> Methinks, I see him stand,
> As at that moment, with a bough
> Of wilding in his hand.[2]

---

[2] "The Two April Mornings", 57–60. *The Poetical Works of William Wordsworth*, 5 vols, eds. E. de Selincourt and Helen Darbishire. Oxford, 1940–49, Vol. IV, p. 69.

"The Danish Boy" ends with two blood-curdling lines:

> For calm and gentle is his mien;
> Like a dead Boy he is serene.

"Lucy Gray", of course, is dead, killed in a storm; while Ruth, though she is not quite dead yet, is piously offered the promise of a Christian burial:

> Farewell! and when thy days are told,
> Ill-fated Ruth, in hallowed mould
> Thy corpse shall buried be,
> For thee a funeral bell shall ring,
> And all the congregation sing
> A Christian psalm for thee.[3]

In "A Poet's Epitaph", he even imagines himself dead. The poor fly, in "Written in Germany, on one of the Coldest Days of the Century", is one of the few survivors from this holocaust; and even his prospects do not seem particularly bright:

> His spindles sink under him, foot, leg, and thigh!
> His eyesight and hearing are lost;
> Between life and death his blood freezes and thaws;
> And his two pretty pinions of blue dusky gauze
> Are glued to his sides by the frost.[4]

Truly, one is tempted to echo the lines "To a Sexton":

> Let thy wheel-barrow alone –
> Wherefore, Sexton, piling still
> In thy bone-house bone on bone?
> 'Tis already like a hill
> In a field of battle made,
> Where three thousand skulls are laid.[5]

With one exception, the love-poem that Wordsworth never acknowledged as his own ("How sweet, when crimson colours dart")[6] every single one of these poems involves at least one corpse or prospect of a corpse – and sometimes more than one. The poet seems to have felt that such a manifold doom would be too much for his readers to swallow. There is no authorised edition in which

---

[3] "Ruth", 253-8.   [4] 21-5.   [5] 1-6.   [6] *The Poetical Works*, II, p. 465.

the Goslar poems are collected together, as the 1798 volume collected the ballads and lyrics of Alfoxden. Even in 1800, they were
insulated from one another by more cheerful offerings from
Grasmere.

The style of the lyrical ballad had been an essentially three-
dimensional articulation of man as a social being, put into situations where social values failed to be relevant. It had been based
on a dialectic of challenge and response (found in its simplest
form in poems like "Anecdote for Fathers") continued to the
point where no further response was valid, save the acknowledge-
ment of humanity existing beyond any conceivable contact. As a
technique, this proved to be too complex and circumstantial for
the new poetry Wordsworth wrote in Germany. In this latter, the
dialectic of *Lyrical Ballads* is stylised and simplified to one moment
only: the challenge is always the loss, and usually the death, of a
loved one, either fancied or in fact. The world outside that loss is
irrelevant – two dimensions are all that are required. Some
technique had to be found whereby the shocks of bereavement
could be registered, and at the same time the proper direction of
response could be indicated, and improper divergences into sentimentality or unreason could be checked. Each poem had to be a precision instrument, compared with which the average Lyrical Ballad
had the lusty awkwardness of a steam locomotive. Pity and terror,
which had provided the emotional drive of 1798, were now
distractions, at the best: for pity is only proper to one who
observes suffering in others, not to him who himself suffers;
while the terror of bereavement is the force that disturbs most of
all the honesty of response that is essential to the unmaimed
freedom of being sane. For sanity, in this new poetry, has moved
into the centre of attention. In *Lyrical Ballads* 1798, the poet had
aimed, one could say, at providing a mature platform for the
values of insanity and unreason. The reader's response to the outcast, the idiot and the child was manoeuvred into magnanimity
and sobering joy. But now, the testing of maturity began in
earnest. Saneness was no longer merely the direction or end-
product of a poem, but its subject-matter as well.

The technique Wordsworth forged for himself relies for its
effects on the precise juxtaposition of variously charged moments
of time. The medium is the quatrain, with its peculiar virtue of

isolating situations, etching them in rapidly, with a minimum of fuss and a maximum of point, and leaving the bare bones of thought uncluttered by irrelevances. One might, perhaps, compare these poems with Eliot's Sweeney cycle. Eliot, it is true, has a very different tone and intention; and he tends to articulate his poems through space, cutting like a film-director from close-up to panorama and back again, whereas Wordsworth articulates his through time. Eliot, juxtaposing spaces, has to preserve the unity of time: Wordsworth, justaposing times, normally keeps to the unity of place. In both cycles, the pressure of unreason is felt as a constant source of psychic disintegration: the sense of loss and death, in Wordsworth, corresponds in this respect to the cultural disaffection and sexual nausea – for example, in "Burbank with a Baedeker: Bleistein with a Cigar" – which were leading Eliot to *The Waste Land* and nervous collapse. The quatrain is a good metre for holding on tight: for one thing, if a stanza doesn't work properly, you can spot it quickly and very likely cut it out. The tightly knit, recurrent structures give you confidence, like links in a chain; whereas a more loose-limbed stanza lets you fall too easily into inconsequence.

3

The comparison between the two poets (as indeed is obvious) must not be pressed too far. Eliot's quatrain-technique is aristocratic, based on the model of Gautier –

> Et la médaille austère
> Que trouve un laboureur
>   Sous terre
> Révèle un empereur –

whereas Wordsworth's derives from the humbler source of *The Babes in the Wood*: he had bought a copy of Percy's *Reliques* in Hamburg, and "Lucy Gray", in particular, betrays the ballad-influence as strong. One can detect the metamorphosis of the ballad into the new Goslar style in what was probably the first of the Lucy poems to be written. It almost certainly began as a lyric about Dorothy at Racedown, similar to the much later "Among all lovely things my Love has been":

Once, when my love was strong and gay,
  And like a rose in June,
I to her cottage bent my way
  Beneath the evening Moon.

Upon the moon I fixed my eye
  All over the wide lea;
My horse trudg'd on, and we drew nigh
  Those paths so dear to me.

And now I've reached the orchard-plot,
  And as we climbed the hill,
Towards the roof of Lucy's cot
  The moon descended still.

In one of those sweet dreams I slept,
  Kind nature's gentlest boon,
And all the while my eyes I kept
  On the descending moon.

My horse moved on; hoof after hoof
  He raised and never stopped,
When down behind the cottage roof
  At once the planet dropped.

Strange are the fancies that will slide
  Into a lover's head,
'O mercy' to myself I cried,
  'If Lucy should be dead!'

I told her this; her laughter light
  Is ringing in my ears;
And when I think upon that night
  My eyes are dim with tears.[7]

This is the version that Wordsworth first sent to Coleridge in a letter from Goslar, which refers to "two or three little Rhyme poems which I hope will amuse you".[8]

Clearly, this is a poem that has lost its way. Wordsworth was probably not satisfied with it, for the simple reason that he could

[7] See "Strange fits of passion have I known", *P.W.*, II, p. 29.
[8] *The Early Letters of William and Dorothy Wordsworth*, ed. E. de Selincourt. Oxford, 1935, pp. 204–6.

not find it a satisfactory ending; and I suspect that this was why, when he came to publish it in 1800, he prefaced it with the rather coy introductory stanza that we know:

> Strange fits of passion have I known:
> And I will dare to tell,
> But in the Lover's ear alone,
> What once to me befell.[9]

This adds nothing of consequence to the poem's content: but it does change the nature of its demands upon us. As it was originally conceived, we may be sure, it would not have needed apology. Apart from the last two lines, the draft in the letter is a far more honest bit of work than the watered-down published text.

However, the juxtapositions at the end are much too cramped. The panic inspired by fancy is followed far too quickly by the final sorrow. As in certain other of these poems (*e.g.* "Three years she grew in sun and shower") death comes too pat to complete the pattern inevitably enough. So, the poet must have argued, if this poem ends in a cul-de-sac, let us salvage out of it what we can. It can be treated as a mere *genre*-piece, a fantasy of Dresden ware, descriptive of a lover's oddities; this is why Jeffrey came to make fun of it. The form of the original, though, had been the typical double-barrelled formula that Wordsworth used for many of his most powerful works – "Guilt and Sorrow", "The Ruined Cottage" and "Resolution and Independence" among them: a journey to some spot is followed by a meeting with someone who tells a story. Here, it is true, the pattern is very considerably curtailed. The reason it fails is because Wordsworth is not yet sure what kind of story it will be, nor even who is the person to tell it. The stylised and simplified challenge that we saw as a development from the complex, three-dimensional dialectic typical of *Lyrical Ballads*, 1798, has wrecked the attempt to encompass its proper response by using merely narrative means.

Wordsworth at this stage was not particularly interested in pathos for its own sake. The Lucy poems are about the lovely object whose loss forms the challenge of Goslar. Lucy is beautifully given her own defining privacy:

[9] "Strange fits of passion have I known", 1–4.

A violet by a mossy stone
Half hidden from the eye!
Fair as a star, when only one
Is shining in the sky.[10]

She is dead, and her presence is one with the earth's – "rolled round . . . with rocks, and stones, and trees". But in this mode (that of simple elegy for the lost one) the proper response to loss can be indicated but not explored. The pathos tends to get in the way; and the pathos is not the point:

But she is in her Grave, and Oh!
The difference to me![11]

What was that difference? And did it abide, like rocks, and stones, and trees, when the temporary shocks of sorrow were done with, and the heart had grown old in joy?

This was the poetic challenge (perhaps only apprehended as such at a subconscious level) that led to the creation of Matthew, a figure compounded of several memories but chiefly derived from his old schoolmaster, the Reverend William Taylor of Hawkshead, who had died in 1786 while the poet was still at school.[12] But as the cycle proceeded, imagination more and more took over from mere memory: with the two final masterpieces, "The Two April Mornings" and "The Fountain", Matthew's identification with Taylor has become irrelevant to the poetry. It would be as absurd to talk of these two poems as if they were merely personal

[10] "She dwelt among the untrodden ways", 5–8.

[11] *Op. cit.*, 9–12.

[12] Mary Moorman, *William Wordsworth: A Biography: The Early Years, 1770–1803*, Oxford, 1957, p. 52, considers that Matthew's identification with Taylor has been too hastily accepted. She thinks Matthew is another metamorphosis of the Packman, who had already inspired the Pedlar in *The Ruined Cottage*. But, though there may be some truth in this, Matthew is after all mentioned always as a schoolmaster; and the memory of the dying Taylor being visited by his boys is obviously behind the "Address to the Scholars", etc. Wordsworth had, of course, already used Matthew in "Expostulation and Reply" and "The Tables Turned": the episodes these were based on were part of Hazlitt's visit to Alfoxden the previous June. There is very little in these two poems, except the name and the location by Esthwaite Water, to connect them with either Taylor or the later cycle of lyrics that we are concerned with here.

tributes to Taylor as it would be to say that "Journey of the Magi" is about Eliot's memory of "six ruffians seen through an open window playing cards at night at a small French railway junction where there was a water-mill".[13]

These two, however, were the final product of a fair-sized mass of elegiac writing, most of which seems to be definitely connected with Taylor. I say most, for there is one poem, "A Poet's Epitaph", which belongs to the series on general grounds, but in which Wordsworth tries to define, in what is almost a mock elegy for himself, the proper response he expected his readers to have to his poetry. It is rather singular that out of this elegiac material no great elegy was ever to emerge. Much of it was left unfinished and unpublished: only one poem, the one that is called "Matthew", appeared with "The Fountain" and "The Two April Mornings" in 1800; another, the so-called "Address to the Scholars of the Village School of ——", was printed in 1842. Two more elegies, overlapping with these in sundry lines and verses, were first printed by Helen Darbishire in 1947.[14] Of the whole series, only "Matthew" itself (apart from "A Poet's Epitaph", which is only partly relevant to the discussion) is anything like a successful poem, though the two posthumous elegies have some of the freshness of a great painter's unfinished sketches.

These elegies differ widely from the Lucy poems which presumably preceded them. For one thing, they mourn publicly a public loss, whereas Lucy had lived unknown to the world and nobody but the poet could know when she died. Wordsworth insists on how well known to the whole community Matthew was, and how well loved. His grief, which is in any case more distanced in time than that for Lucy, is merged in a general mourning. The dirge in "Address to the Scholars" is typical of this unusually choric strain:

> Mourn, Shepherd, near thy old grey stone;
> Thou Angler, by the silent flood;
> And mourn when thou art all alone,
> Thou Woodman, in the distant wood![15]

The reader, also, is invited to share sympathetically in this com-

---

[13] T. S. Eliot, *The Use of Poetry and the Use of Criticism*. London, 1933, p. 148.
[14] *The Poetical Works*, IV, pp. 452–5.   [15] 33–6.

munal contemplation of loss, as embodied in the tablet in the school where the names of all its masters are inscribed:

> — When through this little wreck of fame,
> Cipher and syllable! thine eye
> Has travelled down to Matthew's name,
> Pause with no common sympathy.[16]

And yet, though the mourning is public, it is also personal to the poet. One has the feeling that Wordsworth is trying to isolate a quality in Taylor that he felt was important to his own situation in 1799:

> Remembering how thou didst beguile
> With thy wild ways our eyes and ears,
> I feel more sorrow in a smile
> Than in a waggon load of tears;
>
> I smile to hear the hunter's horn,
> I smile at meadow rock and shore,
> I smile too at this silly thorn
> Which blooms as sweetly as before.
>
> I think of thee in silent love
> And feel just like a wavering leaf,
> Along my face the muscles move,
> Nor know if 'tis with joy or grief.[17]

What emerges from these elegies is a person of infectious gaiety, frolicsome and even wild, playing with children and writing the girl's love-letters for them. Now he is dead, we are told, his schoolhouse no more shall be

> like a play-house in a barn
> Where Punch and Hamlet play together.[18]

He was plainly no conventional schoolmaster:

> Learning will often dry the heart,
> The very bones it will distress,
> But Matthew had an idle art
> Of teaching love and happiness. . . .

[16] "Matthew", 9-12.
[17] 2nd "Posthumous Elegy", 1-12.   [18] *Op. cit.*, 71-2.

> His fancy play'd with endless play
> So full of mother wit was he,
> He was a thousand times more gay
> Than any dunce has power to be.[19]

Yet his gaiety, by itself, is not quite what interests the poet. Nor even is it his kindness, which was vast; nor yet his ability to inspire love. Rather it is a peculiar sadness that existed, as it were, within his frolics – Hamlet, we remember, as well as Punch, played in his schoolroom:

> The sighs which Matthew heaved were sighs
> Of one tired out with fun and madness;
> The tears which came to Matthew's eyes
> Were tears of light, the dews of gladness.
>
> Yet, sometimes, when the secret cup
> Of still and serious thought went round,
> It seemed as if he drank it up —
> He felt with spirit so profound.[20]

The image from Gethsemane, so lightly borne, is enough to assure us that Matthew is not without the sensible sorrow of being human. He is comic, yet not all comic. Sometimes, indeed, he regrets his own levity:

> Yet when his hair was white as rime
> And he twice thirty years had seen
> Would Matthew wish from time to time
> That he a graver man had been.[21]

But we feel this is being over-scrupulous. Without his "wildness", we are made to see, his goodness would not have been so triumphant a virtue; but it is the serious concern that gives life to the frolic, not the other way round.

Grief and joy are mingled in the silent love that Matthew's memory occasions in the poet, as a certain sadness was mingled with his own mirth:

[19] 1st "Posthumous Elegy", 21–4, 29–32.
[20] "Matthew", 21–8.
[21] 1st "Posthumous Elegy", 33–6.

I think of thee in silent love
And feel just like a wavering leaf,
Along my face the muscles move,
Nor know if 'tis with joy or grief.[22]

There is something here to remind us of Cordelia:

patience and sorrow strove
Who should express her goodliest. You have seen
Sunshine and rain at once: her smiles and tears
Were like a better way: those happy smilets
That played on her ripe lip seem'd not to know
What guests were in her eyes; which parted thence
As pearls from diamonds dropp'd. In brief,
Sorrow would be a rarity most beloved,
If all could so become it.[23]

The Matthew of the elegies has not, of course, Cordelia's queenli-
ness, nor her delicacy: she is a tragic figure, he a "grey-haired man
of glee".[24] Nevertheless we can perhaps feel that in a very different
way Wordsworth's mind is moving towards some point of
balance not dissimilar to hers in its richness of response and full
humanity, in its "sunshine and rain at once".

4

But, it must be said, in the elegies this point of balance is only
suggested, not yet achieved. The Matthew of the elegies is still
largely a conventional figure, seen from the outside, and not
wholly unlike one of the gentle and whimsical beings that inhabit

----

[22] 2nd "Posthumous Elegy", 9–12.

[23] King Lear, IV, iii, 17–25.

[24] "The Fountain". Taylor in fact died at the early age of thirty-two, when
Wordsworth was sixteen. In the elegies, Matthew's age is not insisted on,
though in the first posthumous elegy he is represented as sixty or over, with
"hair as white as rime". But in "The Fountain" he is still alive at seventy-two,
and as in "The Two April Mornings", his hair is grey. In the elegies, perhaps,
his age is exaggerated to preserve the age-gap between him and the poet:
sixteen is to thirty-two very nearly as twenty-nine is to sixty. But in the two
later poems, the age of Matthew has considerable significance for our understanding of their meaning, and is therefore very much more precisely
registered.

M

the *Essays of Elia*. Cordelia has a toughness about her, and all the
stubborn unexpectedness of being alive. The elegies are not
inevitable enough, they are too placid about their indecisions. The
emotional tension of great art is lacking – and with it, the tension
of the spirit which alone can justify normality in art:

> I think of thee in silent love
> And feel just like a wavering leaf . . .[25]

– How shocking that second line would be if we said it about
Lear's daughter! Elegy, as we have already remarked, is not a
mode to explore with – pathos, and even sentimentality, are for-
ever in one's way. But now turn to the opening lines of "The
Two April Mornings":

> We walked along, while bright and red
> Uprose the morning sun;
> And Matthew stopped, he looked, and said,
> "The will of God be done!"

This is clearly a poem that means business. There are five finite
verbs in the first three lines; they positively punch the meaning
home. The Matthew of the elegies had no history, only an anthropology. But here, the past definite cuts through the expec-
tations of the imperfect with all the puzzling inconsequence of
immediate events. This particular collocation of circumstances
could only happen once. Anthropologically it is useless, there
are too many variables involved to make it worth describing.
Humanly, therefore, it is normal and exact.

As a matter of grammar, the tension is generated by the close
juxtaposition of verb-forms that are formally identical, yet func-
tionally disparate. Much hangs on the *and* at the beginning of the
third line. If we substitute *but* —

> We walked along, while bright and red
> Uprose the morning sun;
> But Matthew stopped, he looked, and said,
> "The will of God be done!"

– the paraphrasable meaning is virtually the same; yet all the tension has gone from it. Matthew's stopping is now part of a plan,

[25] 2nd "Posthumous Elegy", 9–10.

something deliberately done to break up our walking along. He might almost be being smart. But with *and*, the gestalt is restored: we cannot now say that his stopping contradicts our walking. Rather, the walking and the stopping are parts of one whole, no matter how puzzled we may be by the manner they are experienced together. This grammatical tension, of course, would be meaningless without the real tension inherent in the situation.

For why does Matthew stop so suddenly, look up at the brightening clouds, and be so exorbitantly moved? – how easy it is to expand these four lines into descriptive prose! Why does he break up the agreeable rhythm of the two friends walking in the sunrise, and reveal such a tumultuous resignation – "The will of God be done!" Wordsworth had already tried to handle this type of situation – where an involuntary emotion suddenly catches you by the throat – in the first of the Lucy poems:

> Strange are the fancies that will slide
> Into a lover's head,
> 'O mercy' to myself I cried
> "If Lucy should be dead!"[26]

But even in this first stanza, Matthew's emotion is already richer and more complex than that; and we have seen that the Lucy poem failed to develop. "The Two April Mornings" can develop quite easily, and for a very good reason. Matthew, unlike Lucy, is already at home in a social context – the elegies have seen to that. He is even now walking along with the poet at his side. Wordsworth, therefore, when he is faced with his friend's lapse into discontinuity, can still fall back on what he (and other folk) know perfectly well about Matthew. And he has us on his side. We are as baffled as he is. The next two stanzas accordingly rehearse the anthropology of the elegies; or, in other words, they try to assert the past imperfect of the opening against the past definite which has interrupted it:

> A village schoolmaster was he,
> With hair of glittering grey;
> As blithe a man as you could see
> On a spring holiday.

[26] See "Strange fits of passion have I known", *P.W.*, II, p. 29.

And on that morning, through the grass,
And by the steaming rills,
We travelled merrily, to pass
A day among the hills.[27]

This has the sort of bounce that one gets in the very best eighteenth-century writing about excursions to the country. Even the diction takes on an Augustan air: "steaming rills", for example, is the sort of *mot juste* one finds in Pope's *Pastorals* or Wordsworth's own *An Evening Walk*. It almost sits up and begs to be admired, as part of a polite accomplishment. In this kind of poetry, the implication goes, you do what is expected of you: you do not suddenly stop and say, The will of God be done, for no apparent reason in the middle of a pleasant country walk. You keep your private disconnectedness to yourself, and give other people no cause to be disturbed. To make it explicit, of course, is to make it harsher than it is. The rebuke – if you can call it that – is in fact extremely gentle, and overlaid by a personal friendliness that barely has to make allowance at all for the eccentricities of an old man:

"Our work," said I, "was well begun,
Then, from thy breast what thought,
Beneath so beautiful a sun,
So sad a sigh has brought?"[28]

One can feel the poet's slight awkwardness as he speaks. It is a delicate question to have to put.

Now, in the Lucy poems, this kind of exquisite commonsense would not be possible. It would destroy the poetry altogether. Lucy and her lover exist in a world apart, quite closed against the conventions of the world. Discontinuity, properly speaking, cannot exist in such a world: for, where everything is disconnected, there is nothing to discontinue. The Lucy poems, had they been persevered in, would have resulted in a kind of surrealism, where every happening is as important as every other. Wordsworth, quite obviously, is not going to be very interested in such a non-world as that. But neither is he going to endorse for very long the bland eighteenth-century assumption (represented here by the narrator)

[27] "The Two April Mornings", 5–12. [28] *Op. cit.*, 13–16.

that what seems private, disconnected and unique is *ipso facto* unimportant.

Matthew neither shrugs the matter off, nor apologises for being pre-occupied. Nor does he take it as a chance to display his superior emotional sensibility. He deliberately repeats his strange behaviour, stubbornly resisting the temptation to explain it on any but its own terms. There is a touch of ritual in this next stanza, as though the old man were conjuring up the past for his friend's benefit – the first semi-colon is surely rubric, not punctuation:

> A second time did Matthew stop;
> And fixing still his eye
> Upon the eastern mountain-top,
> To me he made reply:

> "Yon cloud with that long purple cleft
> Brings fresh into my mind
> A day like this which I have left
> Full thirty years behind.

> "And on that slope of springing corn
> The self-same crimson hue
> Fell from the sky that April morn,
> The same which now I view!"[29]

The colours of the sky have a function here very similar to that of the stream in "The Fountain". They manifest what Whitehead calls the eternals, the modes and aspects of reality that persist through all change, not substantially but attributively, appearing and disappearing and appearing again, like the song of Keats's nightingale – "The voice I hear this passing night was heard . . ." Or, as Matthew puts it in "The Fountain":

[29] *Op. cit.*, 17–28. I give the 1800 text of the last stanza because, from 1802 onwards, presumably because he felt it was awkward, the poet changed it to the far more cocksure final version:

> And just above yon slope of corn
> Such colours, and no other,
> Were in the sky, that April morn,
> Of this the very brother.

This seems to me doggerel. One misses the connotations of *springing*, *crimson*, and *fell*; and instead one is given meaningless claptrap about mornings being brothers to one another.

"No check, no stay, this Streamlet fears;
How merrily it goes!
'Twill murmur on a thousand years,
And flow as now it flows.

"And here, on this delightful day,
I cannot choose but think
How oft, a vigorous man, I lay
Beside this fountain's brink.

"My eyes are dim with childish tears,
My heart is idly stirred,
For the same sound is in my ears
Which in those days I heard.[30]

This use of the eternals is characteristic of Wordsworth, as it must surely be of any poet of memory. But what distinguishes the coloured April sky from the sound of the fountain is the far greater particularity of what it evokes. The stream, as so often, stands for the whole life-pattern, from childhood to old age, whereas the coloured sky only evokes, with particular poignancy, one crucial episode. But both, like the rainbow in the poem of that name, serve as talismans to guarantee the continuing worth of the individual response:

My heart leaps up when I behold
A rainbow in the sky:
So was it when my life began;
So is it now I am a man;
So be it when I shall grow old,
    Or let me die![31]

Wordsworth is not simply equating the spontaneity of the child with that of the grown or the old man. The three responses will be different; but all three will be organically related to one another, as the seed is to the plant. The grammatical tension of the opening tenses here takes on a new profundity: organic response belongs to the definite tense, not to the socially habituated imperfect.

But we still do not know why Matthew stopped and said, "The will of God be done!" One April morning has reminded him of

[30] 21-32.
[31] "My heart leaps up when I behold", *P.W.*, Vol. i, p. 226, 1-6.

another April morning thirty years ago: that might be the cause
of a sentimental nostalgia, a *hiraeth* as the Welsh call it, that might
be very real, but still rather deplorable. In "The Fountain" this is
precisely what the stream seems at first to evoke:

> "My eyes are dim with *childish* tears,
> My heart is idly stirred. . . ."[32]

But in "The Two April Mornings", certainly, the complex pain
and resignation of Matthew's exclamation is a very different
matter from simple nostalgia. He proceeds to explain: he says that
on that day thirty years ago he had returned from a fishing
expedition and come into the churchyard where his daughter lay
buried:

> "Nine summers had she scarcely seen,
> The pride of all the vale;
> And then she sang; – she would have been
> A very nightingale.

> "Six feet in earth my Emma lay;
> And yet I loved her more,
> For so it seemed, than till that day
> I e'er had loved before.[33]

If Wordsworth had been interested in mere pathos, he might well
have finished the poem at this point, with a little elaboration of
how fine the girl was, and how much Matthew missed her; and
perhaps, with the narrator nodding his sympathy for the old man,
to cheer him up. We might then have had a poem parallel to the
Lucy poems, with Lucy a daughter instead of a mistress: the "sex-
lessness" of Lucy, which critics have often remarked on, makes
this transition not difficult to imagine. Matthew, after all, has
explained that the colours of the sky are intimately connected in
his mind with the loss of his child – socially speaking, a good
enough reason for feeling sad and being resigned to the will of
God. The harmless sentimentality – it is thirty years ago, remember – would be part of the old man's character, a fair deduc-
tion from the anthropological portrait of the elegies.

[32] 29–30. (My italics.)
[33] "The Two April Mornings", 33–40.

However, the poetry refuses to stop. The concealed clash between the tense-forms of the opening has not been resolved. The imperfect tenses have had it all their own way: the girl *had scarcely seen* nine summers, she *sang* (*i.e.*, used to sing), she *would have been* a very nightingale, she *lay* (*i.e.*, was lying) six feet in earth; and – even more a concession to the imperfect's habit of making us play a role, in this case a sentimental and perhaps self-indulgent role, instead of acting from a truly organic response – Matthew *loved* (*i.e.*, was loving)[34] her more that day than ever he *had loved* her before.

Matthew is freed from this unreal continuum of the imperfect by encountering what W. H. Auden would call a "sacred being":[35]

> "And, turning from her grave, I met
> Beside the churchyard yew,
> A blooming child, whose hair was wet
> With points of morning dew.
>
> "A basket on her head she bare;
> Her brow was smooth and white:
> To see a girl so very fair,
> It was a pure delight!
>
> "No fountain from its rocky cave
> E'er tripped with foot so free;
> She seemed as happy as a wave
> That dances on the sea."[36]

Again, as in the first stanza of the poem, the change from the imperfect to the definite is marked by the sort of *and* that might be a *but* but stubbornly is not – in contrast with the facile *and yet* in the stanza describing the daughter:

> Six feet in earth my Emma lay;
> And yet I loved her more . . .[37]

[34] *To love* (as opposed to *to fall in love*) is nearly always imperfect in meaning, except in the Biblical "Jesus looked at him and loved him". The same goes for *to be*, though Wordsworth often tries to make *was* translate *fuit* instead of *erat*.

[35] W. H. Auden, *The Dyer's Hand*, p. 54.

[36] "The Two April Mornings", 41–52.

[37] *Op. cit.*, 37–8.

Professor Danby describes this vision of the "blooming child" as that of a Lucy still alive.[38] This may be true of the girl as she exists in herself; but her relation to Matthew is quite different from that of Lucy to the poet, and therefore so is her function in the poem. She is anonymous, a girl encountered by chance, or luck, a gift from the gods – ambiguous in her purport, as gifts from the gods always are. In Eliot's phrase, she represents the impossible that is still temptation. On the other hand, she incarnates the eternals – the spring flower, the morning dew, the fountain from the rock, the wave dancing on the sea. She is Lucy, and yet not Lucy. Compared with the pain of this casual encounter with a beauty who is overwhelmingly real, Lucy seems almost cosy. It is impossible not to be reminded of those late Shakespearean heroines, Marina and Perdita and Miranda; and yet she is none of these, for their existence implies that sins will be forgiven.[39] They are real daughters, she is to Matthew only a stranger. Polixenes can accept Perdita, and Alonso can accept Miranda: a new daughter is conferred upon each of them, as part of the discovery of forgiveness. But the only way Matthew can accept this girl for what she is, is to deny her for what she is not. The pain of this denial, we now realise, has passed into the fabric of the man, a vital element in the freedom of his maturity:

> "There came from me a sigh of pain
> Which I could ill confine;
> I looked at her, and looked again:
> And did not wish her mine."[40]

It is the sort of negative we must point to when we define what is most human. It is like Cordelia's "Nothing, my lord". What faced Matthew was a choice, ultimately, between what is real and

[38] *The Simple Wordsworth*, p. 85. My analysis of the Matthew poems is greatly indebted to the chapter on the Goslar poems in Professor Danby's book.

[39] Wordsworth's use of the wave image in the passage quoted above is almost certainly to be connected with Perdita:

> When you do dance, I wish you
> A wave o' the sea, that you might ever do
> Nothing but that.

(*The Winter's Tale*, IV, iv. 140–2.)

[40] "The Two April Mornings", 53–6.

what is not. Everything had conspired at that moment to make him choose wrongly, to become the slave of his own sentiments, to use this girl as a focus for self-pity and self-indulgence: in short, to become unreal. His choice, indeed, was not so dramatic as Cordelia's. It did not involve either a kingdom or a king. Directly, it did not involve anyone except himself. But like hers, it was a choice beyond the choice to do, or not to do, wrong: it was existential, and it was final. One can sin against the new being one has become through making such a choice, but one cannot unmake it, and one cannot be forgiven for it. No one can forgive a man for growing up, or not becoming a priest, or finding out he is a sculptor.

This is why the girl is not a Perdita. In Wordsworth's most typical poetry there is little or no forgiveness of sins. You live by your decisions, good or evil. The girl can never have been Perdita, the lost one. Matthew's daughter indeed is lost, six feet under the earth; but this girl is pure being, pure joy. And as Blake said,

> He who binds to himself a joy
> Does the winged life destroy;
> But he who kisses the joy as it flies
> Lives in eternity's sun rise.

"The Two April Mornings" is about the cost and the freedom of living in eternity's sun rise.

Formally, we have seen it developing in a kind of spiral, reaching back towards this central confrontation. The force that turns this spiral towards its destined focus is contained in the configuration of verbs in the opening stanza. The continuity of the imperfect tense, broken into by the past definite, is yet contained within a single movement with the latter by means of the characteristic use of *and* that we have already noticed. The verbs of the past definite are verbs describing confrontation and ratification of choice: Matthew *stopped*, and he *looked*, and he *said*, "The will of God be done!" This basic syntactic pattern is repeated twice more, each time changing its terms until the central choice is revealed. Thus, at the first repetition of the pattern, what Matthew says is the rest of the poem; and at the second, which takes place within his narrative and relates to events thirty years back, he does not speak at all but makes a purely internal act of renunciation – "I did not wish her mine". The characteristic use of *and* (that might have been *but*, but isn't) also shifts its relative position in this last turn of the spiral. Previously, it had connected the continuum of the imperfect with the definite verbs of confrontation: "And, turning from her grave, I met," etc. Now, however, it connects the verbs of confrontation with the moment of choice. Wordsworth seems deliberately to emphasise this tightening of the screw by his use of the colon at this point:

> "I looked at her, and looked again:
> And did not wish her mine!"[41]

The difference in force between the two *ands* in this couplet should be easily apparent. It is almost as though Wordsworth were counterpointing the weak with the strong usage, almost as though he were punning.

By this time we know why the old man stopped and said, "The will of God be done!" But there is another rhythm in the poem that has not yet been resolved: the rhythm of dialogue, one man questioning another and being answered, an old man talking with one who is much younger. So far, Matthew's own experience has been shown in all its instress and delicacy: but the poet himself, the narrator, has been the merest *agent provocateur* to elicit the information from him. This, besides leaving the poem considerably more than thirty years before the present – for the action was already in the past when the narrative started – also leaves a gap in the organic response that we, as readers, have to make.

Wordsworth solves this problem by, as it were, inverting the spiral into the present:

> Matthew is in his grave, yet now,
> Methinks, I see him stand,
> As at that moment, with a bough
> Of wilding in his hand.[42]

The imperfect, used of the dead, cannot lead to falsity: to be dead is both true to the organic and very continuous indeed. The verbs of confrontation are simplified to the vital one, *to see* – not *to look*, for this is no strenuous ratification, but more like a wise

[41] *Op. cit.*, 55–6.   [42] *Op. cit.*, 57–60.

passiveness on the poet's part. And the confrontation is with Matthew himself, or perhaps with the whole poem of which Matthew is a part. Wordsworth's vision of Matthew, as he remembers him from the past, ratifies the old man's experience, affirms his break-through into reality, and acts as a conductor so that we, the readers, may partake in the "eternity's sun rise" so long after the temporal April mornings in question have been lost to living memory.

A. W. Thomson

RESOLUTION AND INDEPENDENCE

My main concern in this paper is with one kind of resolution which the poem "Resolution and Independence" achieves, and which is evident in its last two stanzas. Recent analyses of the poem have tended to emphasise the resolution which is finally achieved in the last stanza.[1] The very important tensions between the last two stanzas have been sometimes misinterpreted, or not accounted for. This paper may help to redress the balance.

I

There is something of the same kind of flux and reflux in the opening stanzas of this poem as we find in the first part of the Intimations *Ode*. The poem begins with a reference to the storms of the night before, which have been followed by a bright and peaceful morning. Since the early part of the poem tends to move between extremes, we may suspect that behind this there is the suggestion of a night of doubt and self-questioning, or at least wakefulness, and that the present calmness and clearness in Wordsworth as in the morning is a kind of reaction. Perhaps the most striking thing in the opening stanzas is the plainness of the language, which seems almost part of what is seen. Even the gentle lapse of the feminine rhyme which ends the first stanza contributes to this effect, which is largely produced by the sequence of statements in the simple and continuous present.

---

[1] Anthony E. M. Conran, "The Dialectic of Experience: A Study of Wordsworth's *Resolution and Independence*", *P.M.L.A.*, 1960, Vol. LXXV, pp. 66–74. W. W. Robson, "Resolution and Independence", in *Interpretations*, ed. John Wain, London, 1955.

They are short statements, each being given neither more nor less than one line, until we come to the much longer description of the hare at the end of stanza II. It is here that this first movement comes to rest. Until now all we have had is the unseen birds and their voices, but with the hare a glad animal movement, and Wordsworth's interest in it, becomes very evident, and with that the distinction between himself and what he sees begins to be apparent. And in stanza III the change becomes marked. The repeated "I" which opens the first three lines, together with the past tense of the verbs, indicates the loss of this grateful impersonality. The effect is that of a recollection of identity. He is now a Traveller, with something of that word's connotations of detachment. The language is still simple, but the voice of the scene itself, together with that present which seems to take account of no other time, has gone for good. Wordsworth himself is before us, in contemplation of himself. The transparence has become clouded, and the simile "as happy as a boy" suggests, paradoxically, his recollection of the adult self. Once he has withdrawn from the participation long enough to have contemplated himself participating, the withdrawal is nearly complete. The summing up of this participation in the three closing lines is like a conscious recreation of what has just been felt: the closing couplet makes its statement in the negative terms of rejection, and the lingering effect of the feminine rhyme perhaps recalls that of stanza I only to indicate the difference. In stanza III there is the separation inherent in the stated presence of the Traveller and in the use of the past tense; there is the further separation in that consciousness, contained in the simile, of a different self; there is the separating *consciousness* of passivity in "the pleasant season did my heart employ", where the heart is something whose whole being is in response; there is finally that conscious rejection of melancholy which prepares the way for its return. The deliberate recapitulation in III of the experience of I and II is enough to change that experience finally.

What has vanished is not merely a placid contentment, but "the might Of joy in minds that can no further go", and the reaction is explicitly stated in IV.[2] Before the onset of those nameless and

---

[2] "But, as it sometimes chanceth" may contain the faintest of reminiscences of *Hamlet*, I. iv 23. The line before, with line 20, recalls lines 104–5 of Words-

faceless thoughts he tries desperately to recover the joy in which
he began. Not even for a moment, of course, can it be recovered.
Once again there is the voice of an unseen bird, but the element of
recreation is evident in "I heard" and even more evident in "I
bethought me", with its suggestion of something to which he now
has recourse. The progressive abstraction of the hare, from "The
hare is running races in her mirth" to "I saw the hare that raced
about with joy", and then to "And I bethought me of the playful
hare", marks his unwilling return. And this is followed in v by
such an appeal against present reality as occurs in the fourth
strophe of the Intimations *Ode*, in the almost despairing repetition of "I feel – I feel" and "I hear, I hear", just before he is
forced to reconsider what it is that can no longer be felt or heard.

> Even such a happy Child of earth am I;
> Even as these blissful creatures do I fare;
> Far from the world I walk, and from all care.[3]

These lines, where the voice goes higher in the insistence against
facts, repeat something of that movement we have seen before,
from the attempted identification in "such a happy Child of earth"
and "even as these blissful creatures", to that repetitive and
negative rejection in the following line which, as before, means its
opposite. The inevitable descent is swift and, in its immediate
context, final. The first and last of the fears which he provisionally
names in the alexandrine are of particular significance: "solitude"
and "poverty". Having failed to recover that joy in participation
in which he was hardly conscious of self, he is driven now in vi

[3] 31–3.

---

worth's version of Chaucer's *Troilus*: see Anthony Conran, *op. cit.*, p. 68.
Dowden pointed out that Wordsworth's rendering of Chaucer in these lines
echoes *Hamlet* ii. ii. 638: "Out of my weakness and my melancholy" (noted
by de Selincourt and Darbishire, *Poetical Works*, iv, p. 445, eds. E. de Selincourt and Helen Darbishire. Oxford 1940–49). The use of the same rhyme in
"Resolution and Independence" 20–1 as in the *Troilus* stanza, of which the
last line echoes *Hamlet*, may have been responsible for the very slight reminiscence in 22. This would hardly have been worth mentioning if it were
not for the reminiscence of *Macbeth* in the same stanza: "fears and fancies
thick upon me came" (27) is very like the "fear" and "thick-coming fancies"
of *Macbeth* v. iii, 36–8. As is well known, *Hamlet* and *Macbeth*, with *Lear*,
tend to occur at certain moments of crisis in Wordsworth's poetry.

to consider himself against the great adult and social question of
how to live, in its economic as well as its moral sense. The context
is now that of poets, like himself, and of poets who, whatever
their glory, went wrong. The swing from lack of consciousness
of self could hardly be more complete, and it finds an ironic
climax in vii in the statement of his deeper fears: the threat of the
development of moods of dejection into the final impotence of
madness.

Stanza vi (and possibly stanza vii) represents another kind of
abstraction which has more to do with the mode of the poem than
with the mental processes which he has been depicting. The
whole life lived in pleasant thought (the adjective has been used
twice before, in i and iii) is hardly the Wordsworth we know, or
think we know. (It is odd that this fib has failed to horrify those
who cannot bear the thimble-rigging of Dorothy's exclusion from
the poem.) It has been conjectured that his anxieties for Coleridge
made him substitute Coleridge for himself here, and it is true that
the stanzas he began to write as soon as he had finished this poem
contain an idealised description of himself and Coleridge. The
kind of poem he is writing, the kind of moral statement he is
working towards, obviously requires here a stylisation, a more
extreme case of neither toiling nor spinning. (And perhaps, in this
context of mistrust of self and mistrust either of vocation or of his
present understanding of that vocation, the stylisation conceals
something of that attitude unequivocally expressed in the 1802
addition to the Preface to *Lyrical Ballads*: "however exalted a
notion we would wish to cherish of the character of a Poet, it is
obvious, that while he describes and imitates passions, his situation is altogether slavish and mechanical, compared with the freedom and power of real and substantial action and suffering.")
The references to Chatterton and Burns which follow in the
seventh stanza make it likely that Wordsworth also had Coleridge
in mind, though this is of little importance in understanding the
poem. What he is thinking of here is a kind of community in
glory and wretchedness, and in thinking of this he very often has
in mind Chatterton, Burns, and Coleridge. Speaking years later
of Burns and Chatterton, he says that "in [their] temperament
there was something which, however favourable had been their
circumstances, however much they had been encouraged and

supported, would have brought on their ruin".[4] Dorothy's
Recollections for 18 Aug. 1803 similarly links in "melancholy concern" the Wordsworths, Coleridge, and the children of Burns.[5]

The early death and the unrealised power made of Chatterton,
for Wordsworth as for others, a symbolic figure. As Hazlitt said,
replying perhaps to the protests of Keats, we tend to think of
Chatterton's name before we think of any of his poems. The
"pride" Wordsworth speaks of here reaffirms the continually
working imagination of "sleepless", and adds a hint of that un-
willingness to compromise which finally interrupted it: the concept,
ominous enough in this context, of a kind of strength in dying.[6]
The reference to Burns has some odd undertones, which may be in
part the effect of the unfamiliar capital of "Him". But the context
– the references to Matthew 6 in stanza VI, the phrase "walked in
glory"[7] and the references to the plough and to deification which
follow – makes it an unusually suggestive capital. "Walk" on the
analogy of the walk with God occurs several times in *The Prelude*
and *The Excursion*, and Wordsworth uses it in the scriptural sense
of a manner of life in line 33 of this poem. The comment has
been made, with reference to "Resolution and Independence",
that Wordsworth was then approaching the christological age.[8]

[4] Letter of 21 Dec. 1837; *Later Years*, ed. E. de Selincourt, II, p. 902.
Oxford, 1939. See also a letter of April 1816, again linking Chatterton and
Burns (*Middle Years*, ed. de Selincourt, Oxford, 1937, II, p. 845).

[5] The phrase "the ways of men", which occurs in line 21 of this poem, and
means much the same as "world" in line 33, occurs in Burns's *Despondency*, in
a stylised image of retirement. This poem had a particular significance for
Wordsworth during these years: see Mary Moorman, *William Wordsworth: A
Biography. The Early Years, 1770–1803*, Oxford, 1957, pp. 420–1.

[6] Wordsworth's hesitation between "his pride" and "its pride" is of some
interest: see *The Poetical Works*, II, p. 236. In a letter of 21 Apr. 1819, he
speaks of "those powers which [Chatterton] was too impatient and too proud
to develop". For Chatterton's consciousness of his pride, see the letter to
William Barrett: "it is my PRIDE, my damn'd, native, unconquerable Pride,
that plunges me into distraction. You must know that the 19–20th of my
composition is Pride". "Pride" meaning "manhood" or maturity also occurs
in line 6 of the "Balade of Charitie".

[7] *Cf.* Vaughan, "I see them walking in an air of glory" ("They are all gone
into the world of light") and Shelley, "And walked with inward glory
crowned" ("Stanzas Written in Dejection").

[8] Geoffrey H. Hartman, *Wordsworth's Poetry 1787–1814*, New Haven and
London, 1964, p. 203.

Whatever the relevance of this may be, it is almost as if there were at this moment a particular intensification of the idea of redemption. And it may not simply be to contrast his own supposed idleness with the hardships endured by Burns that Wordsworth speaks of him as following the plough. The concept of labour is very important in Wordsworth's poetry: Shakespeare and Milton are "labourers divine", and that vision of an earthly paradise inspiring him to dedication in the fourth book of *The Prelude* finds its climax in the line "And Labourers going forth into the fields" (1805).[9] But the concept of the ploughman here may be more specific. Langland's Piers is seen as Christ, and the Christ-like character of Chaucer's ploughman is evident enough. Northrop Frye, discussing the concept of the ploughman as visionary, points out Spenser's St George.[10] I am not suggesting that Wordsworth had Chaucer's (or anyone's) ploughman in mind: he was thinking of Burns. But there is a moment when the heroic visionary of line 45 ("the Aspirant of the plough", as he is called in "At the Grave of Burns") almost suggests something greater.[11]

The line "By our own spirits are we deified" comes in less oddly, perhaps, than has been argued.[12] There is, however, a curious hiatus before and after it: the rhyme smoothes it, but there is a moment in which it seems to stand out, like a sudden cry. In one sense it sums up (like its counterparts in III and IV) the statement of the first four lines of the stanza, and it is, of course, a kind of

[9] A line, incidentally, which seems to echo Psalm 104. 23.

[10] *The Faerie Queene*, I, x. 66. Northrop Frye, *Fearful Symmetry*, 1962, p. 335. Spenser speaks of himself as a ploughman, in *F.Q.* VI. ix. 1.

[11] The main reason for the capital of "He" is that the heroic figure is named by the action alone, as in Shelley's "If it be He who, gentlest of the wise, Taught, soothed, loved, honoured the departed one" from *Adonais*, or Burns's "There Him at Agincourt wha shone", from *A Dream*, or, for the matter of that, Milton's "Through the dear might of Him that walked the waves", from *Lycidas*. The use of the same form five lines earlier perhaps reflects the stylisation of the figure of innocent and irresponsible trust which is presented. (Pope, presenting an ideal of the poet in his *Imitations of Horace* – the First Epistle of the Second Book, line 342 – has "'Tis He who gives my breast a thousand pains . . .") And perhaps, in line 45, the outbreak of capitals just before ("Boy", "Soul") created a context which required yet another for the reference to Burns. The effect, however, remains oddly suggestive.

[12] W. W. Robson, *op. cit.*, p. 121.

climax in the concept of "the might Of joy in minds that can no further go". But its position, or the form it gets from its position, almost suggests that this recognition is unexpected as well as unwelcome. It is to this that the musing "I thought of" (so different from "I bethought me" a few lines earlier) has led him. The accent falls heavily on "own", and "deified" occurs only to be rejected. The line, in fact, is like the beginning of a statement whose total meaning will be so ominous that Wordsworth shies away from completing it in the same terms. It is completed instead in the analogous recapitulation of the closing couplet, whose deliberate flatness is a kind of bleak and limiting rationalisation.

The hesitation with which the old man is introduced moves from the suggestion of peculiar grace to the explicatory but still speculative "a leading from above", and from there to the factual yet provisional conclusion of "a something given", representing both the importance of what happened and the impossibility of understanding how or why. The moor has suddenly become lonely (the 1807 version speaks of it as "that naked wilderness"), and "striving" perhaps reaffirms the idea of grace: the solitary wrestlings of the Scottish Covenanters among the peat-hags had a particular meaning for Wordsworth, and these words seem to echo such experience. The pool is not simply bare to the sky, or even to the heavens, but to the eye of heaven. And it is here, where nothing can be hidden, that this figure of extreme age inexplicably appears.[13] The figure that appears is plainly human, and as plainly represents something other than human, like the fantasy of the Calais fishwives as Nereids, "in their fretted caves Withered, grotesque, immeasurably old", but without that vision's mockery, or like that other figure of age in *The Pardoner's Tale* (momentarily echoed perhaps in "Simon Lee") that cries to the earth to let it enter. The beginning of the stanza, where Wordsworth is trying to put his finger on the kind of existence which this figure represents, has the same movement as the beginning of VIII: a hesitancy of perception as of utterance, ending in a phrase at once factual and suggesting something beyond fact: "in his extreme old age". The old man is essentially between extremes, neither

[13] The best comment on the similes of IX is Wordsworth's, in the 1815 Preface. See also the reminder of Anthony Conran, *op. cit.*, p. 72.

alive nor dead, neither asleep nor awake. For a moment this is suspended by the phrase "life's pilgrimage". But "rage of sickness", despite the accepted archaism, is again disturbing, with its suggestion of something at once vehement and inhuman. And the alexandrine goes out into something which is once again human, and yet not human: the human endurance of a more than human weight. Obviously the weight – age, and the effects of present pain or past sickness – is more than man can bear and remain upright, but the phrase "more than human" leaves a suspicion that it is more than man could bear at all.

Beside this creature the carefully described staff on which it props itself seems almost reassuringly real.[14] There is even something about the parenthesis of the oddly dispersed "limbs, body, and pale face", thus propped, which implies that though they should make up a human body, perhaps, in this case, they do not. Then, as he approaches, it is an "old Man", and these fantasies seem to be resolved in the image of the cloud. (If "moorish flood" suggests Spenser, the cloud-image is entirely Wordsworthian.) But the cloud too is ambiguous, though its ambiguity is of a familiar kind. There is a subtle combination of reassurance, and the same kind of disquiet as that created by the description in X of a state between life and death, sleeping and waking, the human and the inhuman. The suspicion of movement in the cloud is in the speculation and repetition of the alexandrine, which does for movement and no movement what the alexandrine of x does for the human and inhuman, and what that of viii does for the normally and the abnormally old. (Wordsworth had good reasons for following Milton and Chatterton in lengthening the last line of the rhyme royal stanza into an alexandrine.) The cloud appears to be still, since we can see neither movement nor change of shape. And yet it is moving, perhaps before other winds than those we hear. Like the cloud, the old man is somewhere between stillness and motion, moving perhaps in some way that we cannot understand. And with this Wordsworth, with superb skill, has got the old man, human and yet suspiciously not human, to a point at

---

[14] Like the discharged soldier of *Prelude* IV and the London Beggar of VII, the leech gatherer is "propp'd". The word suggests that these figures are not only out of all normal human movement, but out of all normal human stillness.

which his humanity can declare itself in the simplest of terms: that of movement.

The phrase "himself unsettling" admirably expresses the way in which the figure of the old man came out of this state in Wordsworth's eyes. Almost for the first time he appears unambiguously as a human being. (The obligatory commonplace with which Wordsworth introduces himself also makes plain the oddly striking fact that it is still a beautiful morning.) But it is not an ordinary man he has to deal with. With the reference to the Covenanters or their descendants we understand what kind of company Wordsworth is thinking of. The reference to "religious men, who give to God and man their dues" may suggest that this is precisely what Wordsworth has not done, and that this is how he wants to see the old man and himself at this stage. But the thing which effectively disturbs him now is the climax in xv to its plain statement of poverty and endurance: "an honest maintenance".

There are various references in *The Prelude* to weakness or deceit: self-disgust ("a mockery of the brotherhood Of vice and virtue") in I, cowardice in vi. And here it is this phrase which shocks Wordsworth back into his dream of despair. Nothing that the old man says after "God's good help" and "honest maintenance" matters: their urgency makes what follows only sound. The pious figure of endurance that has replaced the sinister embodiment of otherness is succeeded in its turn by a visionary figure of admonishment. With the renewed consciousness of weakness, his fears return, and in their concentration the verse suddenly takes wings. "The fear that kills" is the spiritual death of despair, and "cold" goes out beyond its immediate context. "Cold, pain, and labour, and all fleshly ills" has far greater force than the "solitude, pain of heart, distress, and poverty" of v which it seems to recapitulate. As before, the despair comes to rest in the image of the defeat of the happiest and perhaps the most complete of men: "mighty poets in their misery dead". And in his renewed and desperate perplexity (his words could hardly be plainer) he returns to that question of identity with which he began: "How is it that you live, and what is it you do?"

These monosyllables have often been misunderstood, but their urgency is plain enough. (Wordsworth later altered some of the lines of the poem to get rid of a preponderance of monosyllables, but he left this line as it was.) To the peculiar excitement of this repetition the old man responds with a smile. Whatever hesitation was there when Wordsworth first asked the question (or a form of it) is hardly there now: he desperately needs to know. All the old man can give is what he said before, except for that statement of endurance in decay in the alexandrine of xviii, where the closing monosyllables are so different from those of xvii. And now it is the endurance rather than the honesty which affects his listener. In xix the phrase "in my mind's eye" and the fact that he is consciously pursuing thoughts within himself shows that this is not the trance-like state of xvi. Something has been understood, and what it is, is given mainly in lines four and five, with their strange repetition and their lapsing rhyme. (As in other stanzas, Wordsworth turns this rhyme to particular account.) There is a perception, beyond personal fears, of the extent of human suffering (Keats's "giant agony of the world") and possibly of the massive strength of human endurance. The deliberate monotony of the last lines of the stanza is relieved by the significant parenthesis of "having made a pause", which is possibly in keeping with what happens in the last stanza. Perhaps we are to understand there that the old man leads the talk away from subjects that disturb this overwrought stranger ("other matter"?) or perhaps that he is simply tired of repeating himself. The "demeanour kind" of the second line might suggest an understanding of his listener's need for reassurance. The main thing is that he is cheerful, and it is this as much as anything else which leads Wordsworth to safer ground. In that sense, the old man has laid the ghost which the sight of him called up in Wordsworth, and seems to have laid several other ghosts besides.

2

Many readers find parts of the poem prosaic and ungainly, and some critics have had harsh things to say about this aspect of it. The explanation which refers it simply to that part of Wordsworth which wanted the factual is probably insufficient. After the simplicity of the opening stanzas, the voice seems to be speaking, with difficulty, in the plainest possible terms. One is conscious of the difficulty experienced in getting to this uncompromising plainness, and perhaps the difficulty is part of the meaning. But the manner obviously suggests Spenser, and much of what seems prosaic is in fact Wordsworth's recreation for his own purposes of a kind of echoing dryness of language which is peculiarly Spenserian.[15] Wordsworth, as I have tried to show, had more use for this alexandrine than Chatterton had in the "Balade of Charitie" or "Elinoure and Juga", or than Milton had in the three poems which he wrote in the same stanza form. His use of some characteristic Spenserian phrasing in the opening stanzas of *Salisbury Plain* has been briefly examined by Geoffrey Hartman,[16] and the effect of the alexandrine of the third stanza of *Salisbury Plain*, for example, is very suggestive. (Incidentally, and for what it is worth, the 1842 revision of the third line of that stanza – "Perplexed and comfortless he gazed around" – echoes the final or 1820 version of line 117 of "Resolution and Independence".) Spenser was very much in Wordsworth's mind about this time. He speaks of "A Farewell" (written in the same month as "Resolution and Independence") as a "Spenserian" poem: the stanza is that of Spenser's June eclogue from *The Shepheards Calendar*, and he may have had in mind the celebration of place with which the Spenser eclogue opens. The *Castle of Indolence* stanzas were begun on 9 May 1802. He worked at "The Leech Gatherer" all day until tea-time, Dorothy tells us, and then after tea tired himself even further by writing "two stanzas in the manner of Thomson's *Castle of Indolence*". This poem was completed on 11 May: its Spenserians are, of course, Thomsonian, and they suggest a deliberate relaxation from what had been attempted in the other poem. For something which is Spenserian as "Resolution and Independence" is Spenserian, we have to go to the fourth book of the 1805 *Prelude*.

[15] The resemblance with the experience of Spenser's Cave of Despair has been noted often enough. One specific resemblance seems to be Spenser's "Fear, sicknesse, age, losse, labour, sorrow, strife, Payne, hunger, cold that makes the heart to quake" (*F.Q.* 1. ix. 44) and Wordsworth's "Cold, pain, and labour, and all fleshly ills" (115). Another may be Spenser's thirty-ninth stanza from the same canto, about passing the flood, and two lines from Wordsworth's first draft: "Who will not wade to seek a bridge or boat, How can he ever hope to cross the flood?" (quoted by Helen Darbishire in *The Poetical Works*, II (1952), p. 540.)

[16] Geoffrey Hartman, *op. cit.*, p. 119.

Book III of *The Prelude*, incidentally, contains a passage which echoes Spenser in quite another way. Lines 564–6 contain a reminiscence of *The Faerie Queene*, II. xi. 28,[17] and a few lines after there is a pageant of corruption and futility whose provenance is unmistakable. The passage – 594–611 – is too long to quote here, but it should be set against the following, also from the third book of *The Faerie Queene*:

> Unquiet Care, and fond Unthriftyhead;
> Lewd Losse of Time, and Sorrow seeming dead;
> Inconstaunt Change, and false Disloyalty;
> Consuming Riotise, and guilty Dread
> Of heavenly vengeance; faint Infirmity;
> Vile Poverty; and, lastly, Death with Infamy.[18]

Compare with this, for example, the movement of such lines from the *Prelude* passage as

> Honour misplaced, and Dignity astray . . .
> Murmuring submission, and bald government . . .[19]

Wordsworth's Spenser, by the way, has been in part strained through Shakespeare: his "Honour misplaced, and Dignity astray" remembers the "gilded honour shamefully misplaced" of Sonnet LXVI, and there are one or two other resemblances between this sonnet and the Wordsworth passage. Shakespeare's bitter little masque or pageant, of course, is all sardonic paradox, which Wordsworth does not really approach until near the end of his own pageant: the brilliantly antithetical movement of Shakespeare's lines has little to do with the leisurely Spenserian accumulation which is the basis of the *Prelude* passage. But this is quite different from that side of Spenser which Wordsworth uses in *Prelude* IV, and which is so close to the Spenser who appears in "Resolution and Independence". The similarities between this poem and the episode of the discharged soldier in *Prelude* IV have been discussed often enough. My only concern here is with four or five lines in the 1805 version.

[17] Noted by E. de Selincourt, *The Prelude*, Oxford 1926, p. 520.
[18] *F.Q.*, III, xii, 25.
[19] *The Prelude* (1805), III, 603, 605.

> He was of stature tall,
> A foot above man's common measure tall,
> Stiff in his form, and upright, lank and lean;
> A man more meagre, as it seem'd to me,
> Was never seen abroad by night or day.[20]

This is how Wordsworth introduces the soldier, and the manner of those lines, with the incantatory repetition of 405–6 and the contribution of the parenthetical "as it seem'd to me" to the peculiar couplet effect of 408–9, is an unmistakable as that of the passage from Book III quoted above. He succeeds in making away with most of this effect in the 1850 text. But it is fairly obvious that at one time he tended to have Spenser in mind in such passages of visionary dreariness,[21] and the invocation of Spenser (perhaps as a kind of distancing) is behind a good deal of what is sometimes taken to be clumsiness.

3

The last stanza of "Resolution and Independence" seems oddly perfunctory, as if it did not fully take account of what had gone before. There has been something like a double vision, of complex doubts and fears on the one hand, and simple human strength on the other, and there is a moment at the end when the moral lesson of the second seems partly obscured by what survives of the first, as if there were something in those visions which could not be met by cheerful endurance. A preoccupation with visionary dreariness may very well make a reader unwilling to accept the relevance of the moral lesson. But setting this aside, I think the appearance of perfunctoriness is undoubtedly there, and that it is an integral part of the effect.

What remains of Sara Hutchinson's transcript shows that there could have been little discontinuity in the first draft of the poem between the uncompromising details of misfortune and hardship which made up so much of the second part, and the final lesson of

---

[20] *Op. cit.*, IV (1805), 405–9.

[21] See Janet Spens, *Spenser's Faerie Queene*, London, 1934, p. 59, for an interesting suggestion of Spenserian influence on Wordsworth in the episode of the child parted from his guide in *Prelude* XII.

the last stanza. Matter of fact in the second part was dominant,
and the simply conveyed moral lesson of the last stanza fitted it.
It is on this element of naked fact that Wordsworth insists in his
Grand Remonstrance to Sara Hutchinson, whether in the significance of "was" rather than "stood" or "sat", or of the impressiveness of lonely and courageous age. But Wordsworth was
capable of listening to advice, and the exasperation of the letter
(the first sentence, if it does not mean that the poem is not a
curate's egg, might almost suggest that if she does not like the
second part, her reasons for liking the first part are probably the
wrong ones)[22] perhaps arises less from impatience with the un-
willingness of others to use their imagination as he did, than from
his recognition of the fact that Sara was right. That the appeal to
the reader to try to see the thing as he saw it is reinforced by a
reference to "The Thorn" and "The Idiot Boy" only makes it
more plain that, although sheer speed may help to carry through
the dramatic intentions behind factual garrulity, they are likely
to be obscured by a slow-moving mode making use of Chaucerian
or Spenserian circumstance. Sara's comments on tediousness
effectively exploded on this occasion Wordsworth's trust in the
imaginative powers of others. Or perhaps they brought to a head
a latent dissatisfaction with the poem. At all events, he seems to
have decided to explore the experience more fully, and in doing so
he wrote a different poem. It is not simply that he dropped the
family misfortunes, together with some of the more obtrusive
neo-Spenserian circumstance, or that he added the stone and
seabeast from the depths and developed and destroyed significant
fantasies. The final version represents, among other things, a
complex interplay between self-communing and communication,
and as such it is essentially a different poem. He continued to
retouch the poem up to 1836. The success of the 1820 emendation
of line 54 is typical: "Beside a pool bare to the eye of heaven"
expresses, far better than the earlier versions, the state of mind or
mental place which he had reached. Line 117 goes through several
versions ("And now, not knowing what the Old Man had said"

[22] "I am exceedingly sorry that the latter part of the Leechgatherer has
displeased you, the more so because I cannot take to myself (that being the
case) much pleasure or satisfaction in having pleased you in the former
part."

. . . "But now, perplex'd by what the Old Man had said") before it reaches in 1820 its final urgency: "– Perplexed, and longing to be comforted". And it is not until 1836 that line 90 finds its final form. The emphasis on the look of surprise which preceded the old man's reply helps to establish his reality for us before his inter-locutor fully understands it. The early reading of "He answered me with pleasure and surprize" becomes in 1820 "He answered, while a flash of mild surprize", and in 1836 Wordsworth, still unsatisfied, changes it to the even more explicit "Ere he replied, a flash of mild surprise".

The last stanza, however, with the exceptions of "cheerfully" and "soon", and the slight additional emphasis of the latter on "other matter", remains very much as it was in the first draft. And the result of this is that curiously perfunctory note in the ending of the poem. In order to understand the full effect of this, we have to consider what happens in the second part, from the appearance of the leech-gatherer. There are really three visions (the word may not be accurate, but it is convenient) derived from the leech-gatherer. The first is the figure of otherness, with all its ambi-guities, which is dispelled first by the movement, then by the speech of the old man. Then, with the unexpected relevance of the words "God's good help" and "honest maintenance", follow-ing on the simply dignity of his utterance, he becomes a visionary figure of admonishment, recreating Wordsworth's fears. By the time the question is repeated, and the old man has answered it, the full understanding of his strength has grown in Wordsworth: there is a significant difference between the gradual manner of this recognition and the shock of the one which preceded it, between the renewal of fantasy in one, and the new understanding in the other. The third and final vision in stanza xix (and here the word is exact) is of endurance in solitude. This vision is not simply what remains of the others after fact has had its way with fantasy. The first vision, or series of fantasies, had relatively little to do with the old man himself, but arose out of Wordsworth's stark melancholy. The second vision, though it had more to do with the old man, and with what he said he did, had even more to do with Wordsworth and with his recognition of the difference between them. But in the third vision Wordsworth, though now quite conscious of what he is doing, is less immediately preoccupied with himself and with his problems. Nevertheless that final vision, which has nothing to do with direct admonishment, and which expresses the human at an almost inhuman distance, has everything to do with Wordsworth. It is the old man as he essentially is – his *gestus*, or essential attitude – and Wordsworth's recognition of that same strength as latent in himself; as well as the actual leech-gatherer, it is enduring humanity, and Wordsworth's mature election, by recognition, of his own part in it.

The first two lines of XIX ("While he was talking thus, the lonely place, The old Man's shape and speech – all troubled me") are a kind of recapitulation, not so much of the other visions as of the circumstances which helped to produce them, with their renewal of the "lonely place" of VIII, of the crooked body of X and perhaps the "whole body" of XVI, and finally of the speech described in XIV, its meaning now fully understood. And with "In my mind's eye I seemed to see", the seeming which has been such a feature of the poem since the appearance of the old man has shifted from the illusion itself ("he seemed") to Wordsworth's clearer understanding of his own part in it. "Troubled" is, of course, a key word. As Bradley said, speaking of this passage, it is a word "not seldom employed by [Wordsworth] to denote the confusion caused by some visionary experience".[23] I cannot agree with W. W. Robson, however (or with Bradley, if, as seems likely from the context, Bradley made the same suggestion) that here it is appropriate to the earlier fantasies.[24] The word has a fairly complex meaning, and seems to act as a kind of pivot. The context is one of recapitulation and readjustment, and "troubled me" is in a sense the climax of the recapitulation of those two lines which introduce the vision. But if "troubled" and what goes before it momentarily recall the fantasies, they are recalled only to be dismissed by "troubled me" and what immediately follows it: the phrase receives from its context a grave finality which makes it indicate not a disturbance of sight or reality, but a new and salutary troubling of the whole man. After what had happened since he first questioned the leech-gatherer, "How is it that you live, and what is it you do" was a reduction to their essence of all

[23] A. C. Bradley, "Wordsworth", *Oxford Lectures on Poetry*, London, 1909, p. 137.
[24] W. W. Robson, *op. cit.*, p. 127.

possible questions, and if "how is it that you live" was more than one question, "what is it you do" was a reduction of this to a stark simplicity. The leech-gatherer's answer was, in effect, that he endured. And similarly the vision of XIX is a reduction to fact out of irrelevance. It is what Wordsworth told Sara Hutchinson he was trying to do: "the figure presented in the most naked simplicity possible".

I suggested earlier that the interplay between self-communing and communication was important. The barren self-communing which follows the failure of his delighted union with nature is followed by an attempt at communication with another man. On one level, this attempt fails ludicrously: as Anthony Conran has pointed out, the characters in this respect resemble those of "We Are Seven".[25] But on another level it is finally successful. It is almost as if the real communication took place at the level of self-communing, and as if one condition of its success on that level was its failure on the other. Looking at it from another angle, we might say that the movement in the first part of the poem between joy and despair, which settled in despair, is followed in the second part by a movement between illusion (which dominated the first part behind the scenes, before coming on stage) and reality. What is of particular interest is where this second movement finally stops, and what the relationship of this conclusion is to the moral declaration of the last stanza. The visionary figures have been gradually humanised: Wordsworth's imagination has worked its way towards fact, and this final vision is part of his mature understanding, not of his immature despair.[26] And being part of his understanding it is not to be dismissed by what follows. The effective optimism of the last stanza, with its exclamation which seems midway between a prayer and a homely oath, is still not enough to contain that embodiment of weariness and endurance which is achieved in XIX. Perhaps the putting of these two side by side was the only possible resolution. What we get in XIX is the other side of the coin from what happens in XX, and this is as near as they can get to each other: on the one hand cheerful human strength in suffering, on the other the disquieting embodiment of

[25] Anthony Conran, *op. cit.*, p. 74.

[26] My interpretation of XIX differs from that of most critics. See, however, Harold Bloom, *The Visionary Company*, London, 1962, p. 165.

countless generations of suffering. The deliberate abruptness of the conclusion is a reflexion of our final inability to understand why this should be so, and of the fact that we know only that it is so. As a resolution, it is as true as anything in the more spectacular recognitions of confusion in Byron or Brecht. The presentation of this great paradox reflects the maturity to which the poem has been tending. It is one of the important culminations of its movements: from the childlike attempt at dismissing all the ways of men, through the distortion of enduring age to thoughts of endurance, and even cheerful endurance, in labour; or from momentary happy unconsciousness of self to unhappy consciousness of immature self, from that to a tormented consciousness of others, and finally to a more sober understanding of self as of others.

There is perhaps something of the same effect in the last stanza as there is in those speciously valedictory lines about love and prayer in *The Ancient Mariner*, which indicate by default the inexplicable nature of what has happened. There a refuge is found in something only partly understood, and there is even a kind of local reassurance in the human limitation. The relation between the two opposing concepts in the Wordsworth poem is that together they represent the human lot, and the understanding of these ways of men, and of Wordsworth's part in them, which has been achieved, is in the fact that they simply appear side by side. In the last line of the "Lines" on the approaching dissolution of Mr Fox ("Then wherefore should we mourn?") the argument is also part of the moment of doubt: it could not be so humanly appropriate if we did not know that the opposite were also true. But here such argument would defeat the purposes of a complete statement which, in its own way, seems to owe as little to any intermediary as the opening stanzas of the poem. The apparent bluntness of the ending may remind us again of Chatterton's "Balade of Charitie", where the abruptness of the moral conclusion is part of the late medieval circumstance. But the surprising and almost offhand simplicity of Wordsworth's ending has another purpose altogether. It is possible that he had in mind this characteristic effect of the Chatterton poem during his own revisions: if so, he turned it to superb account. The problem, the continuing paradox of weakness and strength, decay and endurance, despair and faith, is left where it had to be left: that is, at once very much in the air, and very strongly present. And with that the slight disappointment at the bluntness seems part of it all, as if there could have been no other ending: the poem does not simply end in, but in a sense is completed by silence, by its refusal to comment further.

Bernard Blackstone

THE LIFE OF THINGS: SOME NOTES ON WORDSWORTH'S PERCEPTION

An adequate discussion of "the life of things" in Wordsworth's perception would mean a total survey of his mind and art: the word "notes" in my title is not intended as meiosis. All I shall attempt is to draw out and reconnect two relevant threads, childhood and sensation, and I shall restrict my scope almost entirely to the Great Decade.

I

Blake's emblem book, *For Children: The Gates of Paradise* (1793), presents an amazingly complete panorama of Romantic principles and themes: the first seven emblems (*Frontispiece*: What is Man? (i) I found him beneath a Tree (ii) Water (iii) Earth (iv) Air (v) Fire (vi) At length for hatching ripe he breaks the shell) place Man in his elemental setting, "an equal among mightiest energies".[1] Such elemental affinities were explored by all the Romantics, most productively by Wordsworth, Shelley, Keats, and Landor ("We are what suns and winds and waters make us" – "Regeneration"). The word "thing" is possibly Wordsworth's favourite noun, as "to be" is his favourite verb (in the sense indicated by his own note on "Resolution and Independence"); *thing* stands for the solid object, but also for existence itself in its quiddity:

> I worshipp'd then among the depths of things
> As my soul bade me; could I then take part

---

[1] *The Excursion*, IV, 532. *The Poetical Works of William Wordsworth*, 5 vols., eds. E. de Selincourt and H. Darbishire. Oxford, 1940–49.

In aught but admiration, or be pleased
With any thing but humbleness and love;
I felt, and nothing else; I did not judge,
I never thought of judging, with the gift
Of all this glory fill'd and satisfi'd.[2]

And here the key words are *depths, humbleness, love, felt, judging.* The
early Wordsworth responds without judgment, with a choiceless
awareness; he "feels, and nothing else". He dwells in the depths,
among the existential roots of things. Body consciousness (coenaesthesis) is strong, and response comes from the whole man. At
this period Wordsworth would have agreed with Blake that "the
notion that man has a body distinct from his soul (or soul distinct
from his body) is to be expunged" (*The Marriage of Heaven and
Hell,* plate 14). Many passages in the pre-1800 verse suggest a
naïve pleasure in pure sensation:

Oh! many a time have I, a five years' Child,
A naked Boy, in one delightful Rill,
A little Mill-race sever'd from his stream,
Made one long bathing of a summer's day,
Bask'd in the sun, and plunged, and bask'd again . . .[3]

and lines 87–94 go deeper:

                    Thus long I lay
Chear'd by the genial pillow of the earth
Beneath my head, *sooth'd by a sense of touch
From the warm ground,* that balanced me, else lost
Entirely, seeing nought, nought hearing, save
When here and there, about the grove of Oaks
Where was my bed, an acorn from the trees
Fell audibly, and with a startling sound.[4]

The 1850 *Prelude* omits the "naked Boy" and excises lines 88 to 91.
The senses of touch, taste and smell hardly figure in the post-1800
verse and reference to them is carefully cut out of later revisions
of the *Lyrical Ballads* and the 1805 *Prelude.* Indeed, as one works

[2] *The Prelude* (1805), XI, 234–40. All references in the text and notes to *The
Prelude* are to the 1805 text, unless otherwise stated.
[3] *Op. cit.,* I, 291–5.   [4] *Op. cit.,* 87–94. (My italics.)

o

through the familiar poems in the variorum edition by de Selincourt and Darbishire one gets into the habit of glancing down at
the footnotes in any passage which involves the grosser senses: in
"The Emigrant Mother", for instance (a rather late Great Decade
poem, being composed in 1802) the line "Blessings upon that
soft, warm face" prompts a raised eyebrow, and the footnote
confirms that "soft, warm" was replaced by "quiet" in 1807, to
be restored in 1820.[5] It is difficult to understand why the telling
antithesis of naked crag and southern banks in *Prelude* i. 333–46
should have been denied the 1850 version:

> When on southern banks
> The shining sun had from his knot of leaves
> Decoy'd the primrose flower, and when the Vales
> And woods were warm, was I a plunderer then
> In the high places . . . .
> . . . . Oh! when I have hung
> . . . .
> Suspended by the blast which blew amain,
> Shouldering the naked crag. . . . . [6]

Or why, in the 1850 version of the first passage quoted in this
essay, "As my soul bade me" should be replaced by "As piety
ordained", or "I felt, and nothing else" by "I felt, observed, and
pondered". Difficult – unless (and the conclusion is progressively
forced on one) Wordsworth came to believe that simple sensation
and simple feeling not only were not enough, but were in some
way dangerous and wrong.

2

What I mean by "simple sensation" or coenaesthesis can best be
illustrated from the writings of Coleridge – from the Letters and
Notebooks, in particular, where he was not on his guard as he so
often was in his public utterances.[7] A letter to Humphry Davy

---

[5] The later poems – and revisions – show less fear of touch, taste, smell; as
though a once pressing danger were now overpast.

[6] *The Prelude*, i, 333–46.

[7] Later writers throw some light too: Joyce Cary's Sara, "enjoying the feel
of herself inside her stays" (*The Horse's Mouth*, 15); Virginia Woolf's little

(18 Oct. 1800) tells how he took shelter under rocks from a storm in the mountains: "Here I sate, with a total feeling worshipping the power & 'eternal Link' of Energy", where "total feeling" may stand as no bad translation of coenaesthesis. In a letter of 30 Jan. 1804 to Thomas Poole the factors of unconsciousness and viscerality are included in the totality:

> It should seem, as if certain Trains of Feeling acted, *on me*, underneath my own *Consciousness*, which is all engrossed by vivid Ideas drawn from Nature & Books – & habitually applied to the purposes of Generalization / so that all Feelings which particularly affect *myself, as* myself, connect & combine with my bodily sensations, especially the trains of motion in the digestive Organs, & therefore tho' I feel them *en masse*, I do not & cannot make them the objects of a distinct attention.[8]

Even more interesting is the following, from a letter of 13 Nov. 1802 to his wife:

> As I seem to exist, as it were, almost wholly within myself, in *thoughts* rather than in *things*, in a particular warmth felt all over me, but chiefly felt about my heart and breast; and am connected with *things without* me by the pleasurable sense of their immediate Beauty or Loveliness, and not at all by my knowledge of their average value in the minds of people in general . . . so you on the contrary exist almost wholly in the world *without* you / the Eye and the Ear are your great organs. . . .[9]

Though "total sensation" is something impossible to define and almost impossible to describe, being an inferior state which we cannot *grasp* but rather are *grasped by*, we can at least say of it the following: it is total in three senses, first as being common to the

[8] *The Notebooks of Samuel Taylor Coleridge*, 2 vols, ed. Kathleen Coburn. New York, 1961.
[9] *Ibid.*

George in *Between the Acts*, grubbing at the root of the tree, "all that inner darkness became a hall, leaf smelling, earth smelling of yellow light . . ."; Thom Gunn, *Hot Blood on Friday*, "Expectant yet relaxed, he basks within the body's tight limits, the tender reaches . . ." These illustrate the three characteristics noted in the next paragraph.

*

body as a unity, second as being common to humanity as a whole, and indeed to all existing things, and third as a "Link of Energy" establishing contact between the individual and his world. Phrases which come to mind from Wordsworth are: "Feels its life in every limb",[10] "Joy in widest commonalty spread", "The gravitation and the filial bond". It is characterised by a sensation of warmth, and this may be localised, as may the sensation of slight, pleasurable pressure referred to elsewhere by Coleridge: ". . . the co-operating muscles themselves pray",[11] and again:

> Rais'd by her love the Earthly of my nature rose, like an exhalation that springs aloft, a pillared form, at the first full face of the rising Sun, & intercepting full his slant rays burns like a self-fed fire, & wide around on the open Plain spreads its own splendor & now I sink at once into the depths as of a Sea of life intense – pure, perfect, as an element unmixt, a sky beneath the sky – yet with the sense of weight of water, pressing me all around, and with its pressure keeps compact my being & my sense of being, presses & supports – what else diffusing seemed —[12]

Here love touches off the total sensation, as in Wordsworth's "Vaudracour and Julia". Blake's Song "Love and harmony combine"[13] also presents emotion and coenaesthesis in dynamic counterpoint. Wordsworth usually, and rightly, avoids ascribing any *motive* for recognition of the "total sensation"; it is, after all, a jet of pure energy, sensed before its capture by and channelling into one or other of the emotions; expressed directly in

> Those hallow'd and pure motions of the sense
> Which seem, in their simplicity, to own
> An intellectual[14] charm, that calm delight

[10] This is S.T.C.'s contribution to "We are Seven", if Wordsworth's 1843 note is taken at its face value.

[11] *The Notebooks*, II, 2495.   [12] *Op. cit.*, 3222.

[13] I find it difficult to agree with Donald Davie in "Common and Uncommon Muses" (*The Twentieth Century*, Vol. CLXII, Nov. 1957) that this poem presents no "image". Blake is working on the coenasthetic level where image and sensation are one: the image lies within the reported sensation.

[14] "Intellectual" used for once in its scholastic and rightful sense: the noetic faculty, operating as easily through sense as through intuition.

Which, if I err not, surely must belong
To those first-born affinities that fit
Our new existence to existing things,
And, in our dawn of being, constitute
The bond of union betwixt life and joy.

And the lines that follow picture Wordsworth as a child holding

unconscious intercourse
With the eternal Beauty, drinking in
A pure organic pleasure from the lines
Of curling mist, or from the level plain
Of waters colour'd by the steady clouds.[15]

Wordsworth wrote in the Preface to *Lyrical Ballads* that the poet is "a man pleased with his own passions and volitions, and who rejoices more than other men in the spirit of life that is in him". Coleridge, in a letter of 30 May 1815, remarks: "I supposed you first to have meditated the faculties of Man in the abstract, in their correspondence with his Sphere of action, and first, in the Feeling, Touch, and Taste, then in the Eye, & last in the Ear, to have laid a solid and immoveable foundation for the Edifice (sc. of the great philosophical poem) . . ." There are indications in the early poems that Wordsworth's coenaesthesis was as strong as that of Coleridge or Blake. But it was not long before

spiritual presence gained a power
Over material forms that mastered reason. . . .[16]

Indeed, from the beginning two contrary motions, the expansive and the contracting, are seen at work in Wordsworth's poetry; and they come nigh to tearing him to pieces. There is the Wordsworth of objectless awareness, "Alive to all things and forgetting all",[17] who speaks most eloquently perhaps in the great *Prelude* passage:

The pulse of Being everywhere was felt,
When all the several frames of things, like stars
Through every magnitude distinguishable,
Were half confounded in each other's blaze,
One galaxy of life and joy. Then rose

[15] *The Prelude*, I, 578–93.   [16] "The Widow on Windermere Side", 26–7.
[17] *Poems on the Naming of Places*, I, 1919.

> Man, inwardly contemplated, and present
> In my own being, to a loftier height;
> As of all visible natures crown; and first
> In capability of feeling what
> Was to be felt. . . .[18]

Here "height" is balanced by the implicit depth of "feeling":[19] we have a veritable synthesis recalling the doctrine of interpenetration in the *Gandavyuha*. Energy is not yet geometrised in sterile circles, "wheels without wheels in motion terrific". But coexistent with this *participant* Wordsworth is the Wordsworth whom Coleridge called "spectator ab extra", Wordsworth the surveyor, who taxes the royal saint with vain expense on viewing King's College Chapel (who but Wordsworth would have totted up the builder's bill and balanced it against the roster of white-robed scholars?), who notes of the Prior's Oak in "The White Doe of Rylstone" that it "was felled about the year 1720, and sold for £70. According to the price of wood at that time, it could scarcely have contained less than 1400 feet of timber". And so on. This is the Wordsworth with whom we are all too familiar, the Wordsworth of the "secondary founts"[20] of time and space, number, weight, and measure; Wordsworth the grocer who "arranges his poems in a cunning order so that they shall all be read", as James Smith remarks in an essay I shall refer to later.[21]

3

Man the perceptive instrument is a paradigm that establishes itself over the post-Renaissance centuries, as against "Man the imperial shape" and "Mine own executioner", ancient pre-scientific schemata cognate and antithetic. "The eye altering alters all", Blake said; and those extensions of the eye, the telescope and

[18] *The Prelude*, VIII, 627–36.

[19] The 1850 version omits "In my own being", adds "outwardly" to line 632, and drops the reference to feeling. Height metaphors generally supersede those of depth in the later Wordsworth.

[20] My point of view in the present essay is an extension *inwards*, as it were, of chapter 5, "The Secondary Founts", in my *The Lost Travellers*.

[21] It is not impossible that the deliberate jumbling of old and new, good and bad, has an additional motive of camouflage: a direct sequence, particularly within the Great Decade, would have been too revealing.

microscope, react forward to the visible world and backward to
the perceptive mind. Data demand interpretation; "man the
measure of all things" remains, in this man-made universe of ours,
a valid dictum – but who will gauge the universal measure?
Newton declined the task; Locke and Berkeley, Hume and
Hartley among the philosophers, Darwin, Coleridge, Blake and
Wordsworth among the poets, take it up confidently and elaborate
a variety of anthropologies. Shelley writes, as Apollo: "I am the
eye with which the Universe / Beholds itself and knows itself
divine". Wordsworth's accepted destiny is to be "An eye / That
hath kept watch o'er man's mortality". Blake explores the possibilities of single, twofold, threefold and fourfold vision. Single
vision is *apprehensive* (the word beautifully conveys both grasping
and anxiety, Coleridge's "selfish solicitude"), "binding to itself a
joy"; double vision and its developments are *comprehensive* ("total"
and "understanding"). Among the reasons Wordsworth himself
suggests for the failure of his poetic powers[22] are the "unsouling"
by "syllogistic words" of the "mysteries of passion" ("being",
1850), and a despotism of the eye, a kind of visual greediness,
which led to "a comparison of scene with scene" and a "love of
sitting thus in judgment"[23] explicitly contrasted [24] with Mary
Hutchinson's placid acceptance of the given. Absence of judgment, comparison, preference is a *sine qua non* of the "total sensation"; it cannot co-exist with calculation or desire. Or even with
personal love: Blake's "Little Boy Lost" loves his father and
brothers "like the little bird / That picks up crumbs around the
door"; in Wordsworth's Castle of Indolence the two brother-
poets

<blockquote>
did love each other dear,
As far as love in such a place could be.[25]
</blockquote>

Greed appears in the frequent images of devouring –

<blockquote>
The perfect image of a mighty Mind,
Of one that feeds upon infinity. . . .[26]
</blockquote>

[22] *The Prelude*, XI, 42 ff.   [23] *Op. cit.*, 165.   [24] *Op. cit.*, 199–223.
[25] The Castle is represented as a kind of Abbey of Thelema: Wordsworth's
native impulsiveness is stressed, and we are outside the world of judgments
and adult values, in Blake's State of Innocence.
[26] *The Prelude*, XIII, 69–70.

> . . . spectacles and sounds to which
> I often would repair and thence would drink,
> As at a fountain. . . .[27]

> Thus deeply drinking-in the soul of things,
> We shall be wise perforce; and, while inspired
> By choice, and conscious that the Will is free,
> Shall move unswerving, even as if impelled
> By strict necessity, along the path
> Of order and of good.[28]

Wordsworth was hardly a Sarah Coleridge, but the terms of S.T.C.'s letter ("the Eye & the Ear are your great organs") ring as true of the Triton as of the minnow, and there is a profound sense in which he could be said to "exist almost wholly in the world *without* . . ." Devouring came to take the place of perceiving: there is a steady withdrawal from "total feeling". As James Smith remarked in a brilliant essay in *Scrutiny* as long ago as 1938, "it would almost seem that acute perception was something of which he had learnt to be afraid". Mr Smith's remark is directed to a single poem, the lines on the Simplon Pass; but a close study of the poetry as a whole reveals not merely a decline in both acuteness and range of perception, a gradual stonifying as Blake would call it, but also a positive horror of the more intimate senses of touch, taste, and smell. Along with this rejection of the sense-data which cannot be *distanced* (as can those of eye and ear) goes a repudiation of impulse, feeling, and sensation itself in favour of duty, reason, and thought. The mutilation of original percepts is not confined to *The Prelude*, though it could be documented from that poem alone. It will be interesting to note the ways in which Wordsworth tampered with minor and sometimes narrative poems – poems in which his own "image" is not being directly projected, and for the revision of which the excuse cannot plausibly be offered that the years which bring the philosophic mind have brought also a deeper insight into personal experience.

What we are confronting here of course is the theme of the divided Wordsworth, of the "two consciousnesses" which he himself admitted.[29] This is an immensely complicated and

[27] *Op. cit.*, XI, 383–5.　　[28] *The Excursion*, IV, 1265–70.
[29] *The Prelude*, II, 32.

ungrateful theme best avoided by the critic unless he can add to it something beyond the usual gossip and speculation about Annette Vallon and Dorothy.[30] I think something could be added by an examination of the actual sense-data reported in the poems: in (a) the juvenilia; (b) the works of the Great Decade; and (c) the later works – and by a comparison of the successive revisions of all these. The present paper is no more than an introduction to such a survey, and will confine itself almost entirely to (b) with their revisions. I hope to show that in moving away from his coenaesthesis ("the invisible central power", as Coleridge calls it in *Aids to Reflection*) Wordsworth lost touch with the roots of his being. For the organic primitivism of his original perception he tried to substitute a verbal primitivism (in his theory of diction), and for the sense of unity through "the gravitation and the filial bond" which linked him with the earth he sought to substitute a unity of aspiration. The difference comes out curiously in his critical pronouncements, which progressively prefer an associational account of the creative process to the organic account proffered by Coleridge. Blake commented: "I do not know who wrote these Prefaces: they are very mischievous & direct contrary to Wordsworth's own Practise". Coleridge said much the same thing in *Biographia Literaria*.

4

We can best approach and delimit our subject by relating it to Wordsworth's doctrine of childhood. This has always been felt to be crucial to Wordsworth's "philosophy", but little attempt has been made to define it through a study of its development.[31] Between the Blakean realism of

> Oh! had he but thy cheerful smiles,
> Limbs stout as thine, and lips as gay,
> Thy looks, thy cunning, and thy wiles,
> And countenance like a summer's day . . .

[30] Something has been added recently in the very interesting paper by F. W. Bateson in *Essays in Criticism*, Vol. xvii, No. 2 (April 1967) which reproduces some hitherto unpublished stanzas from Shelley's *Peter Bell the Third*.

[31] There is a valuable paragraph in John Jones, *The Egotistical Sublime*, p. 165.

of "The Emigrant Mother" (1802),[32] and the "Mighty Prophet!
Seer blest!" of the Immortality *Ode* of only two years later the gap
is wide indeed. It is unconvincing to explain this away as the
presentation of babyhood in two contrasting aspects: if it were so
we should have a number of mighty prophets among Wordsworth's numerous pre-1804 portraits, and a number of healthy
Freudian babies from 1804 to, say, 1807. And we haven't. Dora,
in "The Longest Day" (which is outside our period, having been
written in 1817, but it may stand as the terminus of a direction), is
advised first to

> sport, as now thou sportest,
> On this platform, light and free;
> Take thy bliss, while longest, shortest,
> Are indifferent to thee!
>
> Who would check the happy feeling
> That inspires the linnet's song?
> Who would stop the swallow, wheeling
> On her pinions swift and strong?[33]

The answer is, of course, William Wordsworth.

> SUMMER ebbs; – each day that follows
> Is a reflux from on high,
> Tending to the darksome hollows
> Where the frosts of winter lie.[34]

It is too late by 1817, of course, for mighty prophets; but at least
his young daughter can be directed to the service of Duty:

> Follow thou the flowing river
> On whose breast are thither borne[35]
> All deceived, and each deceiver,
> Through the gates of night and morn;
>
> Through the years' successive portals;
> Through the bounds which many a star
> Marks, not mindless of frail mortals,
> When his light returns from far. . . .

[32] 49–52. *Cf.* the Notebook version of *Infant Sorrow.*
[33] "The Longest Day", 13–20.   [34] *Op. cit.*, 29–32.
[35] *i.e.* to Eternity.

> Duty, like a strict preceptor,
> Sometimes frowns, or seems to frown;
> Choose her thistle for thy sceptre,
> While youth's roses are thy crown.[36]

We are as far here from mighty prophets as we are from cunning little wheedlers, but this is what has resulted from the attempt to read the one into the other. The conflation can be made, but not along Wordsworth's upward road.

Rejected lines for "Michael" (1801) show "shepherds' children" as almost losing "the quality of childhood" by a "sanctifying" of their sports in the majestic surroundings of mountain landscape.[37] There is a clear-cut distinction here. However highly Wordsworth may value the quality of childhood he does not equate it with any "brooding o'er the abyss". The child remains a child. "The Danish Boy" (1799) is more "romantic", and the boy is a solitary, "A Spirit of noon-day":

> The Danish Boy walks here alone:
> The lovely dell is all his own. . . .[38]

but he is still seen as "a form of flesh and blood" with a "bloom upon his face": there is no suggestion of deeper relationship between child and environment. Wordsworth has not yet transferred to childhood the relations which existed between an individual child – himself – and the surrounding landscape. That he could do so at all depended on the accident of his acquaintance with Coleridge. Wordsworth had no real friend beside Coleridge: he came to read into a community (one cannot call it an identity) of interest in man-nature-relationship with him a quite fantastic *general theory* of such a relationship. The fact that Wordsworth's "general theory" came to be accepted so widely depended upon an equally astonishing accident, the Darwinian revolution which destroyed orthodox Christianity for the Victorians and left the field wide open for Wordsworthianism.

---

[36] "The Longest Day", 49–56, 65–8. The relevance to my theme of the "Ode to Duty" is too obvious to need stressing.

[37] *The Poetical Works*, II, p. 481.

[38] "The Danish Boy", 21–2.

5

It becomes necessary at this point of our discussion to make some
vital distinctions. My adjective is a descriptive one since they are
in fact distinctions embracing life, existence and being. Wordsworth's poetry is largely concerned with life and the different
levels on which it may be lived; his terminology is, as might be
expected, inexact, but ours cannot be if we are to approach the
subject with any degree of precision. I shall owe a good deal in
what follows to Coleridgean distinctions as expressed in published
works, letters, and notebooks, for this was a subject in which he
was enormously interested. I shall owe something also to that
"philosophy of the east" which Blake said had taught the first
principles of perception. This is dangerous ground, I know, and I
do not wish to be taken in what follows as imposing my schemata
upon the intuitions of Wordsworth or Coleridge. The following
table, for instance, is not intended as a map of Wordsworth's or
Coleridge's thinking about "life": it is drawn up simply to allow
me to talk about the subject more economically than would
otherwise be possible.

A. *Supraconscious:*	BEING	KNOWLEDGE	BLISS
B. *Conscious:*	LIFE	THOUGHT	HAPPINESS
C. *Subconscious:*	EXISTENCE	SENSATION	JOY

Level A is that of "life" as noumenal, unmanifested Sat-Chit-
Ananda, to use the Upanishadic formula exactly translatable as
Being-Knowledge-Bliss; this is the life of what Blake called
"Eternity", and it is unknowable by thought. Level C is the
mirror-image of A in the world of becoming, and it is equally unknowable by thought. In the microcosm, Man, it is the realm of
the vegetative nervous system, Coleridge's "trains of motion in
the digestive Organs" and "total feeling". This is the sphere of
undifferentiated energy which as it ascends to consciousness at B
bifurcates and manifests as feelings, emotions, thoughts, judgments, aspirations, and so on. Level B is the world of consciousness and of the contraries in which life is balanced by death,
thought by emotion, happiness by misery.

The "Wordsworth at Cross-purposes in the Lake District" of
Max Beerbohm's cartoon on "We Are Seven" accurately em-

blematises the oppositions of Levels B and C. Wordsworth
addresses the child on the level of thought and consciousness; the
child is living on the level of existence and sensation. She knows
nothing of death just as she knows nothing of life: existence has
not bifurcated for her. She "feels her life in every limb", the
coenaesthetic sensation;[39] "their graves are green, they may be
seen", the evidences of continued existence are there, and the child
draws no frontiers in "the one life within us and abroad"[40]
between her brother's and her sister's life and that of the grass.
She is not thinking and consequently not labelling: she is
acquainted with death as an event but not as a value.

"Anecdote for Fathers", also a Lyrical Ballad, with the amusing
subtitle "Shewing how the art of lying may be taught", explores
further cross-purposes on the A and B levels. The "boy of five
years old", on a walk with Wordsworth on a perfect spring morning, is jolted from his unthinking pleasure in the season by
questions involving value-judgments. "Would you rather be here
or at Kilve?"

> In careless mood he looked at me,
> While still I held him by the arm,
> And said, "At Kilve I'd rather be
> Than here at Liswyn farm".[41]

Refusing to abandon his unthinking mood of existential pleasure[42]
the child answers at random; but Wordsworth is tenacious, he
pushes him from judgment to explanation:

> At this my boy hung down his head,
> He blushed with shame, nor made reply;
> And three times to the child I said,
> "Why, Edward, tell me why?"[43]

[39] Here and elsewhere "life" = "sensation": Wordsworth makes no consistent demarcation, and of course, the demands of metre wouldn't let him
even if he wished to.

[40] Coleridge, "The Aeolian Harp".

[41] "Anecdote for Fathers", 33–6.

[42] "Pleasure" in our scheme may be defined as joy which has reached the
threshold of individual consciousness.

[43] "Anecdote for Fathers", 45–8.

In desperation the boy looks wildly about him, sees a weather-cock, a *solid object*[44] to which he can cling as a refuge from conceptualism:

> Then did the boy his tongue unlock,
> And eased his mind with this reply:
> "At Kilve there was no weather-cock;
> And that's the reason why."
>
> O dearest, dearest boy! my heart
> For better lore would seldom yearn,
> Could I but teach the hundredth part
> Of what from thee I learn.[45]

The lore Wordsworth learns from the boy is the lore of pure existence, no other than the lore repudiated by "our meddling intellect" which "one impulse from a vernal wood" also provides for him "who watches and receives".

Edward and the little cottage girl are recognisable as human children; they are rooted in the life of nature but they are also integrated with brothers and sisters, with family and with the community. In "Influence of Natural Objects" Wordsworth's own theophany came to him when

> from the uproar I retired
> Into a silent bay, or sportively
> Glanced sideway, leaving the tumultuous throng,
> To cut across the reflex of a star. . . .

but the tumultuous throng of schoolmates is *there* as a society which he momentarily leaves and to which he returns. These are all 1798 poems; with "Lucy Gray; or, Solitude" (1799), the retreat from community significantly begins. The whole complex of "Lucy" poems is a pivot on which we may watch Wordsworth's perception turning from an interest in B and C-level relationship to a preoccupation with B and A. And at this point there enters an obsessive connexion between childhood and death which con-

---

[44] A point needing further elaboration may be noted here: solid objects, "things" in the restricted sense of that word, have for Wordsworth at least two functions: as refuges from the "abyss", and as refuges from "thought". There are more sinister aspects.

[45] "Anecdote for Fathers", 53–60.

tinues through Wordsworth's poetic career. I cannot attempt to
assign a reason or reasons for this shift: that task may safely be left
to the biographers and the psychologists. But the extraordinary
"Fragments from MS. M"[46] which are tentatively ascribed by the
editor to 1802 (a year or two earlier seems to me probable) may
afford a clue to the state of mind behind the shift. The "Fragments" – which compose a perfectly coherent poem, if coherent
in terms better understood in our day than in Wordsworth's –
must be quoted in full.

(i)

I have been here in the Moon-light,
I have been here in the Day,
I have been here in the Dark Night,
And the stream was still roaring away.

(ii)

These Chairs they have no words to utter,
No fire is in the grate to stir or flutter,
The cieling and floor are mute as a stone,
My chamber is hush'd and still,
    And I am alone,
    Happy and alone.

Oh who would be afraid of life,
The passion the sorrow and the strife,
    When he may be
    Sheltered so easily?
May lie in peace on his bed
Happy as they who are dead.

Half an hour afterwards

I have thoughts that are fed by the sun.
    The things which I see
    Are welcome to me,
    Welcome every one:
I do not wish to lie
    Dead, dead,

[46] *The Poetical Works*, IV, pp. 365–6.

> Dead without any company;
>   Here alone on my bed,
> With thoughts that are fed by the Sun,
> And hopes that are welcome every one,
>   Happy am I.
>
> O Life, there is about thee
> A deep delicious peace,
> I would not be without thee,
>   Stay, oh stay!
> Yet be thou ever as now,
> Sweetness and breath with the quiet of death,
> Be but thou ever as now,
>   Peace, peace, peace.

What we have here is clearly – in a different sense from Eliot's – a dissociation of sensibility. Life can be addressed as something pleasant – but dispensable. The piece is indeed a collection of fragments, fragments of consciousness like bits of a disrupted ice-floe which are seeking cohesion; but the resultant synthesis will be something very different from the original. The poem itself is unlike anything else of Wordsworth's. Here for the first and last time the defences are down, the armour is removed, and the quivering nerves laid bare. The lines clearly document a crisis. They were never, of course, published. That they are preserved is an extraordinary piece of luck for the critic.

The death-wish passes very rapidly into the poetry. Indeed, it is there already in 1799, in the otherwise neutral (as between B–C and B–A) "The Danish Boy". The boy is one of the first of Wordsworth's solitaries, but

> A Spirit of noon-day is he;
> Yet seems a form of flesh and blood. . . .[47]

(referable, then, to line 2 of (i) above). He dwells in a spot

> Sacred to flowerets of the hills,
> And sacred to the sky. . . .[48]

which however contains, ominously, two of Wordsworth's

[47] 23–4.   [48] 3–4.

sinister *solid objects*, "a tempest-stricken tree" and "A corner-stone by lightning cut". The boy sits between these two:

> There sits he; in his face you spy
> No trace of a ferocious air,
> Nor ever was a cloudless sky
> So steady or so fair.
> The lovely Danish Boy is blest
> And happy in his flowery cove:
> From bloody deeds his thoughts are far;
> And yet he warbles songs of war,
> That seem like songs of love,
> For calm and gentle is his mien;
> Like a dead Boy he is serene.[49]

Between blasted tree and stone, between the once organic and the inorganic, singing songs of love and war, the Boy is projected into the world of the contraries, which yet fail to affect him, because "Like a dead Boy he is serene".

From now on death is Wordsworth's only protection of innocence from what Keats called "the hateful siege of contraries". The "half hour afterwards" comes, of course, as it came in "The Longest Day"; but "thoughts that are fed by the sun" soon resolve to their climax, "sweetness and breath with the quiet of death". What other refuges can there be? There is idiocy: "The Idiot Boy", "The Emigrant Mother", "Her Eyes are Wild"; solitude: *passim*; the insensibility of old age, attained with the help of these two: "The Old Cumberland Beggar", "Resolution and Independence", pedlars, discharged soldiers and so on in *The Prelude* and *Excursion*. Something has broken down – some vital connexion, "the bond of union between life and joy". Death is a universal solvent. It is *right* that Mary of Buttermere's baby dies. Mary herself

> lives in peace
> Upon the ground where she was born and rear'd;
> Without contamination does she live
> In quietness, without anxiety:
> Beside the mountain-Chapel sleeps in earth
> Her new-born Infant, fearless as a lamb

[49] 45–55.

> That thither comes, from some unshelter'd place,
> To rest beneath the little rock-like Pile
> When storms are blowing. Happy are they both
> Mother and Child![50]

And it is right too that Lucy dies – all the Lucies. What else have they to do? Get entangled with the contraries – with "the passion the sorrow and the strife" of the 1800 fragment? Lucy Gray is a "solitary child"; she passes very willingly out of the ambience of home into the snowy waste, the pall of purity. Wordsworth records of a child seen in a London theatre that he

> hath since
> *Appear'd to me oft-times as if embalm'd*
> *By Nature; through some special privilege,*
> *Stopp'd at the growth he had;* destined to live,
> To be, to have been, come and go, a Child
> And nothing more, no partner in the years
> That bear us forward to distress and guilt. . . .[51]

The italics are mine, and the lines italicised are crucial.

"A slumber did my spirit seal" and "Three years she grew in sun and shower" also belong to 1799. They are prime expressions of stark and decorated embalming. Whether or not, as Coleridge surmised, the first "most sublime epitaph" had its genesis in a premonition of Dorothy's death, it presents with crushing economy the sense of utter loss in a cosmic setting. A dichotomy is first established, a separation of "spirit" from "humanity": not only is Wordsworth's "spirit" sealed in a "slumber", but his "human fears" also are dormant. Spirit slumbers *because* Lucy "seemed a thing": spirit has succeeded in reducing flesh-and-blood to thinghood and fancies there is nothing now to fear; she is embalmed, "stopped at the growth she has", and so *safe*; human fears are redundant. But death steps in with an ironic furtherance of thinghood, a safer sealing: "No *motion* has she now, no *force*" – a naïve dismay is conveyed, like that of a child pleased with blowing up a balloon who is disconcerted with its final bursting. "All gone!" And yet, with the disappointment, comes a certain satisfaction in destruction, as the child feels pleasure in the big bang:

[50] *The Prelude*, VII, 350–9.   [51] *Op. cit.*, 398–404.

> Rolled round in earth's diurnal course
> With rocks, and stones, and trees.[52]

The embalmment is now really final: certain messy possibilities of
growth, emotional involvement, and so on are out of the way.
That this satisfaction could coexist with the sense of utter loss is,
of course, an index of the complexity of Wordsworth's poetry,
and of why it continues to interest us.

The theme is beautifully decorated in "Three years she grew ..."
I suppose this is one of the best-loved of Wordsworth's lyrics,
cunningly disposed as it is towards the indulgence of our basic
irresponsibilities, our nostalgias, our yearnings for escape from
the human condition. The girl is set apart from the outset, kid-
napped by Nature, that cosmic gipsy, and reduced – or exalted –
to the status of "mute insensate things". She grows for three
years "in sun and shower" (no human child could survive such
exposure, of course) and while brief reference is made to her
"sportiveness" in lines anticipating "The White Doe of Rylstone",
it is her projection as flower and tree which dominates the poem.[53]
She is entirely passive to skyey influences, moulded by "the
motions of the Storm", "the stars of midnight", and the dance of
rivulets:

> And vital feelings of delight
> Shall rear her form to stately height. . . .[54]

Vital: yes – but hardly the vitality of human growth. "Stately
height" and "rear" – the terms clash with the next line,

> Her virgin bosom swell;

and our minds go back to the desecrations of *Nutting*:

> the hazels rose
> Tall and erect, with tempting clusters hung,
> A virgin scene! – A little while I stood. . . .

---

[52] "A slumber did my spirit seal", 7–8.
[53] *Cf.* Essay on Epitaphs: "The character of a deceased friend . . . is not
seen, no – nor ought to be seen, otherwise than as a tree through a tender haze
or a luminous mist, that spiritualizes and beautifies it . . ." *The Poetical Works*,
v, 452 (it may be worth noting that the indexes to this edition need revising:
there is no listing of this important essay).
[54] "Three years she grew", 31–2.

I heard the murmur and the murmuring sound. . . .
　　　. . . Then up I rose,
And dragged to earth both branch and bough, with crash
And merciless ravage: and the shady nook
Of hazels, and the green and mossy bower,
Deformed and sullied, patiently gave up
Their quiet being. . . .[55]

It is from this fate that Lucy is saved by death:

> She died, and left to me
> This heath, this calm, and quiet scene;
> The memory of what has been,
> And never more will be.[56]

In yet another Lucy poem the conclusion

> But she is in her grave, and, oh,
> The difference to me![57]

stands as the obverse of "Nay Master, we are seven!"

In "The Two April Mornings" (1799) a thirty years' distancing adds the dimension of "recollection" to death's embalming. The old schoolmaster's daughter had died at the early age of nine: she had been a sprightly child, but her death, clearly, came as something of a relief:

> Six feet in earth my Emma lay,
> And yet I loved her more,
> For so it seemed, than till that day
> I e'er had loved before.
>
> And, turning from her grave, I met
> Beside the churchyard Yew
> A blooming Girl, whose hair was wet
> With points of morning dew.[58]

The living girl is described in all her robust vitality, infinitely appealing – and yet, and yet!. . . .

[55] "Nutting", 19–21, 38, 43–8.

[56] "Three years she grew", 39–42. "Nutting" immediately precedes "Three years she grew . . ." in the 1800 L.B. In Wordsworth's final arrangement all these Lucy poems are broken up. My note 21 may be relevant.

[57] "She dwelt among the untrodden ways", 11–12.

[58] "The Two April Mornings", 37–44.

There came from me a sigh of pain
Which I could ill confine;
I looked at her, and looked again:
And did not wish her mine![59]

Now this is irreproachably parental and affecting, if we read the
poem in isolation; taken in conjunction with the whole movement
of 1798–1800 verse on this obsessive theme, and remembering that
the situation is imaginary, or symbolic, I wonder if we can easily
escape the conclusion that "Be absolute for death!" has by now
become Wordsworth's motto.

6

We have moved far, at any rate, very far, from the

cheerful smiles,
Limbs stout as thine, and lips as gay[60]

of "The Emigrant Mother" to the dehumanised children of
Wordsworth's later years of the Great Decade. "Spirit" gains a
decisive upper hand over "human fears" or human joys in the
Immortality *Ode*. In the "embalmment" poems of the middle
years of the decade the immediacy of existence is side-stepped in
favour of the immediacy of non-existence, Wordsworth's Final
Solution to the problem of physical and emotional mess: but of
course life goes on, and he has to try again, or cease writing. "The
passion the sorrow and the strife", the "fear of life" of the
Fragments from MS. M, have to be faced; the outside world with its
noise breaks into the convalescent world of (ii) in which the
silence of solid objects had "sheltered" him

in peace on his bed
Happy as they who are dead.[61]

The *Fragments*, indeed, *are* the great *Ode* in embryo, in almost
repulsively revealing embryo; the elements are all there, ready to
be transmuted by that uncanny rhetorical skill which Wordsworth
had at command into something sonorous and didactic. The gears

[59] *Op. cit.*, 53–6.   [60] "The Emigrant Mother", 49–50.
[61] *The Poetical Works*, IV, pp. 365–6.

grind to begin with; *Fragments* (i) is better poetry than *Ode* (i) and (ii) with their incredibly schoolboyish "of yore", "By night or day", "beautiful *and* fair", "But yet I know, where'er I go"; but by (iii) he gets into his authentic rhythm, and "Thoughts that are fed by the sun" fertilise (iii) and (iv). "Happy am I" he protests in *Fragments*: "I hear, I hear, with joy I hear!" he insists in the *Ode*; but the *Fragments* collapse into "Sweetness and breath with the quiet of death" and the *Ode* into

> Whither is fled the visionary gleam?
> Where is it now, the glory and the dream?[62]

"Two years at least," Wordsworth tells us, "passed between the writing of the four first stanzas and the remaining part": they are really, of course, two poems, and might better have been published as such, the one a solution to the other. The original *Ode* mediates, if it also conventionalises, the *Fragments*; the seven added strophes of 1804 are a *tour de force* of almost incredible dexterity (considering that Wordsworth was possibly the least "Platonising" of our major poets after Chaucer) in the direction of an otherworldly solution of the life-existence problem; a solution which contradicts every previous datum on which we might set about constructing a "philosophy of Wordsworth". Without Wordsworth's own statement, "Archimedes said that he could move the world if he had a point whereon to rest his machine. Who has not felt the same aspirations as regards the world of his own mind? Having to wield some of its elements when I was impelled to write this Poem on the 'Immortality of the Soul', I took hold of the notion of pre-existence as having sufficient foundation in humanity for authorizing me to make for my purpose the best use of it I could as a Poet," the critic might be led very dangerously astray indeed. As it is, we can salute the Wordsworth of strophes (v) to (xi) as technically the most distinguished of the sons of Gray, admire (x) as a moving pendant to (iv), and (xi) as a valuable exegesis of "Tintern Abbey", and get on with our job of elucidating the original *Ode*.

But there remain strophes (vii) and (viii) for our present survey – outside the original *Ode*, but bearing decisively on the theme of childhood and the three levels. Dr Richards has defended Words-

[62] 56–7.

worth against Coleridge's strictures here: for me they remain valid, aesthetically and doctrinally. In the "chaos of thought and passion, all confused" which is the Immortality *Ode*, these sections are almost pitiably unrealised. Wordsworth seems to be working from line to line, almost from phrase to phrase, unsure of what he will glue on next:

> A wedding or a festival,
> A mourning or a funeral. . . .[63]

(isn't a wedding a festival? isn't a funeral a mourning?) in nervous anxiety to offer some "objective correlative" to the grandiosities of (viii) which present the kind of baby Shelley failed to prod into revelation in that famous encounter on Magdalen Bridge. I can't help feeling that here Wordsworth is making a fool of himself. We all know what babies are, particularly if we are parents; and they are *not* "Mighty Prophets, seers blest". Wordsworth's first child was born in June 1803, Coleridge's seven years earlier. The weight of experience is in Coleridge's favour, and the weight of later evidence: no child of Wordsworth could vie with H.C. in genius. This Immortality *Ode* apotheosis is no more than a confidence trick. And it is a trick which, in the first place, Wordsworth is playing on himself – on the Wordsworth of "The Danish Boy", miserably poised between stone and tree, between existence and non-existence, between organic and inorganic. And it is Wordsworth's confession of failure to maintain the difficult existential poise of the *Lyrical Ballads*, the poise which it was Wordsworth's mission in poetry to maintain and from which he now withdraws in defeat. Coleridge was wrong in thinking it was Wordsworth's role to be a great philosophical poet: it was his role rather to be a great psychological poet, and to prove in particular that "bond of union between life and joy", that umbilical cord which links "our first existence with existing things", the "earthly root" which Keats was to study in *Endymion*. And "existential" is a better word here than "psychological", which is too analytic: Wordsworth's country is on the frontier between consciousness and unconsciousness, on that difficult terrain, that "heath" denuded of every adventitious prettiness (how wrong too Arnold was with his

>   He laid us as we lay at birth
>   On the cool flowery lap of earth!)[64]

where the great archetypes of suffering and *joy through suffering* rove,
and which all must cross (the Brig of Dread) before the trumpets
sound for them, if at all, on the other side.

Strophe (vii) of the *Ode* seems to me so terribly bad that it defies
discussion. Strophe (viii) raises the question, "How old is this
little child, 'glorious in the might Of heaven-born freedom on
[his] being's height' supposed to be?" Pretty clearly he is not the
six-year-old imitator of (vii). The whole strophe is a cradling: the
enormous paradoxes and hyperboles demand a Christmas setting,
an "Immensity cloister'd in thy dear womb", and the Virgin is
Nature: but things fall apart without the Christian framework. At
this point Milton impinges on Wordsworth, to be rejected: homely
nurse as she may be, Nature cannot admit to any "guilty front" or
"sinfull blame", and we are out on a limb; Milton's clear-cut
antitheses are muffled. The Child, *puer aeternus*, is an Eye among
the blind as the Logos "shineth in darkness and the darkness
comprehendeth It not"; Logos, the "Word without a word, unable to speak a word" of Andrewes and Eliot is Wordsworth's
"deaf and silent" Eye reading the eternal deep, "Haunted for ever
by the eternal mind". Plato, Moses, and St John meet here in the
setting of Proclus' commentary on *Timaeus*. But Wordsworth the
embalmer is not absent:

>   Thou little Child, yet glorious in the might
>   Of heaven-born freedom on thy being's height,
>   Why with such earnest pains dost thou provoke
>   The years to bring the inevitable yoke,
>   Thus blindly with thy blessedness at strife?[65]

We are firmly at level A, at the height of Being; from now on the
bond of union between Life and Joy will be sought not in the
hallowed and pure motions of the sense but in the rarefied sphere of
the Michelangelo sonnet of *c.* 1805:

>   Heaven-born, the Soul a heavenward course must hold;
>   Beyond the visible world she soars to seek

[64] Matthew Arnold, "Memorial Verses, April, 1850", 48–9.
[65] 122–6.

(For what delights the sense is false and weak)
Ideal Form, the universal mould.[66]

7

If my conclusions are even marginally valid they suggest a more
complex relevance of Coleridge's Dejection *Ode* to Wordsworth's
Immortality *Ode* than has generally been recognised. While it can
only have been the first four strophes which Wordsworth read or
recited to his friend on 28 Mar. 1802, it is probable, as de Selincourt says, that "he enlarged to C. upon that mood of meditative
ecstasy in which his poem was to close". And the latent development of Wordsworth's mind was at all times more evident to
Coleridge, I imagine, than to Wordsworth himself: he knew just
where Wordsworth was going, and there are signs that he mis-
trusted the direction. When he sat down to write his own
Dejection *Ode* (4 Apr. 1802) it was not simply as a "counterpart"
(de Selincourt's word) but rather as a counterblast, a warning
coming from one who had already recognised of himself that "The
poet is dead in me" (to Godwin, 25 Mar. 1801). Wordsworth's
positions are questioned one by one; even the smug rainbow
epigraph is sharply challenged:

> And I fear, I fear, my Master dear!
> We shall have a deadly storm.

If pupil can speak thus boldly to master it is by virtue of truths
Coleridge has "proved on his pulses".

Wordsworth's first strophe (itself an imitation of lines 9–16 of
Coleridge's "The Mad Monk", written the previous year) and
second strophe make up an elemental complex, glancing from
heaven to earth, from earth to heaven, in which grief though
admitted is carefully distanced and softened to resignation. The
Moon looks round her with delight; the sunshine is a glorious
birth; past and present are embalmed in the moment. Coleridge's
opening strophe breaks up the carefully tailored pattern: Wordsworth's bare heavens are cloudrent, his full moon split into old and
new, the morrow's sunshine threatened by the impending storm.
And it is good that this should be so, that sense should be restored
to its sharpness, even if it is the sharpness of loss. Coleridge is

[66] "From the Italian of Michael Angelo", II, 5–8.

writing primarily, of course, of his own condition of apathy, his "wan and heartless mood"; at the same time he is giving a warning to his friend. This could be demonstrated, if space permitted, by going through the two *Odes* strophe by strophe; here I must keep my concluding remarks to what is relevant to the preceding discussion.

And of course Coleridge is taking in a vaster compass of Wordsworthian sensibility than could be documented from the relatively simple structure of the Immortality *Ode*. In pointing out that the poet

> may not hope from outward forms to win
> The passion and the life, whose fountains are within[67]

his reference is not simply to Wordsworth's strophe (iv), though the forced optimism of that would be evident enough to Coleridge, but to Wordsworth's whole retreat from sensation-in-depth, from "total sensation", towards a sterile aspiration to the heights. No-one knew better than Coleridge (though his addiction had barred the way to his own achievement) that the only access to level A (if I may for the last time refer to my schema) is, for the artist, through the descent to level C, the redemption of the primordial Adam and the achievement, or reachievement, of primordial joy.[68] It is from the reactivated centre alone that the creative contact can be established: this is the meaning of Coleridge's strophes (iv) and (v), too often misinterpreted as Platonic theorising:

> We in ourselves rejoice!
> And thence flows all that charms or ear or sight,
> All melodies the echoes of that voice,
> All colours a suffusion from that light.[69]

In the letter version (to William Sotheby, 19 July 1802) these lines are followed by a short strophe, affirming that Wordsworth *does* enjoy this contact: "Thus, thus dost thou rejoice"; but Coleridge first wrote "mayst", and the omission of this passage on publication (4 Oct. 1802) shows honesty gaining the upper hand.

[67] Coleridge, "Dejection: An Ode", 45–6.
[68] For those readers who will be eager at this point to shout "Jung" I may point out that my reference is to the Creed and that the dirty word "archetype" was used, if not invented, by Blake.
[69] Coleridge, "Dejection: An Ode", 72–5.

SELECT BIBLIOGRAPHY

There are a number of collections of contemporary criticism of Wordsworth, and of Wordsworth and his contemporaries, such as those of ELSIE SMITH, *An Estimate of William Wordsworth by his Contemporaries, 1793–1822*, Oxford (Basil Blackwell) 1932, and *Contemporary Reviews of Romantic Poetry*, ed. John Wain, London (Harrap) 1953. JAMES V. LOGAN'S *Wordsworthian Criticism: A Guide and Bibliography*, Columbus (Ohio State UniversityPress), 1947 and 1961, contains a bibliography which extends from 1850 to 1944. The period from 1945 to 1964 is covered by *Wordsworthian Criticism 1945–1964: An Annotated Bibliography*, eds. Elton F. Henley and David H. Stamm (New York Public Library), 1965. *The English Romantic Poets: A Review of Research*, ed. Thomas M. Raysor (Modern Language Association of America) 1950, revised edition 1956, includes a chapter on Wordsworth by ERNEST BERNBAUM, which was revised by James V. Logan.

The *Cornell Wordsworth Collection*, a catalogue compiled by George Harris Healey, Ithaca, N.Y., 1959, and *The Amherst Wordsworth Collection*, ed. C. H. Patton, Amherst College, 1936, are of considerable value. A *Check List of Master's Theses in the U.S. on William Wordsworth*, Charlottesville (The Bibliographical Society of the University of Virginia) 1962, has been compiled by Elton F. Henley. *The Cambridge Bibliography of English Literature*, Cambridge, 1940, and *Supplement*, 1957, should also be consulted, together with the listings in *The Year's Work in English Studies*, published by the English Association, the *Annual Bibliography of English Language and Literature*, published by the Modern Humanities Research Association, the annual bibliography "The Romantic Movement" (ELH, 1937–49, transferred to *Philological Quarterly*, 1950–), and *English Literature 1660–1800*, a bibliography compiled for *Philological Quarterly*. I have not referred to individual critical studies of shorter poems, whose name will soon be legion, but the

selective listings in the Critical Bibliographies to GEOFFREY
H. HARTMAN'S *Wordsworth's Poetry 1787–1814* will be found to
be very useful.

I. EDITIONS

Literary Criticism of William Wordsworth, ed. Paul M. Zall. Lincoln (University of Nebraska Press) 1966.

The Poetical Works of William Wordsworth, 5 vols, eds. Ernest de Selincourt and Helen Darbishire. Oxford (Clarendon Press) 1940–49.

The Prelude, ed. Ernest de Selincourt; revised by Helen Darbishire. Oxford (Clarendon Press) 1959.

Prose Works of William Wordsworth, 3 vols., ed. A. B. Grosart. London, 1876.

Prose Works of William Wordsworth, 2 vols., ed. W. A. Knight. London, 1896.

II. BIOGRAPHIES

HARPER, GEORGE MACLEAN. *William Wordsworth: His Life, Works, and Influence*, 2 vols. London (Murray) 1916.

LEGOUIS, EMILE. *The Early Life of William Wordsworth, 1770–1798*. London, 1897.

MOORMAN, MARY. *William Wordsworth: A Biography: The Early Years, 1770–1803* (1957). *The Later Years, 1803–1850* (1965). Oxford (Clarendon Press).

III. LETTERS

The Early Letters of William and Dorothy Wordsworth, 1787–1805 (1935); *The Letters of William and Dorothy Wordsworth: The Middle Years*, 2 vols. (1937); *The Later Years*, 3 vols. (1939), ed. Ernest de Selincourt. Oxford (Clarendon Press). Second edition of the Letters, Vol. 1, *The Early Years, 1787–1805*, revised by Chester L. Shaver. Oxford (Clarendon Press) 1967–.

IV. CRITICAL WORKS

ABERCROMBIE, LASCELLES. *The Art of Wordsworth*. London (Oxford University Press) 1952.

BATESON, F. W. *Wordsworth – A Re-interpretation*. London (Longmans) 1954.

BATHO, EDITH C. *The Later Wordsworth*. Cambridge (University Press) 1933.

BEATTY, ARTHUR. *William Wordsworth: His Doctrine and Art in Their Historical Relations*, in University of Wisconsin Studies in Language and Literature, No. 17. Madison (University Press) 1922.

BURTON, MARY. *The One Wordsworth*. Chapel Hill (University of North Carolina Press) 1942.

CLARKE, COLIN. *Romantic Paradox*. London (Routledge) 1962.

DANBY, JOHN. *The Simple Wordsworth*. London (Routledge) 1960.

DARBISHIRE, HELEN. *The Poet Wordsworth*. Oxford (Clarendon Press) 1950.

FAUSSET, HUGH I'A. *The Lost Leader*. London (Jonathan Cape) 1933.

FERRY, DAVID. *The Limits of Mortality*. Middletown, Conn. (Wesleyan University Press) 1959.

GARROD, H. W. *Wordsworth*. Oxford (Clarendon Press) 1927.

HARTMAN, GEOFFREY H. *Wordsworth's Poetry 1787-1814*. New Haven and London (Yale University Press) 1964.

HAVENS, R. D., *The Mind of a Poet: A Study of Wordsworth's Thought with Particular Reference to The Prelude*. Baltimore (John Hopkins Press) 1941.

HERFORD, C. H. *Wordsworth*. London (Routledge) 1930.

HIRSCH, E. D. *Wordsworth and Schelling*. New Haven (Yale University Press) 1960.

JONES, JOHN. *The Egotistical Sublime*. London (Chatto & Windus) 1954.

KING, ALEC. *Wordsworth and the Artist's Vision*. London (Athlone Press) 1966.

LINDENBERGER, HERBERT. *On Wordsworth's Prelude*. Princeton (University Press) 1963.

LYON, J. S. *The Excursion: A Study*. New Haven (Yale University Press) 1950.

MACLEAN, KENNETH. *Agrarian Age: A Background for Wordsworth*. New Haven (Yale University Press) 1950.

MARSH, FLORENCE. *Wordsworth's Imagery*. New Haven (Yale University Press) 1952.

MEYER, G. W. *Wordsworth's Formative Years*. University of Michigan Publications in Language and Literature, xx. Ann Arbor (University of Michigan Press) 1943.

MILES, JOSEPHINE. *Wordsworth and the Vocabulary of Emotion*. Berkeley (University of California Press) 1942.

MARGOLIOUTH, H. M. *Wordsworth and Coleridge, 1795-1834*. London (Oxford University Press) 1953.

OWEN, W. J. B. *Wordsworth's Preface to Lyrical Ballads*, IX. Copenhagen (Rosenhilde & Bagge) 1957.

POTTS, ABBIE F. *Wordsworth's Prelude: A Study of its Literary Form.* Ithaca, N.Y. (Cornell University Press) 1953.

RALEIGH, WALTER. *Wordsworth.* London (Edward Arnold) 1903.

READ, HERBERT. *Wordsworth.* London (Jonathan Cape) 1930.

SALVESEN, CHRISTOPHER. *The Language of Memory.* London (Edward Arnold) 1965.

SPERRY, W. L. *Wordsworth's Anti-Climax*, Harvard Studies in English, XIII. Cambridge (Harvard University Press) 1935.

STALLKNECHT, NEWTON P. *Strange Seas of Thought: Studies in William Wordsworth's Philosophy of Man and Nature.* Bloomington and London (Indiana University Press) 1966.

TODD, F. M. *Politics and the Poet: A Study of Wordsworth.* London (Methuen) 1957.

WELSFORD, ENID. *Salisbury Plain. A Study in the Development of Wordsworth's Mind and Art.* Oxford (Basil Blackwell) 1966.

WORTHINGTON, JANE. *Wordsworth's Reading of Roman Prose.* New Haven (Yale University Press) 1946.

V. ESSAYS AND CHAPTERS

ABRAMS, M. H. "Wordsworth and the Eighteenth Century" in *The Mirror and the Lamp: Romantic Theory and the Critical Tradition.* New York (W. W. Norton & Company Inc.) 1958.

ARNOLD, MATTHEW. Introduction to *Poems of Wordsworth.* London, 1879.

BABBITT, IRVING. "The Primitivism of Wordsworth" in *The Bookman* (U.S.A.), LXXIV (1931).

BAGEHOT, WALTER. "Wordsworth, Tennyson, and Browning; or, Pure, Ornate, and Grotesque Art in English Poetry" in *The Collected Works of Walter Bagehot*, Vol. II (8 vols.), ed. Norman St John-Stevas London (The Economist), 1965.

BLACKSTONE, BERNARD. "The Secondary Founts", in *The Lost Travellers.* London (Longmans) 1962.

BLOOM, HAROLD. "William Wordsworth" in *The Visionary Company.* London (Faber) 1962.

BRADLEY, A. C. "Wordsworth" in *Oxford Lectures on Poetry.* London (Macmillan) 1909.

BROOKS, CLEANTH. "Wordsworth and the Paradox of the Imagination" in *The Well Wrought Urn.* London (Dobson) 1949.

BUSH, DOUGLAS. "Coleridge: Wordsworth: Byron" (Section ii of Chap. II) in *Mythology and the Romantic Tradition in English Poetry.* New York (Pageant) 1957.

CLOUGH, A. H. "Lecture on the Poetry of Wordsworth" in *Poems and Prose Remains*, 2 vols. London, 1869.

CROFTS, J. *Wordsworth and the Seventeenth Century.* Warton Lecture in English Poetry, British Academy, 1940. London (Humphrey Milford) 1940.

CRUTTWELL, PATRICK. "Wordsworth, the Public, and the People" in *Sewanee Review*, LXIV (1956), pp. 71–80.

DARBISHIRE, HELEN. Introduction to *Wordsworth's Poems in Two Volumes, 1807.* Oxford (Clarendon Press) 1914, 1952.

DAVIE, DONALD. "Diction and Invention: A View of Wordsworth" in *Purity of Diction in English Verse.* London (Chatto & Windus) 1952.

—— "Syntax in the Blank Verse of Wordsworth's Prelude" in *Articulate Energy: An Enquiry into the Syntax of English Verse.* London (Routledge) 1955.

DE MADARIAGA, SALVADOR. "The Case of Wordsworth" in *Shelley and Calderón.* London (Constable) 1920.

DE SELINCOURT, ERNEST. "The Early Wordsworth", in *Wordsworthian and Other Studies.* Oxford (Clarendon Press) 1947.

ELIOT, T. S. "Wordsworth and Coleridge", in *The Use of Poetry and the Use of Criticism.* Cambridge (Harvard University Press) 1933.

EMPSON, WILLIAM. "Sense in The Prelude", in *The Structure of Complex Words.* London (Chatto & Windus) 1951.

—— "Basic English and Wordsworth", in *The Kenyon Review*, II (1940), pp. 449–57.

EVERETT, BARBARA. "The Prelude", in *The Critical Quarterly*, Vol. I, no. 4 (Winter, 1959), pp. 338–50.

HOUGH, GRAHAM. "Wordsworth and Coleridge", in *The Romantic Poets.* London (Hutchinson) 1953.

KNIGHT, G. WILSON. "The Wordsworthian Profundity" in *The Starlit Dome.* London (Oxford University Press) 1941.

LEAVIS, F. R. "Wordsworth", in *Revaluation.* London (Chatto & Windus) 1936.

MACLEAN, K. "Levels of Imagination in Wordsworth's *Prelude* (1805)", in *Philological Quarterly*, 38, 385–400.

MORGAN, EDWIN. "A Prelude to *The Prelude*", in *Essays in Criticism*, V, pp. 341–53.

PATER, WALTER. "Wordsworth" in *Appreciations.* London, 1889.

PIPER, H. W. "Wordsworth and the Religion of Nature" and "Nature and Imagination in *The Ruined Cottage*", in *The Active Universe.* London (Athlone Press) 1962.

Sewell, Elizabeth. "Wordsworth and Rilke: Toward a Biology of Thinking", in *The Orphic Voice*. London (Routledge) 1961.

Sharrock, Roger. Introduction to *Selected Poems of William Wordsworth*. London (Heinemann) 1958.

Smith, James. "Wordsworth: A Preliminary Survey", in *Scrutiny*, 7 (1938) pp. 33–5.

Stephen, Leslie. "Wordsworth's Ethics", in *Hours in a Library*, Third Series. London, 1879.

Swinburne, Algernon Charles. "Wordsworth and Byron", in *Miscellanies*. London, 1886.

Willey, Basil. "'Nature' in Wordsworth", in *The Eighteenth-Century Background*. London (Chatto & Windus) 1940.

—— "On Wordsworth and the Locke Tradition", in *The Seventeenth-Century Background*. London (Chatto & Windus) 1950.

Williams, Charles. "Wordsworth", in *The English Poetic Mind*. Oxford (Clarendon Press) 1932.

—— "Blake and Wordsworth", in *The Dublin Review*, No. 417 (1941), pp. 175–86.

VI. Critical Anthologies

Discussions of Wordsworth, ed. J. Davies. London (Heath) 1964.

Tribute to Wordsworth, eds. Muriel Spark and Derek Stanford. London (Wingate) 1950.

Wordsworth: Centenary Studies Presented at Cornell and Princeton Universities, ed. Gilbert T. Dunklin. Hamden (Archon Books) 1963.

INDEX